Solved:
THE RIDDLE OF ILLNESS

Solved:
THE RIDDLE OF ILLNESS

Third Edition

STEPHEN E. LANGER, M.D.
AND JAMES F. SCHEER

KEATS PUBLISHING

LOS ANGELES

NTC/Contemporary Publishing Group

Library of Congress Cataloging-in-Publication Data is available.

Published by Keats Publishing
A division of NTC/Contemporary Publishing Group, Inc.
4255 West Touhy Avenue, Lincolnwood, Illinois 60712, U.S.A.

Printed in the United States of America
International Standard Book Number: 0-658-00293-7

00 01 02 03 04 DHD 18 17 16 15 14 13 12 11 10 9 8 7 6 5 4 3 2 1

To my wife Debi—the wind beneath my wings.
Stephen E. Langer

For my wife Joan with all my love.
James F. Scheer

CONTENTS

ACKNOWLEDGMENTS

A prime mover in clinical research on the thyroid gland for half a century, the late Broda O. Barnes, M.D., Ph.D., was also a prime mover behind the writing of this book, by liberally giving his time, abundant information, encouragement, and inspiration to my coauthor, James F. Scheer, and me. I know of no one else in the world who has done so much as a medical doctor, writer, lecturer, and talk show guest to alert millions to the often hidden causes of illness, as well as to simple ways to stay well for life.

This revised, updated, and enlarged version of *Solved: The Riddle of Illness*—as with the original edition—is intended to carry the Barnes tradition forward—to reveal the unsuspected reasons for illness and sound ways of achieving and maintaining wellness.

Credit for encouraging the writing of *Solved: The Riddle of*

Illness also goes to Mr. George Shutt, of Glendora, California, founder of Shutt Medical Technologies, a division of Bristol-Myers Squibb, and an inventor-pioneer in arthroscopic surgical instrumentation.

For many years, George Shutt served as Dr. Barnes's volunteer publicist. He has made a second career—concurrent and nonprofit—of disseminating information on subnormal thyroid function. By forming a private enterprise, he has realized funding to launch a hypothyroidism foundation to educate the public and the medical profession and to facilitate research efforts in this critically important area.

In addition, thanks go to biochemist Jeffrey Bland, Ph.D. I drew some of the book's material from a talk he gave when we were speakers, with Dr. Barnes, at the Webster-Barnes Foundation in Dallas, Texas.

I am also grateful to William H. Philpott, M.D., from whose superb book, *Victory Over Diabetes*, I used some material with permission from Nathan Keats, founding publisher of Keats Publishing, Inc., publisher of his book and previous editions of this one.

Edward R. Pinckney, M.D., and his wife Cathey, of Beverly Hills, California, prominent medical writers, generously supplied key material from several of their books and other publications for use in *Solved: The Riddle of Illness*.

It's impossible to give enough thanks to two individuals who contributed mightily to the third edition: Mary Shomon and Dr. John C. Lowe. Mary is the author of *Living Well with Hypothyroidism: What Your Doctors Don't Tell You . . . That You Need to Know*, writer-editor of the About.com Web site on thyroid disease (http://thyroid.about.com), and editor of "Sticking Out Our Necks," the thyroid disease news report (on-line at http://www.thyroid-info.com). Don't fail to request subscriptions to her free monthly thyroid newsletters. You can e-mail her for more information at mshomon@thyroid-info.com. Mary introduced us to Dr. John Lowe, who supplied much of the cutting-edge information for chapter 24, "Coping with Fibromyalgia."

Stephen E. Langer, M.D.

PREFACE

In *Solved: The Riddle of Illness*, thyroid gland authority Stephen Langer, M.D., and health editor/writer James F. Scheer show you simple ways to understand and manage your thyroid gland so that you can make the most of your life physically, mentally, and emotionally.

Supercharged energy and a wholesome emotional outlook are basic to living and functioning positively for goal achievement, social adjustment, and happiness—difficult or impossible to achieve if your thyroid gland isn't working properly.

One of the most important books of our time—its first edition was a perennial best-seller—the enlarged and updated edition of *Solved: The Riddle of Illness* reveals in simple and colorful terms secrets of abundant health—physically, emotionally, and mentally.

In this age of astronomical health care costs which threaten to bankrupt the individual as well as the nation, *Solved: The Riddle of Illness* offers new hope, because it deals with underlying causes for a multitude of ailments, rather than just symptoms.

One of the most prevalent basic ailments and one of the least diagnosed—contributing to horrendous medical costs—is hypothyroidism (low thyroid function).

There are more than sixty-four symptoms of low thyroid function, the most prevalent of which are some of today's most common disorders: fatigue and depression.

Among many novel features of *Solved: The Riddle of Illness* is a no-cost, self-administered, temperature test which you can take to indicate whether or not you are hypothyroid. This is called the Barnes Basal Temperature Test. If your temperature runs low, according to given parameters, it is time to see your family doctor to get more extensive and verifying tests.

Dr. Langer and James F. Scheer show you how to reverse a widespread illness that saps your physical vigor, reduces your sexual vitality, steals your ability to think and remember, and undermines your emotional life.

Why is it that normal thyroid function is so key to functioning at 100 percent in this highly competitive world? Every one of your trillions of cells requires thyroid hormone, just as the cylinders of your car require a rapid succession of sparks to ignite the fuel and power them.

Without bright sparks, your car engine falters, runs weakly, or quits entirely. Without adequate thyroid hormone, your cells—and *you*—respond in a similar way.

This third edition of *Solved: The Riddle of Illness* deserves a permanent place on your health and wellness bookshelf, just as it now has on mine!

Dr. Wayne Dyer

PLEASE NOTE!

Solved: The Riddle of Illness suggests a way of life for reaching and maintaining peak health. It is based on the best of the latest research and the best of time-tested methods—some of the latter long forgotten.

Although the medical profession encourages us to take more responsibility for our health, seeking wellness should be done in cooperation with a doctor. More and more physicians are becoming aware of the benefits to be derived from preventive methods—among them optimum nutrition.

This book is not to be considered a prescription. You are unique. You have your own set of individual variations—physical, mental, and emotional. Only the doctor who knows, examines, and treats you can prescribe for you. For this reason, the authors and publishers cannot take medical or legal responsibility of having the contents of this book considered a prescription for anyone.

With regard to case studies used in this book, we have made every effort to conceal the identity of all individuals in order to preserve their privacy. To this end, all names, physical descriptions, and even professions have been changed.

Special Note

The first edition of *Solved: The Riddle of Illness* was written more than a decade ago. Since then it has been found that certain conditions other than hypothyroidism (such as chronic viral infections) can reduce a person's basal body temperature, too.

Therefore, it is incumbent for any practicing physician to perform a complete battery of thyroid tests—T_3, T_4, FTI, TSH, and antithyroid antibodies—in addition to the basal temperature test before prescribing thyroid supplementation.

Happily, with the new, ultrasensitive thyroid tests, a high percentage of patients with low basal body temperature also show abnormalities in their lab workups, and these are the patients for whom I now routinely prescribe thyroid supplementation.

Make no mistake, the Barnes Basal Temperature Test (underarm temperature reading) is often the first indication a person is hypothyroid, and I urge all of my readers to see their family doctors as soon as possible for a complete thyroid evaluation, if the morning thermometer consistently registers less than 97.8.

Stephen Langer, M.D.

A SALUTE

A man who worked medical miracles.

That sums up the life and career of the late Broda O. Barnes, M.D., Ph.D., who worked miracles in the lives of millions of patients—his own as well as those of more than 100 other doctors—and readers of his many books.

This book picks up where Dr. Barnes's writings leave off—actually a little before that. As authors, we—Stephen Langer, M.D., and James F. Scheer—were privileged and blessed to have known Dr. Broda Barnes intimately and benefited from his rich store of knowledge and experience.

After the release of the first edition of *Solved: The Riddle of Illness*, many individuals wrote or asked us for additional personal information about Dr. Barnes. Therefore, we are now delighted to summarize his life—a lot of which is covered in the text of this book—because his accomplishments convince us that he is worthy of the Nobel Prize in medicine and research.

Perhaps you will agree.

Way back in the mists of history, a man named George slew a fire-breathing dragon which had eaten the innocent citizens of a distant city. He was showered with thanks and great acclaim and eventually was sainted. That's how plain George became St. George.

In more recent years, a Fort Collins, Colorado, medical doctor slew a different kind of dragon, which—directly or indirectly—had killed many innocent inhabitants in every land.

Unlike St. George, Broda O. Barnes, M.D., Ph.D., received only limited attention and never stood a chance of being sainted. However, that was all right with Dr. Barnes. He wanted attention drawn not to himself but to the slain dragon, the myth that wholesome and nutritious cholesterol-containing foods should be minimized or eliminated to avoid cardiovascular ailments. He wanted attention drawn to the *real* reasons for clogged arteries, strokes, and heart attacks and to the simple ways to prevent them.

We salute Dr. Barnes for his lifelong studies and discoveries about the thyroid gland and how, when functioning properly, it contributes to preventing heart attacks (as well as cancer, chronic fatigue syndrome, premature aging, and a medical book full of minor to devastating ailments).

His contributions to the health and well-being of people around the world place him among the giants in the modern history of medicine and biochemistry: Drs. Tom Spies, Roger Williams, Hans Selye, the Shute brothers, Albert Szent-Györgyi, and Linus Pauling. You will understand why when you meet Dr. Barnes in the pages of this book.

Just who is Dr. Broda Barnes? What events and information shocked him into the realization that medical researchers were looking at the wrong evidence to solve the riddle of epidemic heart disease and that, of course, they were coming up with the wrong answers?

As we knew him, Dr. Barnes, a stocky, bespectacled, white-haired, small city medical doctor, had a folksy way of talking and an irreverent wit. He was born on April 14, 1904, in a log cabin desperately clinging to a steep and rocky slope of the Ozark Mountains in southern Missouri.

"A couple wheels of my parents' covered wagon broke off there, giving me plenty of time to be born. Ten years later, they had the wheels fixed, and we moved westward," he admitted.

Driven by powerful inquisitiveness as a youngster, he became enchanted with research as a chemistry student at the University of Denver. For two years he taught physiological chemistry at Western Reserve University, where he had received his master of science degree in 1930. At the University of Chicago, he earned a doctorate in physiology in 1931.

It was there, while studying under Dr. Anton J. Carlson, world-renowned physiology professor, that he reluctantly began investigating the thyroid gland.

"My interest in the thyroid gland grew out of necessity, rather than choice," he told us. "Professor Carlson arbitrarily assigned this subject for my doctoral thesis when I entered his department many years ago.

"I would have preferred another subject, but during the Great Depression—actually it wasn't *that great!*—one was happy to find any job permitting the continuation of education. . . .

"As time passed, the wisdom of this great educator's decision was more than justified. He was aware that many secrets of this tiny gland remained undiscovered, but I'm sure he had no idea that this humble beginning would solve such an incredible range of medical problems. Neither of us foresaw the solution of the major health problems of the century through proper care of the thyroid gland: everything from overwhelming fatigue to the devastating diseases—heart and artery ailments and cancer—and, least suspected, common emotional disorders such as depression."

Dr. Barnes taught physiology at the University of Chicago for five years, then studied for his medical degree, completing this work in 1937 at Rush Medical College (Chicago), interning at Illinois Research Hospital. He began practicing medicine while serving for two years as assistant professor of medicine at the University of Illinois.

The brilliance of his research papers on thyroid function led to his being named chairman of the Health Education Department at the University of Denver. He served in the military between 1943 and 1946 and intermittently until 1951. Then he was appointed professor affiliate in the department of physiology at Colorado State University (1963–1968).

During more than forty years in private medical practice, Dr. Barnes was decades ahead of his time in stressing prevention of illness, rather than just treatment. Although a general practitioner, he always specialized in the thyroid gland, because its insufficiency and improper function were the unsuspected causes of a host of illnesses.

More than 100 of his publications on the thyroid gland and related topics appeared in leading medical and scientific journals throughout the world and in three books.

Without the contributions of Dr. Broda O. Barnes, millions of individuals would be energyless, living vegetables, old far before their time, emotionally disturbed without understanding why, unable to think or remember (believing that they had Alzheimer's disease) and being treated for symptoms, rather than for the easily correctable, underlying condition responsible for sixty-four common medical ailments suffered by an estimated 40 percent of the population.

You may be among that 40 percent.

After reading this book, you will understand fully why Dr. Barnes is worthy of a Nobel Prize!

1

"NOTHING ORGANICALLY WRONG"

"*D*r. Langer, I hate sex!"

Tears glistened in the eyes of the attractive thirty-year-old woman seated across the desk from me.

"Maybe it's my fatigue," she continued. "Half awake, in a mental fog, I drag around the office. At home in the evening, I collapse, exhausted, when my husband wants me most. Yet how can I even think of having sex when my body cries out just for survival?"

Particularly upsetting to this patient, whom I'll call Connie, was the assessment of her condition by previous doctors: "There's nothing organically wrong."

Allison's problem was somewhat different. She enjoyed sex but usually turned off her mate with icy cold hands and feet.

1

Tired, drowsy, anxious, often depressed, she caught every cold that came her way, and had frequent sinus and upper respiratory infections and severe headaches.

"My doctor can't find a thing wrong," she told me. "He calls me the world's foremost hypochondriac."

Eloise had no complaints about her sex life, only her sex. Difficult menstruation, which had started prematurely at age ten, caused her to miss school and, now, time from her prosperous advertising agency. To cope with exhaustion and with being cold, she drank mug after mug of hot coffee. She often experienced acute anxiety and occasional feelings of doom.

"My former doctor—and I do mean *former*—made me furious during my last office visit," she explained. "He told me, 'I advise you to take a more wholesome view of your health, because there's nothing organically wrong.'"

Like these women, Phil, a brilliant twenty-nine-year-old computer circuitry designer, had a mixed bag of problems—sudden inability to perform sexually, increasing difficulty producing innovative ideas, and minimal energy and endurance.

"My sexual failure is humiliating," he admitted, "but mental sluggishness and lack of energy are threatening my income and career. Coffee and pep pills don't do a thing for me. It's as if somebody pulled the plug on my power source."

His previous physician had tried a series of testosterone injections, which had given him only a minor charge and no improvement in his sex life or performance in business. Too young to be old, Phil was naturally dejected.

The four patients had two things in common: frustration and the same basic ailment. During their individual consultations with me, I informed them:

"Your thyroid function needs checking."

Their reactions could be summed up in the words: "Not *another* test!" All of them had gone through exhaustive tests, including one for thyroid function, at a cost of hundreds of dollars.

"This won't cost you a cent," I assured them. "You can do the Barnes Basal Temperature Test yourself at home."

They were puzzled. Who had ever heard of a no-cost test? Then I explained how to do it.

"Before going to bed tonight, shake down a thermometer.

Leave it on the bedside table. As soon as you wake up in the morning after a good night's sleep—no later—tuck the thermometer snugly in your armpit for ten minutes as you lie there.

"If your thyroid function is normal, your temperature should be in the range from 97.8 to 98.2 degrees Fahrenheit. If it's lower, you are probably hypothyroid—your thyroid gland is underfunctioning—and your physical problems and related ones have probably been caused or at least influenced by that. The test should be done on two consecutive days."

To the women, I said, "You get the most accurate readings if you're not menstruating (temperature fluctuates at this time) or on the second or third days of menstruation."

Reported results confirmed my suspicions: all were indeed hypothyroid. The treatment—natural desiccated thyroid supplement—brought gratifying results: freedom from their ailments in less than two months. Eloise was ecstatic about painless menstruation and normal body temperature. Appreciative husbands of Connie and Allison told me that thyroid had saved their sex lives and marriages. Phil went even further. He said, "It saved my whole life."

Over sixteen years as a medical doctor, I have been privileged to help many Connies, Allisons, Eloises, and Phils. In fact, I seem to specialize in patients whose symptoms are not readily diagnosed—persons who have been through the traditional system and possibly have been rejected as psychosomatic cases or as hypochondriacs.

A graduate of the New York College of Medicine at Buffalo, I spent some time studying medical psychology before realizing that I couldn't accept one of the basic assumptions of traditional Western allopathic medicine—the sharp cleavage between mind and body. I was troubled that patients should be branded as "psychological problems" or as having "psychogenic problems," as opposed to having "ailments of the body." It seemed that the twain would never meet.

In my frame of reference, mind and body are two expressions of the same thing. As I moved out of medical psychology, I realized another key fact about my professional stance. I couldn't build a shrine before the double-blind approach so highly revered in medical schools. It is certainly valid, but it is just one belief system among many. Belief systems should be used pragmatically, not be regarded as sacred. They should be continually transcended if something better comes along—even if that something doesn't fit into the tidy training mold of medical doctors.

Because of this position, I can draw upon the best of today's medicine and still think and act independently. Therefore, if patients have no clinical findings to back up a laundry list of complaints, I don't automatically conclude that they are hypochondriacs, neurotics, or psychotics. After an examination and the taking of a thorough history (which may not reveal reasons for their problems), I still do not paste a negative label on them. After all, no medical system or doctor is infallible. Often there is a physical basis for many symptoms, a cause not always apparent within the framework of traditional clinical medicine.

One major basis frequently overlooked is hypothyroidism—underfunctioning of the thyroid gland. Even a seemingly slight deficiency in thyroid hormone can cause an incredible number and variety of sabotaging physical, emotional, and mental ailments.

For the benefit of my patients and the expansion of my professional horizons, I am thankful that I stumbled across the monumental research in this area of Broda O. Barnes, M.D., Ph.D., one of the world's foremost authorities on the thyroid gland. This wealth of information revolutionized my practice of preventive health maintenance more than any other single factor.

Speaking from almost fifty years of clinical experimentation, Dr. Barnes stated that no less than 40 percent of the adult population of the United States suffers from an often hidden condition known as hypothyroidism. In medical school we saw a few cases, but no one paid much attention to them. The 40 percent figure struck me as a gross exaggeration until I followed the Barnes method in my practice and found the percentage running slightly higher.

Lecturing to physicians and laypeople worldwide, Dr. Barnes warned that serious hypothyroidism was going virtually undetected, because of doctors' almost total reliance upon laboratory blood tests. Why should millions suffer needlessly from the insidious effects of hypothyroidism when a simple, accurate thyroid function test was available to everyone? After all, his underarm test had been painstakingly checked for accuracy against basal metabolism results in thousands of persons in the late 1930s and early 1940s and a paper on the subject had been published in one of the most prestigious medical journals.

His hypothesis was interesting enough for me to investigate it. Why not give it a fair trial? Obviously, Dr. Barnes was not out to sell something, because thyroid hormone is one of the cheapest substances on the market. He did not claim that an underactive thyroid was the sole cause of a host of ailments, only that it played a role in them, and that many traditional treatments for chronic degenerative diseases would not work smoothly—or at all—until the thyroid gland was properly tested, and, if necessary, supplemented. Certainly he never claimed that thyroid hormone was a panacea.

About this time, I began appearing as a guest on television and radio talk shows, as well as conducting my own question-and-answer radio show in the San Francisco area, and I set up a phone interview with Dr. Barnes, then practicing medicine in Fort Collins, Colorado. For two hours, Dr. Barnes answered my questions and those from the audience so directly, factually, and convincingly that I was prompted to take my own basal temperature; I found it somewhat low. Shortly after I started using a small daily dosage of natural desiccated thyroid supplement, remarkable changes occurred: my energy shot up, my ability to concentrate improved dramatically, and many minor nagging symptoms disappeared.

Then I judiciously began using the Barnes Basal Temperature Test on a number of problem patients and, when it was indicated, prescribed the thyroid supplement. Their quick, positive response made me a believer. Soon I found that this test is the key to treating a number of chronic degenerative illnesses that I couldn't touch by conventional methods. I learned what most doctors know: that there is always a population of people who defy many of our best clinical approaches. My surprise was in seeing how large that population is.

Unusual success and satisfaction with Dr. Barnes's methods stirred up questions in my mind. How did he discover that temperature is a more reliable indicator of thyroid function than the pride of modern medical technology, lab tests? How did he learn that even slight hypothyroidism—often not detectable by conventional measuring devices or systems—can cause or contribute to serious ailments in women, men, and children?

Once I became well acquainted with Dr. Barnes, I learned firsthand the fascinating facts which have helped me treat the neglected gland of hundreds of patients in a proper manner so that they could become revitalized. Here is how he tells it:

In the early 1930s, even before planning to become a physician, I was assigned to study the thyroid gland for my doctorate in physiology at the University of Chicago, under Dr. Anton J. Carlson, a giant in the field.

Soon I had a Ph.D. after my name, and Dr. Carlson assigned me to teach endocrinology to future physicians. One of my duties was to show a motion picture to demonstrate the powerful influence of the thyroid gland on every living cell of every body system.

Students were shocked at the rapid deterioration of a small rabbit after removal of its thyroid. Previously warm at room temperature, active, and alert, the animal now shivered with cold, moved in slow motion, drugged with fatigue—as if old and feeble. Its fur was dry, its skin was scaly, its mucous membranes were infected—particularly in the respiratory system—and its heartbeat and muscles were weak. My respect for the tiny thyroid gland increased with every class.

Striving to increase my effectiveness as an instructor, I completed the medical curriculum, not realizing that I would soon do more doctoring than teaching. Upon completion of my internship in 1937, I took the Hippocratic oath, and the philosophy of Hippocrates, the Father of Greek medicine, is still branded on my brain, particularly the following statement:

"It is not to be expected that he should know the remedies of illnesses who knows not their origin."

Treating the symptoms, the usual approach in modern medicine, was not enough. I wanted to probe to the roots of illnesses, to causes. Now, licensed to practice, I had an immediate opportunity.

Charlotte, my wife, who developed tuberculosis, became my first patient. Galen, the celebrated physician of the second century, had said, "If you develop tuberculosis, go to the mountains and buy a cow."

We did both, settling in the then clean-air countryside near

Denver, where we not only drank fresh milk but picked and ate ripe vegetables and fruit from our garden and trees. Charlotte and I took a small amount of thyroid daily to compensate for hypothyroidism. Her rapid recovery and my boundless energy and endurance demonstrated the value of natural, nutrient-packed food—a major part of the foundation for good health—and thyroid supplementation.

Lessons learned from the rabbit helped with my first paying patient, a clubwoman who had complained of female problems, coldness, lack of energy, anxiety, low blood pressure, and one infection after another. She had been thoroughly examined and treated in a world-renowned midwestern clinic, where no physical reason for her symptoms could be found.

"Doctor, I spent a small fortune there and came away with no satisfaction. What makes me indignant is that they think I'm a hypochondriac."

I put her on a daily grain of natural thyroid extract and she soon improved, recovering completely in seven weeks.

That rabbit continued to make me look good. This grateful woman sent me friends who had one or more similar complaints with no apparent measurable causes: sexual dysfunction, little or no sensation in the vagina, feeling cold, excruciating menstrual pain (then commonly treated with aspirin and bedrest), too frequent periods, too copious blood flow, acute headaches, fatigue, irritability, hair-trigger temper, and infections (mainly in the vaginal and urinary channels).

Small doses of natural desiccated thyroid improved or eliminated these conditions. Husbands began coming to me. Spectacular recoveries of women and men enlightened and puzzled me. Surely so many of my patients would not have been helped by thyroid if it had not been necessary. Yet other doctors had given them comprehensive physical exams, including a basal metabolism test (the then accepted measurement of thyroid function), without detecting hypothyroidism. Could it be that thyroid deficiency too slight to be recorded contributed to or caused many illnesses? Could the basal metabolism test be so far wrong that it actually concealed hypothyroidism? Could known symptoms of low thyroid function be a more reliable indicator than the basal metabolism test?

Searching for answers—even clues—I paged through countless journals in the Denver Medical Library and found a revealing, detailed description of the first acute hypothyroid patient who had symptoms similar to those of my patients, though far more exaggerated.

In 1877 Dr. William N. Ord, a brilliant London clinician, had made a milestone discovery while performing an autopsy on a mature woman. Medical records disclosed that she had been constantly cold and exhausted, prone to fall asleep if not moving around, incapable of thinking or speaking without extreme effort, unable to sew because of numb and clumsy hands, and inclined to suffer frequent headaches and menopausal problems, as well as infections and a kidney ailment causing bloody urine.

He was fascinated by her unsightly physical degeneration—a moon face too swollen to change expression (a feature of cretinism) and body skin and connective tissue bloated with fluid. When Dr. Ord cut into her skin, expecting water to run off (as in kidney failure), a thick, glue-like substance called mucin remained fixed there. To give a name to this condition, he took the Greek word for mucin, "myx," and wedded it to "edema," the description for water-logged tissue, calling it "myxedema."

The woman's arteries showed advanced atherosclerosis. Coronary, kidney, and brain arteries were almost clogged. He was amazed at the sight of the woman's thyroid gland, so overgrown and choked with fibrous tissue that it had stopped functioning. He concluded that this was what had caused myxedema and atherosclerosis.

Mulling over the woman's list of symptoms, I found six common denominators in my far milder cases of hypothyroidism: subnormal temperature, fatigue, drowsiness, depression, female problems, and infections.

Despite exhaustive study of the thyroid gland, I still thought it incredible that this tiny, lightweight (less than an ounce), coral-colored bow tie semicircling the windpipe under the Adam's apple could be so critical to living and to the quality of life. Yet numerous well-designed experiments had already shown that production of thyroid hormone can make or break a person's health.

All of your blood—approximately five quarts—circulates through the thyroid gland once every hour, bringing iodide, the material your thyroid needs to make hormones, as well as a hormone from the anterior pituitary gland to stimulate production from the thyroid. Your thyroid also stores and discharges thyroid hormone in the bloodstream for delivery to your cells where and when needed.

Too little thyroid hormone (in hypothyroidism) causes your

motor to run sluggishly. Heartbeat slows, blood pressure drops, circulation becomes lazy (contributing to discomfort from cold, particularly in the hands and feet), energy and endurance are low, digestion slows down, constipation is common, headaches occur frequently, hair becomes lifeless and falls out more readily, nails are brittle, wounds heal slowly, thinking is slow, memory undependable, and sex urge weak or dormant. The effects of hypothyroidism are felt in each of your trillions of cells in every organ and tissue of your body.

Too much thyroid hormone, in hyperthyroidism, makes your motor race; heartbeat increases, blood pressure rises, blood volume swells; you flush from overheating, often to the level of a mild fever; you perspire profusely, are nervous and sleepless, and you may have diarrhea. (Similar symptoms may occur if a hypothyroid is given too much thyroid supplement.)

Teamwork of the thyroid and pituitary glands in infants, children, and youths encourages growth of the skeleton and sexual organs and contributes to eruption of teeth and development of the brain.

One of the most succinct and colorful summations of the dramatic function of the thyroid (which I happened upon considerably later) is in the writings of endocrinologist Herman H. Rubin, M.D.: ". . . a few grains of thyroid may be the main difference between a captain of industry and the office boy who is always dragging his feet."[1] Then he added that a close and sympathetic relationship exists between the thyroid and sex glands of men and women, that sexual function really is an expression of energy. Due to the fact the thyroid is the governor of our uses of energy, we shouldn't be too surprised by the association. Alertness, animation, fire, and sparkle result from a properly functioning thyroid. These qualities show themselves particularly in glamor and sexual attractiveness.

In my reading, I came across another succinct summary on the critical importance of the thyroid gland by the late Louis Berman, M.D., world-renowned endocrinologist:

"Without thyroid, there can be no complexity of thought, no learning, no education, no habit formation, no responsive energy for situations, as well as no physical unfolding of faculty and function. No reproduction of kind with no sign of adolescence at expected age and no exhibition of sex tendencies thereafter."[2]

With no thyroid gland, you and I would not be human at all—we'd be vegetables!

In a continuing search of the literature, I noticed that subnormal temperature appeared to be a common denominator in hypothyroidism. Many decades of pioneering research in England had demonstrated that if metabolism is low, temperature is also low. Each hypothyroid patient who came to my office was a verification of this fact.

Could temperature give a more accurate indication of hypothyroidism than the basal metabolism test? I decided to find out. In my private practice and, later, as professor of Health Education at the University of Denver, I took the oral temperature of hundreds of male and female patients and students and also gave them the basal metabolism test, making sure that no subjects had an infection, which would have caused a false reading.

I then compared results of both measurements with known symptoms of hypothyroidism and learned that temperature was the more accurate indicator by far.

In a subsequent study of 1,000 college students, reported in the August, 1942, issue of *Journal of the American Medical Association*, I again found that the relationship of subnormal temperature to accepted major symptoms of hypothyroidism was significantly greater than to basal metabolism readings.

Dr. Joseph Ehrlich and I, while U.S. Army medical officers in Kingman, Arizona, during World War II, refined the test, taking oral, rectal, and armpit temperatures of 1,000 soldiers. We found that, barring sore throats, sinusitis, or colds, which raise oral temperature, mouth and armpit temperatures are nearly identical.

Out of these experiments came the Barnes Basal Temperature Test, which, for many years, has been listed in the *Physicians' Desk Reference* (the *PDR*). Many physicians now rely on this test because by using it they have discovered tens of thousands of hypothyroid individuals who were rated normal by conventional tests. But even though the temperature test's accuracy has been abundantly demonstrated, we do not lean exclusively on its results. We verify them with classical symptoms of hypothyroidism and the patient's thorough medical history, carefully correlating and interpreting data.

Any less painstaking procedure can lead to possible error. A Mayo Clinic study by Drs. Joseph C. Scott, Jr., and Elizabeth Mussey made this point clearly when they found that a patient can be regarded as mildly hypothyroid by one physician and normal by another, based on results of just one office interview or test. "No single test or procedure will define the status of the thyroid gland," they write. "Further, any combination of methods may lead to erroneous interpretation or to inconsistent results.

The clinician must have the faculty of correlating the clinical appearance of the patient with laboratory findings."[3]

Despite the validity of this position, present-day doctors, enchanted by the laboratory test, often make it the sole and final authority. Is this wise or otherwise?

You be the judge.

The Centers for Disease Control routinely sends out specimens to 980 licensed laboratories—some 7 percent of all laboratories in the United States. Between 8 and 25 percent of the tests yield erroneous results, according to an article in *American Medical News*.[4] These labs process all kinds of tests, including critical ones for thyroid function.

Edward R. Pinckney, M.D., former associate editor of the *Journal of the American Medical Association*, wrote an earthshaking article for the *Archives of Internal Medicine* on the accuracy of medical testing. It says, in part: ". . . Hardly a week goes by when the FDA [Food and Drug Administration] does not recall several in-use laboratory reagents that are contaminated, defective, or inaccurately labeled. Other surveys have reported that one out of every two sphgymomanometers [the common blood-pressure checking device] gave erroneous readings, that thousands of ECG [electrocardiogram] machines were found to be improperly calibrated, and that hundreds of X-ray machines, often operated by inadequately trained technicians, were producing thousands of useless roentgenograms [X rays]."[5]

Dr. Pinckney reveals that in an American Medical Association survey, three out of four doctors admitted ordering X rays, ECGs, and a multitude of laboratory and other procedures for the sole purpose of having a better defense in the event of a malpractice suit.

"The American College of Physicians is in the throes of evaluating the usefulness of medical tests," writes Dr. Pinckney. "To date, it has declared some fifty tests to be of no proven value, unreliable, or obsolete."

Admitting that medical journals are constantly reporting controversy, confusion, and contradictions about the significance of tests, Dr. Pinckney advocates the old-fashioned approach to doctoring: comparing results of medical tests against the physician's clinical judgment. If the doctor doesn't do this, what good are his or her training and experience?

"In three separate but similar studies, one conducted at the Mayo Clinic, the physician's history and physical examination detected twice as many alcoholics as did detailed laboratory data," writes Dr. Pinckney.

As early as 1959, a nationally recognized authority on the thyroid gland, Dr. A. S. Jackson, had published a paper in the *Journal of the American Medical Association*, declaring that low thyroid function is the most common disease entering the doctor's office and the diagnosis most missed.[6] The situation is much the same today, except that there are more tests, more misdiagnoses, and more people.

Like Drs. Jackson and Barnes, I continue to see numerous previously undetected cases of hypothyroidism. For this reason, it was no surprise to learn that biochemist Roger J. Williams, discoverer of pantothenic acid (one of the B vitamins), says: "There are doubtless a great many people who are mildly deficient in thyroid hormone and would be benefited by taking it orally but are not ill enough to see a physician."[7]

The findings of Dr. James C. Wren, reported in the *Journal of the American Geriatric Society*, bear out those of Dr. Williams, as well as those of Drs. Barnes and Jackson.[8] In a five-year research project with 347 atherosclerotic patients—174 women and 173 men—only 31 were shown by laboratory tests to be hypothyroid. Yet when thyroid supplements were given to all subjects, measurable improvement was shown in a significant number of patients. Further, their mortality rate was less than half that of the run of this category of untreated patients. Why were results of thyroid treatment apparent across the board if only thirty-one subjects—9 percent—were hypothyroid according to conventional laboratory tests? (Later chapters will offer additional revealing data on how hypothyroidism relates to heart and artery diseases.)

A nationally known physician and author, New York City–based H. L. Newbold, M.D., who has successfully used the Barnes Basal Temperature Test for years, agrees with Dr. Barnes in his book, *Dr. Newbold's Revolutionary New Discoveries About Weight Loss*, that many people have borderline or subnormal thyroid output and can enhance their health with modest amounts of thyroid supplement.[9]

In an article, "Hypothyroidism: A Treacherous Masquerader"

(*Acute Care Medicine*, May, 1984, pages 34–36), Dr. Gerald S. Levey, an endocrinologist and chief of medicine at the University of Pittsburgh School of Medicine, warns that hypothyroidism is often such an extremely subtle disease that physicians can misinterpret its symptoms.

The correct diagnosis is often missed, because a broad range of symptoms is not generally associated with hypothyroidism, he says: severe muscle cramps, particularly at night; persistent low back pain; blood abnormalities (easy bruising, minor bleeding, heavy blood loss in menstruation, and anemia); excessive blood uric acid; stiffness of joints (mild arthritis); and a decrease in heart contractility.

These conditions can be improved or relieved by thyroid hormone therapy, he says. Dr. Levey feels that traditional routine screening for thyroid function may leave something to be desired, inasmuch as many factors—among them drugs and certain systemic states—can distort results of such tests.

Various researchers have estimated that one-fourth of the United States population is hypothyroid—considerably under the forty-plus percentage of my new patients.

You may be among them.

Now, however, you don't have to wonder whether you are or aren't. You can gather the evidence through the Barnes Basal Temperature Test, a careful review of your medical history, and a check of your symptoms against the following telltale physical and emotional signs: (1) weakness; (2) dry, coarse skin; (3) lethargy; (4) slow speech; (5) swelling of face and eyelids; (6) coldness and cold skin; (7) diminished sweating; (8) thick tongue; (9) coarse hair; (10) pale skin; (11) constipation; (12) gain in weight; (13) loss of hair; (14) labored, difficult breathing; (15) swollen feet; (16) hoarseness; (17) loss of appetite; (18) excessive and/or painful menstruation; (19) nervousness; (20) heart palpitation; (21) brittle nails; (22) slow movement; (23) poor memory; (24) emotional instability; (25) depression; and (26) headaches.

If your temperature, medical history, and symptoms indicate that you are hypothyroid, report to your doctor with the facts and request treatment. Most physicians are now familiar with Dr. Barnes's method of treatment and his extensive list of publications in medical journals.

It is not my intention to indicate that additional thyroid hormone is a cure-all for anything or everything that might ail you. This would be simplistic, narrow, and possibly inaccurate, ignoring many other considerations, including biological and biochemical differences which make you and me individuals with varying needs.

What I am saying is that a broad and serious blind spot exists today in physical diagnosis, one that needs immediate recognition. The purpose of this book is to serve as a newly ground, polished set of lenses to bring all parts of this area sharply into our visual fields.

Awareness of widespread hypothyroidism and the three-way approach to its accurate diagnosis will enable you to do one of two things: rule it out entirely or get proper treatment for it. This condition is too important to go ignored and untreated. It only worsens. Remember that the thyroid—the neglected gland—can have a mild to profound effect on every aspect of living: energy, endurance, body heat, sexuality, mind and emotions, resistance to colds and other respiratory ailments, and condition of hair, skin, and nails, as well as protection against diabetes and diabetic complications, heart and artery diseases, and cancer. It affects how long and how well you live!

2

WHY SO MUCH HIDDEN HYPOTHYROIDISM?

*O*ften patients, viewers of my *Medicine Man* TV program, or readers of my newspaper column ask, "How can hypothyroidism possibly be so widespread with iodized salt available to everyone?"

An important question deserves a good answer.

Iodized salt was never intended to prevent hypothyroidism, just one manifestation of it: goiter, enlargement of the thyroid gland on the front and sides of the neck. It would not be practical or healthful for us to increase salt use in an effort to get all the iodine necessary to assure normal thyroid function. Overuse of salt is implicated in a host of ailments—insomnia, obesity, stomach ulcers, edema, high blood pressure, and heart disease, among others.

The daily Recommended Dietary Allowance (RDA) of iodine is 100 micrograms (mcg) for women and 120 mcg for men, although up to ten times that amount has not produced toxic effects in persons with a normal thyroid. Residents of Japan thrive on nearly 4,000 times as much iodine as Americans, all from large amounts of seafood, kelp, dulse, and sea lettuce. (Warning: it could be hazardous to health, if not fatal, to ingest so much iodine in supplement form.)

Goiter, premature gray hair, and symptoms of hypothyroidism are rare in Japan. Is it any wonder? Much of the nation's population lives near the coast, and both soil and water are iodine rich at or near seashores. So are vegetables, fruit, and grains grown there, as well as readily accessible seafood and ocean plants.

Although we require only a minute quantity of iodine for our thyroid glands, the world's goiter belts supply just one-seventh of that amount. Goiter belts are found in mountainous or inland regions, such as the Alps, Carpathian, and Pyrenees mountains of Europe, the Himalayas of Asia, the Andes mountains of South America, and various parts of North America, including the valley of the St. Lawrence River, the Appalachian mountains, the Great Lakes basin, and westward through Minnesota, South and North Dakota, Montana, Wyoming (and adjoining areas of Canada), the Rocky Mountains, and into the northwest (parts of Oregon, Washington, and British Columbia).

Over the course of many centuries, soils of mountain and inland areas become iodine bankrupt because rain washes this trace mineral away into streams and, eventually, into the oceans. Low iodine content in the soil, however, is not the sole reason for subnormal thyroid function. Another weighty factor is inheritance. Several studies show that goiters and hypothyroidism without goiters run in families, many of whose members are hypersensitive even to minute iodine lack. Individuals prone to hypothyroidism are often revealed to have subnormal thyroid function, despite what appears to be an adequate intake of iodine.

Why did 7 percent of 8,000 schoolchildren with adequate iodine intake, surveyed in the early 1970s in Georgia, Kentucky, Michigan, and Texas, have goiters? Why did the 1968 to 1970 study of individuals in ten states—from California to Massachusetts—by the Centers for Disease Control end up with almost the same results? Again, more than 99 percent of those surveyed reported an acceptable intake of iodine.

A research project by Eduardo Gaitan of the Veterans Administration Medical Center and University of Mississippi Medical School, Jackson, leads him to believe region-specific environmental factors are often to blame. Returning to his native Colombia, South America, he studied this problem in the Cauca-Patia Valley area of the Andes mountains.[1] In 1948, more than half of all schoolchildren there had goiters. The correct amount of iodine was added to the daily diet, but a 1978 survey revealed that 15 percent of the population still had goiters. Gaitan wanted to know why within this 800-kilometer-long valley the goiter incidence ranged from 1 percent to 42 percent.

His investigation permitted him to rule out insufficient iodine intake, other dietary shortcomings and socioeconomic factors. "It is certain chemicals in the water supply," he told an American Chemical Society meeting in Seattle, and elaborated his reasons for this belief. He had found a high-goiter area and a low-goiter area in Candelaria, a nonindustrial city in the Andes with a population of 8,000. This confused him until he learned that two different wells supplied the sections. Gaitan had water samples analyzed by an impartial testing laboratory, and the chemical culprits emerged in water from the high-goiter district—10 to 100 parts per million of resorcinol and phthalate esters. Resorcinol has a documented reputation as a goiter causative. The phthalate esters (normally added to various plastics to give them flexibility) also contain substances which encourage goiters. No resorcinol and negligible amounts of phthalates could be found in the water samples from the low-goiter area.

What puzzled Gaitan is how resorcinol and phthalates could enter the water supply, inasmuch as they are common products of the industrial world, and Candelaria has no industry. Pipes from the well with the high level of contaminants were not made of plastics and plastic containers were not used in gathering or storing water samples. Gaitan finally concluded that these chemicals came from organic soil constituents 200 feet down.

For self-protection, it would be well for us to avoid or minimize our consumption of beverages stored in plastic containers and to check with officials of the municipal water supply to make sure it does not have a harmful content of resorcinol or phthalate esters from industrial wastes.

While Gaitan's findings may well apply to previously unexplained goiter prevalence in areas amply supplied with iodine, individual variation in size and capability of thyroid glands may also play a big part.

Dr. Roger J. Williams, whose studies on the size and functional variation of human organs have revolutionized physiology and biochemistry, writes in his book *Free and Unequal* that, among what are called normal individuals, thyroid glands vary in weight from 8 grams to 50 grams. Undoubtedly size and activity of one's thyroid gland make a difference.[2] Heredity is also an important factor.

One would have thought it possible that, in the course of several generations, marriages between hypothyroids and persons with normal thyroids would decrease hypothyroids in the population. Actually, there appear to be few such intermarriages, as many physicians conversant with problems of the thyroid have observed. Hypothyroids usually attract other hypothyroids for a basic reason: they have low energy and high sleep requirements in common. Even when short, impulsive courtships bring hypothyroids and those with normal thyroids to the altar, these couples soon realize their glaring energy mismatch and, in time, may end up in the divorce court.

In my early days of prescribing thyroid, I discovered it was a serious mistake to treat just one person of a hypothyroid couple. One of my patients was a pudgy, sluggish, no-energy man who hardly made it through a workday, mechanically munched a TV dinner with an equally dragged-out wife, then collapsed heavily into a sexless bed. A daily grain of thyroid and a diet without junk foods brought about a remarkable change in him in less than three months. He lost weight, gained energy, slept less, and began going out at night, insisting that his weary wife join him in going to parties and attending concerts and the theater. Their contrasting energy levels triggered repeated quarrels. Rather than let them live unhappily ever after, I insisted that the wife take her basal temperature. Learning that it was way below par, I prescribed natural desiccated thyroid. Now this couple has made new breakthroughs in marital harmony.

The growing population of persons with subnormal thyroid glands is not entirely due, however, to the procreation of hypothyroid couples. Medical ingenuity has something to do with it. Antibiotics have made hypothyroids less susceptible to infectious diseases which in years past would have annihilated them. Less than a century ago, almost 50 percent of all children died before becoming adults. Only those who could resist infectious diseases survived. At that time, medical science contributed little to the ability to survive. Today, over and above those who are normally infection resistant, there is a new population segment—hypothyroids with low resistance to infectious diseases, who are kept alive by the physician's arsenal of antibiotics.

Dr. Barnes draws a sharp focus on the historic battle to survive in pointing out that humanity is constantly threatened by a grim competition of diseases: "Smallpox led the pack for many years, wiping out babies and children. Then an obscure physician, Edward Jenner, discovered that smallpox could be prevented by vaccination. Soon the champion killer was dethroned, and a larger segment of the population could live longer. Then a new menace moved in, tuberculosis, which, for more than two generations, decimated young adults, until bedrest, improved diet and, particularly, antibiotics knocked it out. Again, life expectancy rose, making the biggest advance in medical history. One disease or another keeps proving our mortality. Due to our longer life through the conquest of many infectious diseases, another killer has now claimed the championship—heart and circulatory ailments," he says.

Like Dr. Barnes, other medical doctors, clinical researchers, and scientists over more than eight decades have found that thyroid supplements have won skirmishes, battles, even wars, against myriad ailments in addition to the so-called hypochondriacal conditions: fatigue, physical and sexual coldness, infectious diseases, every kind of female problem, emotional illnesses, migraine headaches, skin abnormalities, heart disease, arthritis, diabetic complications, and cancer.

It is time for medical researchers and doctors to take a fresh look at the thyroid—the neglected gland—at present laboratory tests for thyroid function and at treatment of its subnormal function.

Often I am asked by patients or audiences why, if they are

revealed to be hypothyroid, they cannot correct their condition simply by supplying more iodine to their thyroid glands through seafood or kelp. Sometimes they can. In first-generation hypothyroidism, such compensation often proves helpful. However, in most cases, hypothyroidism has persisted for generations, so iodine supplementation may be too little, too late. This is not my finding alone. Dr. Barnes and more than one hundred of his physician followers have discovered the same phenomenon. Through experience, we have discovered that natural desiccated thyroid supplement helps make sure that enough thyroid hormone is available. It takes less than 1/100,000 ounce of this substance to keep us healthy.

A commonsense approach now assists doctors in administering thyroid supplement safely and effectively. The fear of prescribing it, so prevalent from the start of this century to the 1940s, is slowly disappearing. The secret is to balance the amount of the supplement with the amount of hormone secreted by the thyroid gland, so that an oversupply does not lull the gland into complacency and stop it from working. When the blood level of thyroid hormone drops below normal, the hypothalamus gland in the brain senses this and discharges thyroid-releasing hormone (TRH). TRH influences the pituitary, the boss of the glandular company, to release thyroid-stimulating hormone (TSH), which tells the thyroid to get to work. Once sufficient thyroid hormone has been produced, the pituitary puts the thyroid gland on hold.

A thyroid whose function is limited by lack of iodine, by a hereditary flaw, or by a tumor or some other defect can't carry out the orders of the pituitary gland. Then it needs help from the outside.

When the subnormal working of the thyroid results from the gland itself, this is called primary hypothyroidism. When under-production is caused by imperfect function of the hypothalamus or the pituitary gland, this is called secondary hypothyroidism. Both kinds usually respond to thyroid hormone supplementation.

I start hypothyroid patients with a moderate daily dose of natural thyroid—¼ to ½ grain of Armour desiccated thyroid preparation—and increase their dosage in ¼ to ½ grain increments every seven to ten days until I obtain a dosage that achieves desired clinical results.

Usually, a child under age three requires no more than ¼ grain until he or she reaches age six, at which time ½ grain is most frequently the optimum amount needed. Teenagers generally work up to a full grain, and adults go as high as several grains. I monitor patients carefully, and if symptoms disappear, I keep them at this level.

I also advise that patients take a multivitamin and mineral supplement rich in B vitamins, inasmuch as, according to Murray Israel, M.D., a pioneer in thyroidology, B vitamins are essential to efficient transport of oxygen inside the cells. Originally, Dr. Barnes used thyroid hormones alone—with success—but, impressed by Dr. Israel's results, he added vitamin B–rich brewer's yeast tablets to his treatment.

Dr. Israel's career in recognizing and managing widespread, unsuspected hypothyroidism also helped focus my attention on this much-neglected area of medicine. Startling results with his first case in 1934, as described at the 1966 annual meeting of the American College of Endocrinology and Nutrition, left an indelible impression on me.[3]

Called in to treat an elderly woman so far gone that her family had brought in a priest to administer the last rites, Dr. Israel found her breathing shallow, heart sounds faint, blood pressure high, coronary artery severely atherosclerotic, and hypothyroidism pronounced. She had stark white hair and her pale face was flecked with dead skin. Fresh out of internship, Dr. Israel had a critical decision to make. From the standpoint of conventional medicine, the woman had two incompatible conditions, atherosclerosis and hypothyroidism. The usual treatment was to remove the thyroid gland surgically. The easy way out would have been to do nothing, but Dr. Israel decided to do something. Surgery would only make her hypothyroidism worse, so he administered 10 milligrams of thyroid along with brewer's yeast three times daily. (Brewer's yeast was then the best available vitamin B–complex source.)

He continued this regime, and in a few days, the patient turned the corner. Within two weeks, she was mentally alert and perky and walked to church. Soon her dead, pale skin peeled off, leaving her complexion pink and smooth. Black strands of hair eventually began to replace some of the white. She lived actively and enthusiastically for another twenty years.

This milestone case set a pattern of treatment for Dr. Israel, which, over the course of many years, he used successfully in over a thousand similar cases. In addition to alerting modern medicine to a more effective approach for managing coronary atherosclerosis and hypothyroidism, his triumphs spared patients with these ailments the harmful, unnecessary, and costly removal of the thyroid gland and showed doctors that judicious supplementation with natural desiccated thyroid can be helpful *and* safe.

What excited Dr. Israel particularly was that the thyroid treatment had an apparent rejuvenative effect on patients. These results also intrigued a young medical doctor, Nathan Masor, who later joined Dr. Israel's research staff. After injecting Dr. Israel's formula into elderly atherosclerotic patients each week for a month, along with supplements of vitamins C and B-complex, he noticed marked physical and emotional improvement: more energy, faster movements, more endurance, better sleep, and less irritability, anxiety, and depression.

Encouraged, Dr. Masor did additional research, eventually concluding that organic and functional diseases are intertwined, showing two basic manifestations—fatigue and anxiety—which, in turn, cause myriad satellite symptoms, among them headache, hot flashes, depression, drowsiness, insomnia, irritability, loss of memory, inability to concentrate, impotence, guilt, and inferiority feelings.

In his book *The New Psychiatry*, Dr. Masor states that symptoms of hypochondria can mimic those of any organic disease, that when fatigue and anxiety begin to disappear, so do satellite symptoms in varying degrees.[4] He explained his thyroid-vitamin therapy to the Second International Congress for Psychiatry in Zurich, Switzerland.

Dr. Masor is skeptical about the accuracy and helpfulness of the usual laboratory tests for thyroid function and asks if it isn't possible that such modern tests are incapable of detecting every case of malfunctioning thyroid gland. "This is strongly suspected in the condition of metabolic insufficiency (hypothyroidism)," he says, "wherein all tests prove normal, but the individual may suffer from a fully developed fatigue and anxiety state."[5]

On the same subject, Dr. Israel's findings are even more decisive than those of his protege. In almost forty years of practice, studies and experimentation at the Vascular Research Foundation in New York, which he founded, he observed that laboratory tests failed to uncover even a minute fraction of hypothyroids.[6] Standard tests indicated that 85 percent of his patients had normal thyroid function. Yet all of them showed marked and consistent benefits from thyroid supplementation, including comfortable body temperature and increased energy and vitality.

With so much undiagnosed hypothyroidism, it is no wonder that patients with legitimate emotional, mental, and physical symptoms are sometimes written off as hypochondriacs and, even worse, left untreated, living fractional lives.

3

CARE AND FEEDING OF
THE THYROID

*D*on't take your thyroid gland for granted! Even if it is now normal, it may not stay that way unless properly fed, as one of my patients learned.

Mark's subnormal temperature, symptoms, and medical history indicated hypothyroidism.

"How can that be?" He was genuinely surprised. "I take kelp tablets for iodine."

Mark had been a vegetarian for a few years, eating raw and lightly cooked vegetables, with an emphasis on carrots, sweet potatoes, spinach, tomatoes, rutabagas, cabbage, and turnips.

After carefully examining a list of his daily foods, I observed,

"Your diet seems short on protein and on at least three vitamins necessary to keep your thyroid working normally, particularly vitamin A."

That puzzled him.

"Something's wrong here, Doctor. I get plenty of vitamin A in carrots, sweet potatoes, spinach, and tomatoes."

"That's not true. What you get in these vegetables is carotene, a precursor of vitamin A. An underactive thyroid gland cannot efficiently convert carotene to usable vitamin A. In addition, vegetables such as rutabagas, cabbage, and turnips, eaten daily, suppress thyroid function even more."

That was just the surface aspect of Mark's thyroid deficiency. I pointed out that he lacked vitamins B_2, B_6, and B_{12}, the former two further reducing his thyroid gland function. He rejected the idea of eating liver, which would have satisfied requirements of the B vitamins, so I recommended almonds, milk, wheat germ, and brewer's yeast for vitamin B_2; bananas, barley, wheat bran, wheat germ, and brewer's yeast for vitamin B_6 and, inasmuch as he wouldn't eat meat, the best other sources of vitamin B_{12}—eggs, American and Swiss cheese, and two kinds of fish, haddock and sole. I also put Mark on a grain of natural thyroid until the new diet could return his thyroid function to normal. Several months later this happened, and he is healthy again.

Although Mark's case was quite straightforward, that of Kathleen, a girl in her early teens, had mystified several other doctors and now challenged me. Once rather plump, ridiculed by schoolmates, she had opted for vegetarianism, despite parental objection, and had shed 34 pounds. Now she suffered from daily diarrhea, extreme sluggishness, and a seeming wasting away of muscles. She wore sunglasses even in my office.

"Is the light too bright?" I asked.

"Yes."

"Do you have any other eye problems?"

"It's a little hard for me to see at night," she replied.

"On a vegetarian diet, unless you work at it, it is difficult to take in enough protein—and enough of certain vitamins—to sustain you."

"My parents make me take a protein supplement twice every day," she responded.

That stopped me for an instant. However, her case triggered

recall of a fascinating study done some years ago in India. Mass suffering from the protein deficiency disease kwashiorkor by tens of thousands of children prompted an American medical relief team to fly in to correct the situation. In kwashiorkor, the most prominent symptoms are wasting tissues, physical and mental sluggishness, swollen bellies, eye ailments—sometimes blindness—and even mental retardation. Immediately, the medical team fed the children a good grade of protein—powdered skim milk—expecting a reversal within weeks. Nothing beneficial happened, however, and they were baffled. Weeks ran into months, and the children grew steadily worse.

A second medical team flew in to help—doctors expert in eye ailments. Noting the myriad eye problems, they added vitamin A—a vitamin essential to good health of eyes—to the protein-enriched diet. Eye ailments began clearing up, and the children recovered from symptoms of protein deficiency. These doctors then ran painstaking tests and evaluated results, concluding that vitamin A must accompany protein to make it available to the body.

Kwashiorkor is a common disease in countries like India and parts of Africa and South America, where poverty prevents millions from eating enough protein and vitamin A–rich foods such as meats and milk. Now how could a teenage girl in California show some of the symptoms of kwashiorkor? Apparently by following a diet not too different from those of kwashiorkor victims. I told my patient what had happened to the children in India, got her agreement to add milk products and eggs to her diet, gave her a good vitamin A supplement, vitamin B-complex, and half a grain of thyroid to compensate for a malnourished thyroid gland. She did an amazing about-face. Today, she is a beautiful, slim, healthy young woman.

You may conclude from these cases that I do not favor a strict vegetarian diet; that is correct. Unless one is an experienced biochemist or nutritionist and knows the pedigrees of vegetables and fruits—that is, how they are grown, where, and with what kinds of fertilizers—it is difficult to secure enough protein and B vitamins.

Many years ago, Dr. William J. Albrecht of the University of Missouri investigated protein and vitamin content of commercially available vegetables and found that their food values had declined steadily because growers did not replace all the elements which the plants remove from the soil. Numerous more recent studies have shown the same alarming trend. Furthermore, vegetables and fruits contain only a negligible amount of vitamin B_{12}. Most of us require just an infinitesimal amount of vitamin B_{12} daily—one microgram (one-millionth of a gram). If we don't get that much, however, we run the risk of pernicious anemia and possibly death. If my patients insist on strict vegetarianism, I tell them to proceed at their own peril, urging them to add milk, other dairy products, and eggs as dietary insurance.

Not long ago I ran across a chilling item in the nationally syndicated newspaper column of Dr. Lawrence Power that demonstrates the hazards of uncompromising vegetarianism better than I can. Dr. Power cited a hospital report on twenty-five infants born in a religious community which adheres to a strict vegetarian diet. Twenty-five deathly ill babies were rushed to the hospital. Three were dead on arrival. Five more died a few hours after admittance, all from malnutrition. The remaining seventeen—severely malnourished—were returned to good health by more complete nutrition. Upon entry into the hospital, the surviving infants had enteritis, pneumonia, and anemia. Nine had acute rickets. The remainder showed involuntary muscle twitching.

I see too many risks in the Spartan vegetarian diet. Most vegetarians are opposed to eating red meat, but I see no reason why they can't include poultry and fish in their diets, or at least dairy products and eggs. (More about the value of eggs in the chapter on the heart.) The great peril of the strict vegetarian diet is suppression of the protective and life-giving thyroid function by minimizing the intake of essential vitamins.

In one of the most comprehensive published surveys of the effects of nutritional substances on thyroid health and function, Isobel Jennings of the University College, University of Cambridge, England, says in her biochemistry classic, *Vitamins in Endocrine Metabolism*, that carotene, the vitamin A precursor, is not easily translated into vitamin A.[1] Vitamin A is far better absorbed than carotene from vegetable sources, which is probably converted to vitamin A in the liver.

The malnutrition in the case of the babies mentioned earlier probably came about because infants (as well as adults with gastroenteritis) have a much reduced capacity for converting carotene to vitamin A. In hypothyroids and diabetics, this ability is nearly completely blocked. Without enough vitamin A, the infants could not make their limited protein supply available to their bodies.[2]

Just how do certain vitamin deficiencies affect the thyroid gland and its function? Studies cited by Isobel Jennings show that when animals are shortchanged on vitamin A, their ability to produce thyroid-stimulating hormone (TSH) is limited. Vitamin A–deficient cattle and sheep show degeneration of pituitary gland basophils, the cells where TSH is synthesized.[3]

In the world of glands, the pituitary is king; it controls the structure and output of the thyroid gland by means of TSH and makes sure that there is enough thyroid hormone circulating in the blood to service the living cells. When this level has been reached, thyroid hormone (TH) shuts off production of TSH and inhibits the release of added TH. Vitamin A deficiency also influences the thyroid gland directly in two ways. The rate at which this gland can take up its major nutrient, iodine, is reduced, along with the amount of TH secreted.

A Danish researcher, B. Palludan, found that after two weeks of severe vitamin A deficiency, thyroid secretion of pigs was reduced by 40 to 50 percent. In other experiments, when thyroid glands were removed from rabbits, they developed bulging eyes, a condition called xerophthalmia. Administration of vitamin A corrected the eye disorder; carotene did not. Researchers have concluded that without a functioning thyroid—or adequate supplementation—vitamin A can be metabolized, but carotene cannot.

Like vitamin A, vitamin B_2 (riboflavin) exerts a powerful influence on how well or how poorly the thyroid gland works. Animal experiments reveal that in a vitamin B_2 shortage, function of the ovaries or testes is often depressed, and that changes occur in all glands—particularly in the thyroid and adrenals—which fail to secrete their hormones.[4]

Another powerful member of the vitamin B family, B_3 (niacin), helps assure the good health of your thyroid and other glands. All living cells require niacin, since it assists in respiration and in the metabolism of carbohydrates, proteins, and fats.[5] This vitamin is essential for keeping your cells—including those of your endocrine glands—in efficient working order.

A thyroid gland starved of vitamin B_6 (pyridoxine) cannot utilize its iodine raw material efficiently in the making of hormones that are a matter of life or death to us. Physiologists are not sure if this action is directly on the thyroid or on the pituitary gland, in which it may block the synthesis and release of TSH.[6]

Unless we feed the thyroid gland properly, we can't efficiently absorb another critical vitamin, B_{12} (cyanocobalamin). In laboratory tests, rats without thyroid glands could not absorb vitamin B_{12} at all.[7]

Earlier we mentioned that acute vitamin B_{12} deficiency could bring on death from pernicious anemia. Other serious symptoms are mental illness, various neurological disorders, neuralgia, neuritis, and bursitis. This vitamin is one of the most temperamental of the B family. It can't be manufactured in our intestines and therefore must be ingested in foods or supplements. Some of us are not well enough supplied with what is called "the intrinsic factor," which makes it possible to absorb vitamin B_{12}. Subnormal thyroid function is undoubtedly a little-known reason why many of us cannot make the best use of the vitamin B_{12} in our diets.

Although I do administer vitamin B_{12} shots to patients desperately low in this nutrient, I prefer to make certain that their thyroids are normal to assure proper absorption. Then, for non-vegetarians, I recommend the richest sources of B_{12}: beef liver, beef kidney, and beef round. Fortunately, many good vitamin B_{12} supplements are sold in nutrition stores. Hypothyroids usually show dramatic uptake of vitamin B_{12} once their blood levels of thyroid hormone are raised with natural desiccated thyroid supplement.

The thyroid gland is also hypersensitive to too little vitamin C (ascorbic acid) in the daily diet. When guinea pigs, which, unlike most of the lower animals, cannot synthesize ascorbic acid from other food substances, were made deficient in this vitamin, capillaries in the thyroid gland began bleeding, a condition which became even worse in acute scurvy. Additionally, in long-standing vitamin C deficiency, normal cells of the thyroid gland multiply at an abnormal rate—a condition called hyperplasia—and secrete too much hormone, as if the governing influence of the pituitary gland had been nullified. Once the guinea pigs were well supplied with vitamin C, all three negative conditions disappeared.

As is the case with depletion of ascorbic acid, experimental animals (rabbits) deficient in vitamin E showed unnaturally rapid multiplication of normal thyroid gland cells, as well as too little TSH synthesized by the pituitary gland.[8] Rats demonstrated the same basic response to deficiency of vitamin E, and in, addition, they transmitted hyperplasia to litters born to them. Most of the young failed to survive.[9]

A sense of horror comes over me when I think of the true significance of the last two experiments mentioned, namely, that a shortage of vitamins C and E brings about a condition which appears to be hyperthyroidism—overproduction of thyroid hormone and a racing of the metabolic motor. What appalls me is that, from the turn of the century until the late 1950s, it was standard surgical procedure to remove the thyroid gland that was over- or underproductive. A great number of such operations might have been avoided merely by compensating for certain vitamin deficiencies.

To sum it all up, it is possible in many instances to correct unbalanced thyroid hormone production—too much or too little—merely by compensating for certain vitamin deficiencies. *Some* cases of hypothyroidism can be successfully treated even without taking thyroid supplements.

Certain facts of life about nutrition and the thyroid have been known for the past twenty or thirty years. Yet they have never seen print in anything but medical publications, and there only rarely. One of this book's missions is to fill in the broad knowledge gap—to make you and your doctor aware that how and what you eat may be slowing down or speeding up your thyroid or even injuring it.

Individuals who have been proved to be hyperthyroid usually have part of their thyroid gland removed by surgery or by radiation. Some, however, are given chemicals such as thiouracil or thiourea to counteract overproduction of hormone. Doctors who are not nutritionoriented don't always realize that thiouracil and thiourea are thyroid antagonists, as Isobel Jennings points out. These drugs prevent conversion of carotene into usable vitamin A. Therefore, strict vegetarians suffer.[10] If the patient fails to take preformed vitamin A—not the carotene—he or she soon depletes vitamin A stores in the liver and kidneys. Then, because dietary protein cannot be used, the patient slowly declines into malnourishment. However, Isobel Jennings indicates that if the doctor prescribes thyroid supplementation to overcome the vitamin antagonists, carotene can be converted into vitamin A and assimilated, making protein absorption possible once more.

The overactive thyroid gland of the hyperthyroid individual has a hunger for vitamin B_1 (thiamine), using much and excreting much. Therefore, a high intake of this vitamin is necessary.[11] Likewise, demand for vitamin B_6 (pyridoxine) is high in hyperthyroidism and also when protein intake is generous. Depletion of this vitamin in hyperthyroidism is sometimes so great that only daily injection can prevent a common ailment, muscle weakness.[12] Other vitamins, too, are drawn upon heavily in hyperthyroidism, particularly vitamin C, which is literally drained from the tissues.[13] Some experimenters have found that the taking of vitamin D by hyperthyroids counteracts the usual rapid excretion of calcium, and the blood level of calcium returns to normal.[14] Higher intake of vitamin E is often needed as well to counteract the great amounts depleted from the system by this condition.[15]

Hyperthyroidism stimulates the metabolism of essential fatty acids (EFA), which the thyroid gland requires to function normally. Rats deprived of EFA become hyperactive with excessive thyroid hormone production. Experimenters do not yet know why this happens.[16]

A deficiency of EFA and vitamins is not the only cause of an unbalanced thyroid. Certain drugs and chemicals can suppress it as well. In a number of studies, sulfa drugs and antidiabetic agents interfered with the formation of thyroid hormones by inhibiting iodine uptake. It has been shown that prednisone should be used judiciously in known or suspected hypothyroidism, because, in pharmacologic doses, it indirectly worsens already abnormal thyroid function. So does estrogen in pharmacologic doses, an important consideration for women on birth control pills or hormone replacement therapy.

The next chapter will serve as a red flag to warn you of hidden hazards and danger in the water you drink, the air you breathe, and the food you eat—environmental saboteurs of your thyroid gland.

4

WHAT'S SABOTAGING YOUR
THYROID?

There's more to keeping your thyroid healthy than an ample amount of iodine and other nutrients just mentioned—as crucially important as they are. Chapter 2 *(Why So Much Hidden Hypothyroidism?)* touched lightly on some key factors.

Studies of Eduardo Gaitan, chief of endocrinology at the University of Mississippi School of Medicine, reveal that an estimated four hundred million people worldwide have from slightly enlarged thyroid glands to full-fledged goiters—some as large as the belly of a pregnant woman. Such conditions indicate reduced thyroid gland function.[1]

One-quarter of these individuals—one hundred million people—have goiters that can't be traced to a lack of sufficient dietary iodine. They may be victims of goiter-producing geological factors, states Gaitan.

Like what?

Environmental pollutants in drinking water tend to limit thyroid function and cause goiters. In certain Appalachian coal-mining areas of Kentucky "as many as 37 percent of the children have large goiters," writes Gaitan—this, despite an adequate intake of iodine.

He notes that children are more susceptible to goiter than adults. And this condition is especially harmful to children, because they are in the formative stage. Therefore, they can suffer both physical and mental problems if this condition is not treated.

An extreme example of this is cretinism, defined in *Webster's Collegiate Dictionary* (Tenth Edition) as "a congenital, abnormal condition marked by physical stunting and mental retardation and caused by severe hypothyrodism." Adult cretinism is attributed to the cumulative damage from low thyroid function over many generations.

Studies by Gaitan and associates in these Kentucky regions revealed resorcinol, a well-known thyroid inhibitor, present in much of the well water there.

"We also found other compounds in the water—phthalates—which, under the action of bacteria, can be transformed into dihydroxy benzoic acids: thyroid inhibitors," Gaitan told *Science News*.[1] He also reported finding them in his research in high-goiter areas of Colombia, as stated in chapter 2.

Why are these substances that apply the biochemical brakes to thyroid function so prevalent in the Kentucky regions mentioned? Both resorcinol and dihydroxy benzoic acids are waste materials in the coal-mining process, says Gaitan. So, it is likely that they may be present in any coal-mining areas of the world.

Other harmful chemicals discovered by Gaitan in drinking water in high-goiter areas of Kentucky, but not Colombia, are methoxy anthracene and bromoform. In investigating children in these Kentucky regions, he and associates found that one-third of affected children "make antibodies against their own thyroid glands"—a serious disorder called autoimmune thyroiditis.

Citing studies by other researchers, Gaitan mentions that buffalo rats given methoxy anthracene and bromoform develop autoimmune thyroiditis, a condition more fully covered in a later chapter.

Another key piece in the goiter jigsaw puzzle was a discovery made some years ago by Sir Robert McCarrison, a noted English medical doctor who traveled worldwide searching for environmental sources of goiter.[2] He found that, although people in Hunza, high in the Himalaya mountains in northern Pakistan, were eminently healthy and living long, with no goiters, inhabitants in nearby areas where climate, soil (and its iodine content), and water were similar, suffered goiters, other forms of hypothyroidism, and less than ideal health.

Why? Sir Robert observed that the Hunzas were close to pure water sources, pristine white snow and ice, and kept their drinking water clean in roofed tanks and cisterns, protected from environmental contamination and animals.

However, near Hunza, nine villages on the mountainside, one below the other, share water that rolls down through an open channel. This water is used for drinking, bathing, washing clothing and household utensils, crop irrgation, and to drain off manured fields, wrote McCarrison. Each village receives pollution-laden water from villages above, and the last one suffers the most accumulated pollutants. Other researchers have found that such contaminated water usually contains the poison cyanide, a well-established thyroid depressant. McCarrison's census of goiters shows a steady increase from the highest village to the lowest.

However, contaminated water is not limited to people in Third World countries. It exists in many parts of the United States. Government surveys reveal that goiter is nearly always more prevalent in rural areas. Many, if not most, wells yield polluted water. So individuals who escape to rural areas for freedom, home-grown food, and well water may be little better off than residents of the nine Himalayan villages.

During floods, brooks and rivers fill up with organic matter and chemical fertilizers. When a drought follows, the contaminants become more concentrated, and the cyanide content of the water increases. This is when goiter epidemics usually occur.

Ever since 1854, it has been known that fluoride is one of the most potent inhibitors of thyroid function, particularly in areas where soils and water are iodine deficient. Individuals who drink fluoridated water regularly and show a low temperature on the Barnes Basal Temperature Test may experience thyroid suppression—an excellent reason for using pure, bottled, spring water. In most instances, eliminating flouridated water restores thyroid function to normal.

Certain drugs and chemicals suppress thyroid function. Many barbiturates contain cyanide and produce hydrocyanic acid in the body. In a number of studies, sulfa drugs and antidiabetic agents interfered with the formation of thyroid hormones by blocking iodine uptake. As indicated previously, it has been shown that prednisone should be judiciously used in known or suspected hypothyroidism, because in pharmacologic doses, it indirectly worsens already subnormal thyroid function. So does estrogen in pharmacologic doses, an important consideration for women on birth control pills or hormone replacement therapy.

Various medications can contribute to hypothyroidism—among them some cough medicines, amiodarone HC1 (Cordarone) and lithium (used as an antidepressant or for treating bipolar disorder)—by blocking the secretion of both major thyroid hormones: T_4 and T_3. Dopamine and corticosteroids suppress the pituitary gland's secretion of thyroid stimulating hormones (TSH), essential for proper functioning of the thyroid gland. Corticosteroids also decrease thyroxine-binding globulin (the carriers of this hormone to the body's trillions of cells) and block the conversion of thyroid hormones T_4 and T_3.

Many doctors who have their patients take an aspirin or two a day to prevent blood clotting and to protect the heart may not be aware that aspirin and other salicylates—painkilling drugs—can contribute to hypothyroidism. The main ingredient in oil of wintergreen used in rubbing liniments to soothe muscles, salicylates may interfere with the binding of T_4 to its transport proteins and decrease the amount of T_4 in the blood.

Heavy smokers and those who share their polluted environment with nonsmokers should be aware that cigarette smoke contains thyocyanide (among its arsenal of other health destroyers), a fairly strong thyroid gland inhibitor. However, it isn't just noxious chemicals in the air we breathe and the fluids we drink, and additives in processed foods which some of us eat that suppress thyroid function. (There are thousands of food additives whose relations to thyroid function have never been studied—a good reason for eliminating processed foods from our diets, or at least for minimizing them.)

Certain otherwise wholesome foods—some of them found to contain anticancer substances—lower thyroid gland efficiency by reducing the amount of iodine available for synthesizing of two thyroid hormones: T_3 and T_4. Cabbage, cauliflower, kale, kohlrabi, mustard greens, rutabaga, and turnips are most noted for this action in that they contain progoitrin, which is transformed by the body into goitrin. However, unless the person eats large amounts of these vegetables frequently and lives where iodine is deficient in the food and water, there's little chance of thyroid suppression from them.

A clue to the damage caused by excessive eating of cabbage and turnips was observed by food researchers in Europe as early as World War I. During that time of limited food supply, isolated pockets of individuals subsisted only on cabbage and turnips. Soon most of the people there developed goiters.

To test these findings, researchers fed animals a diet almost exclusively made up of cabbage and turnips, and most of them developed goiters. Inasmuch as there are trace amounts of cyanide in these vegetables, they concluded that cyanide was the cause of suppressed thyroid function.

Other of the best-known food contributors to low thyroid function are soy products and walnuts—that is, if eaten frequently and in large amounts. Certainly, they should be minimized by individuals who are hypothyroid, at least until their condition is corrected or supplemented with thyroid hormone.

Millet, a highly nutritious breakfast food and a staple in developing nations, now appears to diminish thyroid function.[3] Data from researchers Robert Cooksey and associates at the Veterans Administration Medical Center in Jackson, Mississippi, the University of Alabama (Birmingham), and the National Research Council of Canada (Saskatoon) reveal that substances in the hulls of millet are changed into resorcinol (mentioned earlier) by intestinal bacteria. Additionally, it is broken down to what is called "substituted resorcinol," dihydroxy benzoic acids, ferulic acid, and thiocynate—all powerful thyroid suppressants.

Cooksey believes that heavy and frequent intake of millet in

Third World countries may explain, at least in part, why there is so much hypothyroidism—indicated by the high incidence of goiter—in these parts of the world. In most instances, moderate and occasional eating of millet brings many health benefits and should not prove harmful to anyone but extreme hypothyroids. However, in Third World nations, it is often eaten daily, sometimes more than once a day.

A further alarming discovery by Cooksey and colleagues is that when millet is cooked and stored—not an uncommon practice in developing nations where refrigeration is almost non-existent—its thyroid suppression increases sixfold.

It is important to know and avoid environmental enemies, because in undermining the thyroid gland's function, they lower body temperature enough to bring on myriad illnesses.

5

BODY HEAT

r. Barnes's breakthrough research in hypothyroidism was due in large part to his observations that patients with thyroid deficiency were frequently cold even when people in the same room were comfortable. Their cold hands and feet created problems in social situations and in many instances severely hampered their ability to have a harmonious sex life.

In addition, Dr. Barnes found that low body temperature inhibits the ability of these patients' bone marrow to produce both red and white blood cells properly. Red blood cells are responsible for transporting oxygen to the rest of the body for food metabolism, energy, and heat. Red blood cell disturbances lead to lower metabolic activity and still lower temperatures.

Ability of the marrow to produce white blood cells—soldiers of the immune system army—is reduced, too, making hypothyroids vulnerable to repeated colds, flu, sinusitis, sore throat, pneumonia, and other respiratory ailments.

While a physiology instructor at the University of Chicago many years ago, Dr. Barnes witnessed a dramatic demonstration that normal body temperature is essential to the production of sufficient blood cells. A Ph.D. candidate was puzzled as to why red and white blood cells were being formed only in the bone marrow of certain bones—the ribs, spine, pelvis, and long bones nearest the body. "He suspected that it was a matter of temperature, body organs being warmer than the extremities (the arms and legs)," explains Dr. Barnes.

"To test this hypothesis, he devised a special needle in whose hollow he inserted a small, thin thermometer to check bone marrow temperature in a white rat. He found only yellow, non-bloodmaking marrow in the rat's long tail, which had a temperature lower than that of the blood-producing backbone.

"Then he curved the rat's tail, and made a small incision in the animal's belly, temporarily inserting and suturing the tail there. Soon the marrow in the tip of the tail, now warmed by the body, was transformed into blood-producing red marrow, while the marrow of the bony structure of the tail's curve remained yellow and unable to make blood cells."

Years later in his medical practice, this graphic demonstration helped Dr. Barnes understand why anemic women often remain dragged out, pale, and depressed, even after having been administered extra iron. Several hundred sickly patients regained a new, fuller life when he gave them thyroid supplementation, which raised their temperature and increased their bodies' ability to produce blood cells, particularly red corpuscles.

Supplemental iron therapy is usually only temporarily useful in the treatment of hypothyroid anemia, because it treats the symptoms, rather than the cause, which is well taken care of by thyroid hormone therapy. Foods rich in iron—liver, fish, fowl, meats, fruits, green vegetables, raisins, and brown rice—are of limited value in a person whose anemia is caused by a hypothyroid condition.

At best, the body absorbs little more than 10 percent of available iron. Vitamin C (ascorbic acid) greatly aids the absorption of iron from the digestive tract. Research done by Drs. Paul R. McCurdy of Georgetown University School of Medicine and Raymond J. Dern of Loyola University Stritch School of Medicine revealed that between 200 and 500 mg of ascorbic acid made it possible for the body to absorb twice as much iron (ferrous sulphate, 15 to 120 mg) as without this vitamin.[1] An accompanying dose of 500 mg of vitamin C resulted in a much higher absorption of iron from the gut than when smaller doses of this vitamin were given. A Swedish study, in fact, revealed that the United States government's recommended daily allowance (RDA) of 60 mg of vitamin C will do nothing to help absorb iron.[2]

Once absorbed, iron is constantly recycled by the body to manufacture new red blood cells from worn-out ones. Women, however, lose iron with their menstrual flow, and must therefore replace it in their diets. After absorption, iron must be assimilated by the cells in order to manufacture the hemoglobin necessary to carry oxygen throughout the body. To enable this to happen, another essential mineral, copper—found in liver, other organ meats, bonemeal, legumes, molasses, nuts, raisins, and seafood—must be present.[3] If, as is often the case, copper is in short supply, the blood's oxygen-carrying efficiency may be sharply diminished.

Hypothyroidism may reduce the uptake of copper from the gastrointestinal tract. In addition, a decreased body temperature, common to an underactive thyroid, can cause brain wave changes which may be misinterpreted by a clinician as neurological damage, but which will in most instances be entirely reversible when thyroid therapy is instituted.

Slower reaction time is caused by lowered body temperature, as illustrated by polar explorers subjected to extreme cold who develop hypothermia. Anyone who is hypothyroid may have similar complaints.

Emanuel Donchin, a psychologist, and Noel K. Marshall, an electrophysicist, both of the Cognitive Psychophysiology Laboratory at the University of Illinois, discovered, not long ago, that seemingly small daily changes in body temperature—one or two degrees below normal—reduce certain brain responses in test subjects.[4] Their findings showed that even slightly depressed body temperatures slow down our movements and our higher thought processes. Although we may not be aware of it, our brains respond more slowly to sound.

Brain wave peaks have a readily recognizable pattern. Nerve damage in the brain is a good possibility if wave peaks either don't appear or come later than they should. In hypothermia, the brain wave peaks are markedly delayed. Yet when the temperatures of these subjects are normalized, the brain waves speed up and become normal.

Donchin and Marshall caution doctors diagnosing such cases to consider body temperature of patients before concluding that they have irreversible brain damage. This recommendation was based on their experiments with fifteen test subjects. They discovered that even small temperature changes caused changes in their test subjects. The efficiency of sensory processing and coordination dropped with subnormal temperatures and rose when temperatures reached normal.

These scientists relate their findings to those of G. A. Kerkhof and his colleagues at the University of Leiden (Netherlands), who discovered that body temperatures actually do influence the brain in a manner that correlates with how subjects rate their performance of various tasks.[5]

Sometimes we put ourselves into categories—as "morning" or "evening" people—according to our work efficiency. Kerkhof discovered that temperatures were normal at peak performance times and lower than normal at other times. Not only was execution better at peak times, but subjects could also concentrate longer when working.

Experiments by Kerkhof and Donchin and Marshall offer laboratory proof of the handicaps of those individuals with a chronically low temperature, as in hypothyroidism. Frequently hypothyroids register temperatures from 1 to 2½ degrees below normal, as I have observed many times in my practice.

Now we can better understand why persons with extremely low thyroid function—and correspondingly low temperatures—show some of the following symptoms: slow-motion response, thick-tongued speech, poor coordination, impaired memory, and a slowing of mental activity.

If, indeed, 40 percent of the American population suffers from hypothyroidism, an incredible amount of mental and physical potential is being lost needlessly, because no condition can be more readily and inexpensively treated than hypothyroidism. Yet none is more frequently untreated and, even worse, unsuspected. Unless this condition is corrected, the thyroid gland, in partnership with the adrenal glands, cannot properly operate the body's heat-regulating system.[6] That is why, as indicated earlier, so many hypothyroids are cold when everybody else in the room is warm.

Not only do these glands regulate body heat for everyday living, they raise the body's temperature in disease states to produce a fever, which protects us from infection. Ever since the first thermometer was invented, there has been a difference of opinion about fever. Is it a friend or an enemy? The only point doctors have agreed on in the past hundred years is that fever is a sign of illness.

In the early twentieth century, the eminent physician Sir William Osler labeled fever as one of the three great scourges of mankind, the other two being famine and war: "By far the greatest, by far the most terrible is fever," he concluded.[7] However, even the eminent can be wrong. In 1960, two scientists, I. L. Bennett, Jr., and A. Nicastri, did a thorough review of medical literature and, although not as extreme in their judgment as Sir William, they found no convincing evidence that fever benefits us in our continual warfare with microbes.[8]

Then researcher M. J. Kluger and his associates blasted this opinion with a stunning discovery on infected lizards. Lizards do not have a built-in fever-generating system such as ours and must find fever-inducing sources on the outside.[9] The Kluger team learned that sick lizards have an instinct which makes them seek hot environments in order to raise their body temperatures to fever level when they are sick. Infected fish, too, swim to warmer water to raise their temperatures and combat illness.

Various experimenters have discovered that fever encourages quick inflammation in the immediate area of an infection and keeps it from spreading. Apparently fever is triggered in the brain first by a hormone-like substance from macrophages, immune system cells that attack invading germs. Then the thyroid gland and adrenal glands work together to speed up metabolism to produce extreme heat.

Experiments by G. W. Duff and S. K. Durum showed that at 2 degrees centigrade of fever, certain immune system defenders—T-cells and antibodies—increased by 2,000 percent over their number at normal body temperature.[10] Similar findings were reported by another research team. Antibody production in the spleen cells has been found to increase dramatically during a fever. Scientists have concluded that the hormone-like substances, called interleukin-1, set off body defense cells to fight infection and also send the brain signals to increase body temperature to provide an ideal climate for the multiplication of defense cells. Many physiologists believe that human beings are equipped with a temperature regulation system which puts a ceiling on fever at approximately 41.11 degrees centigrade (106 degrees Fahrenheit). In heat stroke and malignant hyperthermia, temperature breaks through to killing levels.

How is fever controlled? Scientists are not sure. Some believe that fever lingers as long as the infection lasts and recedes when there is no longer need for it.

If fever increases our ability to fight diseases, do subnormal temperatures make us more susceptible to them? Very likely. Hypothyroidism and its accompanying subnormal temperatures are stresses which lower the body's innate ability to fight off infection.

We are always under attack by infectious agents—bacteria and viruses. Countless invisible enemies mass on the skin, in the mouth and throat, and in the intestinal tract. Yet that is only half the bulletin from the war zones. Our built-in resistance, our own defense network, is the other half. If we keep our resistance high enough, the enemy cannot win the battle. He is neutralized until some stress weakens us and permits him to multiply and grow stronger.

Low thyroid function is far from the only stress that invites attack. Devastating emotional shock, long exposure to extreme heat or cold, physical exertion, inferior nutrition, and insufficient sleep are other common causes of weakened resistance. But, hypothyroidism is definitely a major stress. Subnormal body temperature and too little thyroid hormone can reduce the strength and resistance of every cell, including the billions involved in the immune system. One of the most common results of hypothyroidism which I see daily in my office is recurrent colds, throat and nose infections, and other respiratory ailments.

Between sniffles and a hacking cough, a patient named Beverly let out all her frustration on the first visit to my office.

"Dr. Langer, I feel as if the common cold was invented exclusively for me. I'm sick at least four times a year—winter, spring, summer, and fall. I've had every respiratory ailment through the alphabet from A to Z."

Beverly's sardonic humor fascinated me, because it seemed too vigorous in contrast with her many symptoms typical of hypothyroidism: low energy, cold extremities, an assortment of respiratory ailments, tight, masklike facial skin, and a more-than-plump figure.

A Barnes Basal Temperature reading of 96.4 degrees confirmed my suspicion. I started Beverly on a grain of natural thyroid, 2 tablespoons of brewer's yeast (taken an hour before breakfast and lunch in grapefruit juice to prevent flatulence), and 10,000 units of vitamin A, plus 3,000 milligrams of vitamin C daily. Several weeks later, she returned, looking great, weighing 6 pounds less, all smiles and no sniffles.

"This treatment seems to have broken my monopoly on respiratory ailments," she proudly announced.

And she was right.

Another new patient, whom I'll call Diane, had a similar problem but one with sad social overtones. A natural auburn-haired woman in her midthirties, she would have been striking, except for many symptoms of respiratory problems—a slightly swollen, reddish nose, watery green eyes, and a nervous habit of continually clearing her throat.

"Doctor, I simply can't shake this cold, no matter what cold remedies I take." She covered a sneeze with Kleenex. "I go through a big box of Kleenex every other day. I'm desperate. I don't know what to do."

Diane's condition depressed her, because, with her frequent sneezing, nose blowing, throat clearing, and headaches, men avoided her.

"Nobody wants me and my cold," she said. "I'm like Typhoid Mary." Tears of frustration began rolling down her cheeks.

Diane had so many obvious symptoms of hypothyroidism that I didn't delay giving her a grain of natural thyroid even before getting a report on her temperature, which, it turned out, was 2 degrees subnormal. Nothing dramatic happened for three weeks.

Then Diane phoned to say the mucus was clearing from her head. "I'm beginning to feel like a human being." After three months, she was a total human being, and an extremely beautiful one. The headaches and respiratory ailments had all disappeared. She hadn't had any symptoms of a cold for weeks and felt great.

"You probably don't recognize me without a wad of Kleenex in my hand," she said during her last office visit, when she promised to stay on thyroid supplementation for the rest of her life. I haven't seen Diane for years. I know I would have if she weren't feeling well. What a pleasure to lose a patient to good health!

Diane's case is not uncommon. Often I have found unyielding colds and related respiratory ailments interfering with patients' love lives. The same goes for headaches, a frequent symptom of hypothyroidism. Many headaches in the bedroom are not just bedroom headaches. They are real ones. I have helped hundreds of patients get rid of them without aspirin.

Every part of the body suffers when insufficient thyroid hormones are available, including the skin and even the erogenous zones. A poor complexion is often a revealing sign of hypothyroidism, although far less dependable than subnormal basal temperature. Sophisticated electronic measuring devices have shown that in extreme cases of low thyroid function, the skin may be deprived of 75 to 80 percent of its normal blood supply, severely reducing the amount of nourishment delivered to the cells and delaying the removal of harmful waste products.[11] All sorts of strange, embarrassing skin conditions can result, disorders damaging to social and sexual acceptance: blackheads, whiteheads, pimples, boils, carbuncles, acne, eczema, icthyosis (fish skin), and psoriasis, among others. Thyroid therapy brings about almost unbelievable improvement, often complete disappearance of these conditions, because circulation has been stepped up. Further, the sensitivity of erogenous zones to touch and friction is heightened, making sex more enjoyable. Conditions which make sex less enjoyable—fatigue, headaches, respiratory ailments, and being physically cold—tend to diminish or vanish with thyroid supplementation.

To the hypothyroid with low body heat and a string of related physical problems, survival is higher on the priority list than lovemaking. But in time, thyroid supplements may be able to effect a remarkable change in priorities!

6

THYROID AND SEX—
FOR WOMEN

*O*ut of the memorable Broadway musical *Flower Drum Song* came an exuberant song, "I Enjoy Being a Girl," which unfortunately does not express the sentiments of many women just before and during the menstrual period. Ever since Eve, women have agonized each month, losing valuable time from work, education, social activities, recreation, and sports, while the male-dominated medical profession had done little or nothing to help.

Likewise, ever since the bedroom went public in the sexual revolution, women—and men—have developed inferiority feelings about their contributions to lovemaking, comparing them to survey results and fictional standards. I know this from my own practice in preventive medicine and from discussions with numerous physicians, including gynecologists.

Few women *or* men know that a properly functioning or supplemented thyroid gland can bring new excitement to their sexuality. Even fewer know that the Pill, an effective birth control method, can cause severe bodily damage in hypothyroidism.

In this chapter I will discuss menstrual disorders, sexual problems, sexual enjoyment, and birth control as they relate to proper thyroid function.

To help women cope with menstrual problems, I have administered, although unwillingly, painkillers, aspirin, relaxants, and tranquilizers. These are alien chemical substances which can be harmful, and therefore I prefer to use natural means. By administering desiccated thyroid, I have seen the correction or at least the lessening of such menstrual disorders as inordinate pain, irregularity, too copious flow, or premature or delayed menses.

Dr. Broda Barnes managed almost two thousand such cases successfully by this method and gave me access to his findings. He told me that he almost felt like shouting "Eureka!" when he first found thyroid supplementation to be helpful for these problems.

"I experienced the exultation of a pioneer until medical history revealed that, as early as 1899, Dr. Eugene Hertoghe, of Antwerp, Belgium, had discovered that many female problems result from mild to acute thyroid deficiency," he admitted. "He cured hundreds of women with thyroid supplements. Incidentally, his grandson is achieving the same success today, as I learned not long ago while lecturing on thyroid to a group of physicians in Belgium." The Hertoghe method spread to the United States in the early 1900s, bringing welcome relief to tens of thousands of women.

Early medical textbooks and journal articles mentioned the effectiveness of thyroid supplementation in problems peculiar to women. In the 1950 Curtis-Huffman *Textbook of Gynecology*, the authors wrote that even medical conservatives accept that thyroid substance has definite value.[1] It is helpful in promoting conception, in stopping functional uterine bleeding from various causes, in improving gynecological disturbances in many patients with a low metabolic rate, in correcting delayed onset of menstruation in adolescents and, most especially, in adjusting disorders of menstrual flow.

Taylor's *Essentials of Gynecology*, published in 1969, states that in myxedema (acutely subnormal thyroid function) premenopausal patients may show menstrual excesses and this condition may be corrected with thyroid extract.[2] Dr. Taylor relates that one researcher (Lerman) discovered that the hypothyroid patient has a loss of normal follicle-stimulating hormone (the substance which spurs growth of cells surrounding the eggs in the ovaries) preceding menopause. In patients past menopause, Lerman found that follicle-stimulating hormone levels were lower than in normal patients of the same age. He also learned that treatment of hypothyroidism with thyroid hormones was accompanied by a rise in follicle-stimulating hormone.

"Occasionally, amenorrhea [interruption of normal menstrual periods] will be a complication of hypothyroidism," wrote Dr. Taylor. "With correction of the hypothyroidism, regular menstrual cycles will follow."

In a study of fatigued hypothyroid women with menstrual disorders, Mayo Clinic researchers administered thyroid hormone to bring their metabolism to normal range.[3] Numerous gynecological conditions improved: amenorrhea improved in 72 percent of the women; aligomenorrhea (deficient menstruation) in 55 percent, and menorrhagia (excessive blood flow) in 73 percent. A bonus value was an improvement in the health of 75 percent of the women, including higher energy levels.

A recent experiment reported in the *International Journal of Gynecological Obstetrics* illustrates that just one component of the thyroid hormone, thyroxin, helps restore menstruation in women with low-normal thyroid function. Regular menstrual cycles were restored in ten of seventeen test subjects.[4] An article published in another international journal, *Problems of Endokrinology*, revealed that in a study of twenty-three infertile female hypothyroids with amenorrhea and lactorrhea, most were returned to normal by thyroid therapy.[5]

A third article, this one in the *Journal of Endocrinology*, established a "distinct relationship between thyroid function and that of the ovary ..." in a bird experiment.[6]

Thyroid hormones, too, are essential to the proper development of the breast, as shown by animal experiments. They help to regulate the growth and development of the mammary gland.

By decreasing the levels of thyroid hormone in the blood, researchers were able to retard the growth of key parts of the breast.[7]

Although hypothyroidism contributes to many kinds of female problems, the most widespread in my practice are menstrual, even though I am not a gynecologist. This was also true for Dr. Barnes, who scanned his office files on 2,051 adult female patients with a complete menstrual history and was amazed to find that 1,980 of them (80 percent) had some kind of female problem. Of these, 1,590 had had menstrual cramps; 883 had had irregular periods, usually accompanied by cramps; and the remainder had undergone occasional flooding or had had an early or late onset of menstruation.

Those with menstrual distress experienced moderate to severe pain (a day or two of school or work lost each month), although some patients endured more excruciating pain than often accompanies having a baby, with no baby to show for it.

Individuals whose menstrual periods started later than the average age of twelve numbered 438. The oldest was eighteen. Those whose periods started too early numbered 260, the youngest being a five-year-old who also developed mature breasts and pubic hair. Immediately recognized as hypothyroid, she was treated with low-potency natural desiccated thyroid and in a month menstruation stopped, the breasts started regressing, and pubic hair disappeared until puberty.

In most of Dr. Barnes's cases—and in mine, as well—painful menstruation, irregularity, too copious flow, and premature or delayed menses normalized with administration of thyroid supplementation. The type of uterine bleeding brought about by low thyroid function runs to opposite extremes—excessive flow to sparse flow. A word of caution: abnormal blood flow may be a sign of uterine cancer, so it makes sense to be checked by a gynecologist.

If thyroid function is normal and menstrual irregularities continue, certain vitamin deficiencies may be the cause. A lack of vitamin B_{12} or folic acid has been found to bring on irregularity, sparse flow, or no flow, conditions which are corrected when the missing vitamins are supplied.

A heavy menstrual flow for three or four days has often been corrected if the patient takes 600 international units of vitamin

E daily for thirty days. Sometimes a damaged liver—which cannot inactivate hormones which govern menstruation—may cause a too-copious flow. Liver damage can result from alcoholism, a diet high in sugar or other refined carbohydrates or saturated fats, or from deficiencies of calcium, magnesium, or protein (particularly the amino acids cystine and methionine) or vitamins A and C, which, with choline, are protectors of the liver.

Like menstrual problems, sexual dysfunction (once called frigidity, an insensitive, finger-pointing word) can arise from one or more factors: fatigue, illness, dyspareunia (pain during the sexual act), guilt feelings, self-consciousness, and emotional tension with one's mate, to name some of the common ones. A spectrum of supercharged emotional problems can contribute, too: indelicate treatment in the first sexual encounter, rape, a hangover from childhood conditioning to taboos of sex, a lingering attachment to a parent. Some can be so traumatic and unyielding that they need psychological or psychiatric treatment. Physical problems, some common, some not so common, can contribute, too: irritation or infection of the vulva or vagina, the injured remainder of the hymen, the bruised tissue from abortion, or crudely executed surgery in the mouth of the vagina to aid delivery in difficult childbirth.

Even seemingly insignificant factors can bring on discomfort in intercourse. A patient with a sinus infection complained of secreting too little lubrication for enjoyable sex. Inasmuch as antihistamines are drying agents, I told her to stop taking them, cleared up her sinus infection, and soon she was again forming ample lubrication.

Both physical and emotional obstacles to sexual enjoyment—fatigue, vague illnesses, and even childhood conditioning against sex—are often overcome by thyroid supplementation.

A patient we'll call Linda told me bitterly, "I don't feel a thing during lovemaking."

She showed a low score of 96.8 degrees on the Barnes Basal Temperature Test. Clinical symptoms and her medical history told me plainly that she was hypothyroid, and I prescribed the natural desiccated thyroid supplement.

"Thyroid? How can that possibly help?" she asked incredulously.

I explained that the electrocardiogram (EKG) of hypothyroid

individuals shows reduced nerve stimulation of the heart muscle, causing blood to be pumped in lesser quantities and less forcefully. Reduced nerve conduction influences not only the heart but many other parts of the body, often desensitizing the sex organs.

This patient's response to thyroid supplementation was cheering: a temperature rise to normal and ecstatic reaction to lovemaking including, for the first time, sexual climax.

Another satisfying case was that of a young woman named Ardis.

"Doctor, I'm cold physically and sexually. I'm never spontaneous in bed," she confessed. "It's probably my puritanical upbringing. My husband wants to trade me in for a better model." She paused with a sigh. "Maybe I should be seeing a psychiatrist."

I shook my head. "No. You came to the right place."

The armpit test showed her to be markedly hypothyroid, so I prescribed a grain of thyroid daily. During her fourth visit, Ardis beamed:

"My hands, feet, and the rest of me are warm now," she bubbled. "How I enjoyed sex last night! I wasn't at all self-conscious."

Thyroid supplementation has fanned many fires, banishing bedroom headaches and guilt feelings. Aside from its values in heightening sexual urge and the enjoyment of sex, thyroid therapy helps marriage become more productive. One authority told the Section of Obstetrics and Gynecology of the American Medical Association that 30 percent of sterile women with low thyroid function conceived while on thyroid supplements.[8]

Before thyroid treatment was pushed into the background by the plethora of drugs from the arsenal of the pharmaceutical industry, a gynecology textbook by Emil Novak, of Johns Hopkins Medical School, stated that, in hypothyroids, thyroid therapy will usually correct menstrual disorders, infertility, and miscarriage.[9] In these times, however, less accent is put on sex for procreation. Most patients seem more interested in birth control, in finding the elusive, foolproof way of avoiding pregnancy. The Pill currently enjoys the greatest popularity, because of its effectiveness and convenience.

The Pill distributes its two major ingredients—estrogen and

progestin (synthetic female hormone) throughout the body's cells, acting to prevent the ovaries from producing eggs. Among other things, it creates a hostile environment for pregnancy, thinning the endometrium (uterine lining) while decreasing its secretions.

I am unenthusiastic about the use of drugs which are not absolutely necessary, especially powerful ones with well-documented side effects, such as the Pill, which is contraindicated for women with asthma, cystic breast disease, a family history of breast cancer, diabetes, blood-clotting disorders, high blood pressure, heart, kidney, and liver disease, exposure to DES before birth, elevated blood serum cholesterol or triglycerides, epilepsy, fibroid uterine tumors, gallbladder disease, menstrual abnormalities, migraine headaches, and the habit of smoking.

In addition to women with these problems, I flatly refuse to prescribe the Pill for anyone older than age thirty-five. The momentum of risk gains dizzying speed with each year after that age. I prescribe it only if would-be users are safeguarded against blood-clotting disorders by adequate thyroid function or by thyroid supplementation. Of more than 100 patients in my practice who took the Pill for less than five years, not one developed any of the wide range of common side effects: blood-clotting disorders, high blood pressure, strokes, heart attacks, migraine headaches, eye ailments, and liver tumors, among others.

I have been well guided by a report which Dr. Barnes wrote for *Federation Proceedings* (a copy of which he gave me for my patients' benefit and for use in this book) called "Making the Pill Safer with Thyroid."[10] In it he states:

> The most serious complication from oral contraceptives has been a seven- to tenfold increase in morbidity and mortality due to thromboembolic diseases reported in Great Britain. . . .
>
> Since these changes are characteristic of abnormalities found in thyroid deficiencies . . . it would appear that a careful scrutiny of thyroid function should be made in all cases before initiating the Pill. The Basal Temperature has been found to be the most satisfactory test. If a woman has any symptoms of thyroid defi-

ciency and/or a subnormal Basal Temperature, adequate thyroid therapy is maintained as long as she is taking the Pill.

In my large general practice, no case of thrombophlebitis has occurred, and few patients have complained of water retention. Thyroid is an excellent diuretic in hypothyroidism. A few cases have been seen in which thrombophlebitis developed under administration of the Pill from other physicians.

In each instance, evidence of thyroid deficiency was present before the contraceptive was started. Thyroid prophylaxis for thromboses in those taking the Pill seems to be as effective as it is for the prevention of coronary disease.

Obviously, there are hazards in almost every form of birth control. However, if the ground rules are adhered to with the Pill, this method seems to have many advantages. Most birth control methods are not fair, in that they place the responsibility entirely on the woman. But now there is a way that men can share responsibility—not just by the obvious means of vasectomy, a surgical procedure which some males live to regret. This will be discussed in the next chapter.

7

THYROID AND SEX—
FOR MEN

I thought I had heard everything when a new patient, twenty-six-year-old Clayton, sole owner of a small manufacturing company, admitted to using the headache alibi when his wife wanted sex more often than he could deliver. In this liberated society, bedroom headaches are no longer the sole prerogative of women!

Already a workaholic, Clayton avoided embarrassment over the test of his maleness—"or lack of it," as he put it—by also taking refuge in long hours of work in his plant. As the story unfolded, the problem came into sharp focus. Within five years, Clayton had translated a patent into a thriving production firm through the usual entrepreneurial formula: a clear-cut goal—wishing to become a millionaire through his inventiveness—

little capital, and many long, grueling hours. To Clayton, the first one at the plant early each morning and the last to leave late at night, weekends were just two more weekdays. Obviously, he had not only worked at a sprint but could have made the *Guinness Book of World Records* for rapid eating. He bolted two-minute meals from the lunch wagon, gulped eleven cups of coffee daily, and chomped endless glazed donuts, sweet rolls, and cookies "to get me through the day and night."

Fear of bedroom failure and embarrassment compounded Clayton's intermittent impotency. Diagnosis? Emotional causes compounded by physical ones: exhaustion (never calculated to enhance sexuality), little sleep and relaxation, junk foods (as nourishing as wartime prison camp fare, which rendered many men temporarily incapable sexually), and subnormal thyroid function.

I advised Clayton to level with his wife—to tell her that he was under doctor's orders not to have sexual demands placed on him until his total recovery—and also to delegate tasks, to stop suicidal fourteen- to sixteen-hour workdays, to take weekends off, to get more sleep, and to cut out junk foods. I told him to improve his diet by adding more protein, fresh vegetables, and food supplements: brewer's yeast, desiccated liver, and wheat germ, plus a high-quality B-complex supplement and vitamins C, D, and E, essential fatty acids (in the form of evening primrose oil), and the minerals selenium, calcium, magnesium, and potassium. After finding that his basal temperature was 96.2 degrees, I put Clayton on a daily grain of natural thyroid. This regime turned him around in three months. Then the power of his sex drive overcame his self-consciousness and fear of failure, and he recovered completely.

Like Clayton, many men feel their masculinity being tested, even threatened, by the increased aggressiveness of women in initiating sex—a good reason for them to make sure that their thyroid function is normal and that they are in peak condition otherwise.

Aside from wanting to feel equal to sexual demands on them, male patients appear to be assuming more responsibility for birth control, as evidenced by a growing number of vasectomies. Because of the difficulty of reversing vasectomy, many men want to know if there is an effective means of contributing to birth control without surgery.

I tell them about something promising on the horizon. Not long ago, British medical researchers accidentally discovered an efficient birth control product. While taking heart medications called beta blockers, men complained to doctors that they couldn't make their wives pregnant. To investigate, researchers put a drop of the drug into vigorously swimming sperm. Within ten seconds, the sperm lay dead. After testing is done to determine if all men can use the drug safely, and after governmental approvals are secured, men may be able to assume responsibility for birth control.

As interesting as this subject is, most men are mainly preoccupied with making sure that their sexual ability meets or exceeds demand. This fact did not come to light immediately relative to a new patient of mine, a bright, thirty-one-year-old insurance salesman whom I'll call Jerry. His problem was irregular heartbeat.

I was perplexed. Jerry had no history of illness. The diet sheet he had filled out revealed no clue. My questions turned up nothing helpful except that occasionally he seemed hesitant, guarded. Obviously, he was holding out on me. Sometimes patients did that when asked about their sex lives.

"Look, Jerry, you came to me with a problem," I said bluntly. "You're not telling me things that could let me help you."

He flushed.

"Tell me, what have you been doing differently in the past month or so that might account for your problem?"

"I'm having trouble with my sex life," he admitted.

It turned out he was having a problem getting an erection. Sometimes it didn't stay hard for more than a few minutes. Once it softened on him during sexual intercourse, and he was humiliated.

"What did you do about it?" I asked.

"I began taking zinc. That's supposed to be the sexy mineral."

I agreed with him silently. The prostate gland and its secretions have a high content of zinc, as do the sperm cells. Potency and fertility disorders often yield to supplementation with zinc and its vitamin companion, B_6. Zinc is essential in the formation and function of a number of sex hormones, including gonadotrophin, which excites and stimulates the sex glands of males and females. One medical paper had shown that without zinc, no gonadotrophin could be produced.

"Zinc certainly contributes importantly to sex drive, enjoyment, and fulfillment," I told him.

"I felt I couldn't get enough zinc from my diet," he said. "I read in an article that zinc content of grains—corn, oats, and wheat—has dropped 10 percent or more in recent years."

"True. Some studies show that zinc and other trace minerals are being taken out of the soil year after year and not returned. What is happening to farmland is similar to what is happening to money values through the invisible larceny of inflation."

"My zinc supplement helped me sexually to a degree," he went on.

"How much zinc are you taking daily?"

"Just a small amount, about 100 milligrams."

This remark upset me.

"*Just* 100 milligrams a day? Jerry, that's a lot. You can't take trace minerals in the liberal amounts that you can many vitamins."

Then I remembered a talk given by Jeffrey Bland, Ph.D., Professor of Nutritional Biochemistry at the University of Puget Sound. He and I, along with Dr. Barnes, had been speakers at a symposium for medical doctors in Texas on the subject of hypothyroidism. Dr. Bland had done some original research on zinc and copper and their relationship to low thyroid function and had studied the literature on this subject for many years. Something Dr. Bland had said told me what Jerry's trouble was. He had probably upset the natural ratio of zinc to copper in his body.[1]

Quickly, I skimmed over Jerry's food chart to confirm my opinion.

"I don't find seafood on your chart."

"I don't eat it too often."

"How about organ meats—kidneys, brains, sweetbreads, liver?"

"Never."

"How about nuts?"

"Once in a while."

"Those are copper-containing foods. What I suspect is that

you've disturbed your zinc-copper ratio. Many biochemists feel that we get all the copper we need from our foods and don't have to supplement. Therefore, if we increase our zinc intake as you have—and the ratio for most individuals is eight parts of zinc to one of copper—we throw off the relationship. You can't safely bring your copper level up with the very high intake of zinc, because you would be risking copper intoxication."

I told him that Dr. Bland had found that irregular heartbeats, premature beats, and other EKG abnormalities were caused in animals by a diet deficient in copper and had been corrected by the addition of minute amounts of copper in their diet.[2] Dr. Bland had cited similar results in human test subjects.

I asked Jerry to reduce his zinc intake to no more than 30 to 40 mg daily and to add 4 mg of copper. Within two weeks his heart irregularity stopped. I found his thyroid function a bit low and added a grain of thyroid to his daily regimen.

Not long ago, Jerry told me, "My sex life is great again, and my heart is fine."

So many thanks that I get from patients should actually go to thyroid pioneers like Dr. Barnes and to biochemical pioneers like Dr. Jeffrey Bland.

Copper and zinc are important trace minerals, vital in a number of bodily functions including the sexual ones. I remembered clearly that Dr. Bland had mentioned that the list of symptoms for zinc and copper deficiencies was almost identical to that for hypothyroidism. He had also said that trace minerals within human beings act as coenzymes. Enzymes are molecules which cause biochemical changes without being changed themselves. They cause carbohydrates to be split into simple sugars, fats to be broken into fatty acids, and proteins into amino acids. There are, in addition, thousands of other enzymatic actions.

Some enzymes can't act on their own—metalo enzymes, for instance. They have to become bound to trace minerals such as zinc and copper to work. So if there is not enough zinc or copper or any other trace mineral to go around, certain enzymes can't become attached to them and do their proper job. Metalo enzymes work in the brain, the liver, the heart, and every other body organ and tissue.

One kind of copper-containing molecule is necessary to oxidize iron and change it to a form acceptable in hemoglobin molecules—that which carries oxygen throughout the arterial system.

"There are many people in our population with an anemia that doesn't respond to iron supplementation," says Dr. Bland. "They are truly suffering from copper insufficiency."[3]

Without another kind of copper-containing enzyme, the skin could not accept pigmentation. One of the first signs of copper deficiency is called "subtle albinism," and extremely white skin, which tans poorly and sometimes develops white spots. Still another copper-containing enzyme concentrates heavily in the adrenal gland, which could not synthesize norepinephrine, one of its key hormones, without this enzyme.

Two more copper-dependent enzymes guard against body deterioration: superoxide dismutase (SOD), a compound well known for protecting individual cells from attack by free radicals (chemicals which cause our bodies to age), and a metalo enzyme which forms elastin, one of the integral parts of the artery walls.

Likewise, five zinc-bound enzymes make life-or-death contributions. One of them controls the rate of protein synthesis, cell growth, cell repair, hair growth, and white blood cell production. A second zinc-bound enzyme is an important part of the first step in metabolizing alcohol. A third zinc-containing enzyme contributes to the manufacture of retinaldehyde, a pigment which makes night vision possible. Still another one enables us to enjoy a full sense of smell and taste. Zinc-deficient people often lose the ability to smell, or objects give off a strange odor to them. The fifth zinc-attached enzyme helps to clear lactate from muscles and joints. In shortages of this trace element, muscle and joint pains are more acute.

On this subject, Dr. Bland mentioned a little-known fact based on an authoritative published paper which says that many symptoms of old age are really not the results of the aging process, but rather the results of malnutrition, including a deficiency of trace minerals.

These metallo enzymes create many symptoms similar to those of hypothyroidism, but do they in fact have a direct influence on thyroid function? They do in several ways. Before going into them, it might be well to mention again that the thyroid gland is activated, first, by thyroid-releasing hormone (TRH) from the hypothalamus gland by way of the pituitary gland, which gives off thyroid-stimulating hormone (TSH) to urge the thyroid into releasing its hormones into the bloodstream.

According to Dr. Bland, "neurotransmitters in the brain and the TRH from the hypothalamus and the TSH from the pituitary are controlled by copper nutrition." How well the thyroid hormone thyroxin (T_4) is metabolized in our trillions of cells depends on the proper ratio of zinc to copper in all these sites.[4]

"What does this mean?" asks Dr. Bland. "There are two direct relationships between zinc and copper nutrition and thyroid status. One is to the production of T_4 and, potentially, to T_3 and to the metabolism of these hormones in the cells where their activity will be used."

Dr. Bland reminds medical doctors that there are at least two ways to approach the patient with the symptoms of hypothyroidism.

"One way is the pharmacological approach, supplying larger doses of thyroid hormone through supplement. The second is normalizing the pituitary-thyroid and peripheral cell system by restoring the zinc-copper status in the individual deficient in these trace minerals."[5]

Such approaches often return the slipping male to full sexual potential, as many doctors who are experienced in thyroid hormone and trace mineral replacement are aware.

Hypothyroidism can diminish sexuality directly and indirectly. Fatigue and low endurance reduce both men and women to the survival level, where sexual activity plunges to the bottom of the priority list. Sex life automatically improves when general health is better.

Sex drive, potency, and sexual sensitivity and enjoyment rise with a normal thyroid or one which is adequately supplemented. In hypothyroidism, insufficient pituitary hormone is synthesized and, as a result, the level of the sex hormone testosterone is low. Brain levels of dopamine are also low, which further diminishes sexual desire. Animal experiments show that thyroid hormones administered to the hypothyroid raise dopamine to normal levels.

Sluggish blood flow to the sex organs in hypothyroidism also can lessen sexual performance, as it can in atherosclerosis (narrowing of the arteries), a condition encouraged by subnormal thyroid function. (Atherosclerosis and hypothyroidism will be covered extensively in several later chapters.)

Hypoglycemia, whose symptoms are similar to those of hypothyroidism, often is present in the latter condition, resulting in zero energy and not much interest in sex.

One cause of hypertension, or high blood pressure, is hypothyroidism. Males who take hypertensive drugs over a protracted period sometimes lose their sex drive. Addiction to alcohol, narcotics, and tobacco can also neutralize sex drive.

As in the case of Clayton, stress of various types can result in lower sex drive. An experiment with young male soldiers under the severe physical strain of a five-day combat course without sleep was reported in the *European Journal of Applied Physiology*.[6] After the first twenty-four hours, one of the thyroid hormones, thyroxine (T_4), increased (apparently to compensate for stress). However, the other thyroid hormone, triiodothyronine (T_3), did not. Within forty-eight hours, T_4 had declined to normal, and T_3 had gone lower.

The blood serum level of TSH went down throughout the experiment. Other hormones related to sexuality, prolactin and testosterone, also declined. Sleep helped reverse downtrends, particularly in prolactin and testosterone. Thyroid hormone production did not respond as readily. This experiment, in almost complete agreement with a previous study, points out the harmful effects of physical stress on general health and sexuality.

A less obvious stressor in many instances is low thyroid function. Sidney C. Werner, M.D., coeditor of *The Thyroid*, one of the most respected books in its field, states that sexual urge and potency are definitely reduced in extreme hypothyroidism.[7]

Among authorities who claim that decreased sexual drive is the most common reproductive abnormality of hypothyroid men is Peter Singer, M.D., Associate Clinical Professor of Medicine and Director, Thyroid Disease Diagnosis Center, Hospital of the Good Samaritan, Los Angeles.[8]

This, too, has been my repeated experience with patients. In psychological circles, it has been the custom to say that impotence is "all in the mind." Don't you believe it. It is also in the glands, starting with the thyroid. That is also where overconcern and immobilizing fears about potency may originate, as well as a host of emotional problems in areas other than sex.

8

BETTER SKIN, BETTER LIVING

Whether to make yourself more desirable for sexual, social, or career purposes, it is critically important to put your best face forward. And that means presenting a complexion that's appealing.

In her early twenties, auburn-haired Melissa would have been a striking and lovely young woman, if her face hadn't been peppered with blackheads and whiteheads and reddened with pus-filled pimples and boils. Hers was as severe a case of acne as I had ever seen. Her first words shocked me:

"Dr. Langer, when I look in the mirror, I want to commit suicide." She nervously clasped and unclasped the pale hands in her lap. "I almost did last week. Thank God a friend told me you could probably help!"

I had never before met Melissa, but I had met her condition on the faces and necks of dozens of other patients in my years as a medical doctor. Many of them had responded to treatment with natural thyroid.

Before her next office visit, I checked results of her Basal Body Temperature Test and thyroid function tests and saw that my suspicion was correct.

Melissa was definitely hypothyroid. I started her with a half-grain of natural thyroid, and her skin appeared to be better within three weeks.

"Look at the improvement!" she exclaimed during her next office visit. "My depression has lifted, too," she continued. "For the first time in years, I feel there's hope."

Indeed there was. I increased her thyroid gradually over the subsequent months until she was taking two grains daily, her skin condition improving with each office visit.

As with many such disorders, Melissa's took almost seven months to clear up, and her skin was so clean, smooth, and healthy looking that she refused to wear makeup. She didn't have to.

One of my unusual cases was a six-month-old baby boy, named Zack, who suffered severe eczema. From birth, he had endured incessant itching and soreness from eczema all over his body.

"No matter where I've taken Zack—clinics, hospitals, offices of dermatologists—no treatment has helped," his mother, one of my patients, told me.

I explained that I don't usually treat infants or children, but Zack's mother pleaded:

"I can't stand by and let him suffer."

Neither could I. Inasmuch as many abnormal skin conditions result from low thyroid function, I consented to see Zack at once. His tests indicated a hypothyroid condition, so I pre-scribed thyroid. As with Melissa, improvement started immediately, but it took almost eight months to clear up the skin lesions, bleeding, and itching. It was a great relief to Zack, and a joy to his mother and me.

Even more extraordinary than this case was that of Jo, a thirty-year-old hair stylist. She had dry, scaly skin (called icthyosis or fish skin), brittle, pitted nails, and patches of baldness, which she hid with a brunette wig.

"Doctor, I'm sick with embarrassment. I can't stand the sight of myself. My skin itches like fire and, of course, I can't scratch myself in the beauty salon," she sighed deeply. "Starting today, I'm taking a month's leave of absence, because I can't try to beautify someone else when I can't beautify myself."

Ichthyosis, poor nails, and hair loss are not uncommon in hypothyroid individuals, as I told her. I rushed her lab tests through and made a special appointment for her on the day I received her test results, which indicated severe hypothyroidism.

On thyroid hormone supplementation, her turnaround was remarkable *within two weeks!* Her skin had begun to soften and the scaliness was less visible.

"Jo, in time, your hair will fill in, too," I promised.

There was no miracle within the month, but her appearance had improved enough for her to return to work. Several months later, the fish scales were replaced by soft, clean, pliable, and pink skin. Her nails were coming in smooth and hard. And a stubble of new, healthy, black hair had begun filling in the bald spots.

Within a half year, Jo looked so stunning that I hardly recognized her. Supplementing a weak thyroid function had worked again!

Throughout the two decades of my practice, I have seen astonishing reversals in the skin of patients through supplementation with desiccated thyroid. Sometimes various other skin abnormalities clear up with this form of treatment: acne, eczema, fish skin—as indicated—and cellulitis, erysipelas, impetigo, lupus erythematosus, and psoriasis.

Rarely is an acne patient suspected of thyroid deficiency. Yet, hypothyroidism is at the root of many acne cases. When hair follicles on the skin surface become filled with dirt, makeup, or oil from the sebaceous gland, skin eruptions soon appear—blackheads, whiteheads, pimples, and boils.

Infection then sets in, and cysts may form, some leaving unsightly scars. A change of diet, scrupulous facial hygiene, and frequent washings with antibacterial soap are often recommended by dermatologists. They help, but not enough. Thyroid hormone supplementation usually clears up the condition.

This is no surprise. Two factors are responsible for correcting all the serious skin ailments: improved blood circulation and return to normal metabolism due to thyroid supplementation.

Electronic equipment monitors the efficiency with which blood circulates to our trillions of cells. Hypothyroidism causes low readings, meaning that the heart isn't pumping forcefully enough, so, consequently, circulation is reduced. In advanced cases of low thyroid function, sensitive measurements show that extremities such as the skin may get delivery of only 20 to 25 percent of their required blood supply.

That is only part of the story. With reduced blood supply, the skin cells are oxygen and fuel deprived. Further, waste products of skin cells are not entirely removed—a sort of skin constipation.

Such an unhealthy skin cannot resist invading enemy bacteria that multiply and cause infection. Result? Pimples and boils erupt and refuse to leave.

Bacteria such as staphylococci establish beachheads in sebaceous glands and at the bottom of hair follicles. Then come unsightly skin blemishes and merciless itching.

Treatment with antibiotics brings temporary relief and skin improvement, but soon the negative condition returns, because the cause—low thyroid condition—has not been corrected. Many such cases I have treated respond to natural thyroid, a B-complex supplement, and a reduction or elimination of junk foods.

Like acne, eczema is one of the most torturing skin conditions. It can involve any part of the body, causing itching that can bring on emotional trauma in some patients. Further, the skin becomes scaly, often swelling, blistering, and oozing. Scratching may cause excessive bleeding and infection.

Use of thyroid supplementation to correct eczema is not new. In fact, an English doctor discovered it in the 1890s when he treated a sixty-five-year-old woman with eczema for her major complaints: low energy and cold extremities.[1]

The eczema disappeared. Now the doctor's curiosity was aroused. He stopped the thyroid, and, sure enough, the eczema returned. After renewed treatment, this disorder again disappeared.

Almost any skin ailment can have its basis in hypothyroidism, although this isn't always the main cause.

Cellulitis is a swelling of the skin and tissues under the skin, which brings on redness and pain. These symptoms are accompanied by chills, fever, headache, and low energy. Cellulitis is caused by streptococci, staphylococci, or other unfriendly bacteria which take advantage of the skin's inability to defend itself and the body it encloses against invaders.

This condition is not taken lightly by physicians or knowledgeable patients. In its most deep-seated and advanced form, it can cause tissue-destroying abscesses to form. Cellulitis is particularly dangerous when it breaks out in the scalp, because it can cause brain damage and serious complications.

One of the worst complications I have seen is cellulitis of the mouth. Sometimes surgery is required. However, antibiotic treatment saved my patient until his condition could be managed with thyroid hormone.

Erysipelas, with a frightening name that sounds somewhat like a social disease, is a streptococcal infection that brings on hot, red skin blotches—as well as a fever, fatigue, and an often depressed state. Unless this ailment is checked, it can poison the system through invading bacteria and the toxins they introduce into the blood (septicemia), kidney inflammation, pneumonia, and even rheumatic fever. Before we had sulfa drugs and antibiotics, erysipelas often killed the patient. Today, it is again dangerous, because there is so much new antibiotic resistance. In many instances, erysipelas indicates hypothyroidism.

Like erysipelas, impetigo also can kill. It seems just a superficial skin disorder at the start, brought about by the invasion of streptoccoccal or staphylococcal microorganisms. Its symptoms are pustules half an inch in diameter to small, hot-cake-size, crusty, pus-swollen blisters which often break. These are localized in a small area or cover the entire face, neck, and body and may evolve into ulcers or boils.

Toxins can spread throughout the whole system to poison vital organs and cause death. Antibiotics usually control the condition, but, again, hypothyroidism should be suspected and, if present, treated. Otherwise, this condition can return.

Lupus erythematosus, too, is a serious disorder, most frequently affecting the skin only. However, it can also attack the internal organs. In its initial stage, it causes butterfly-shaped, red flushing on the nose and cheeks. Sometimes it manifests as hard, red lesions covering the ears, scalp, and mucous membranes of the mouth and/or throat.

When this condition seizes upon internal organs or joints, it becomes especially critical. Lupus erythematosus is characterized by deposits of mucopolysaccharides in connective tissue and elsewhere. As mentioned in previous chapters, such depositions are caused by a deficiency of thyroid hormone. So lupus has much in common with rheumatic arthritis, rheumatic fever, amyloiditis (deposits in internal organs which undermine their function), and necrotizing arteritis (inflamed arteries), among other connective tissue ailments.

Lupus usually responds to thyroid supplementation. It rarely, if ever, attacks a person whose bloodstream contains sufficient thyroid hormone.

One of the most difficult skin disorders to control by conventional methods is psoriasis, recognizable by bright red outbreaks laced with silvery scales. Although the red patches can appear anywhere on the body, they usually manifest on the arms, legs, palms of the hands, elbows, knees, buttocks, and scalp.

Often psoriasis accompanies rheumatoid arthritis, an added misery. As with lupus, mucopolysaccharides invade connective tissue. One of the most successful treatments for psoriasis is thyroid supplementation, but it is not consistently effective.

In the history of thyroid supplementation, sometimes psoriasis responds well. Sometimes there's no improvement of the condition. My experience with psoriasis is somewhat limited. However, with thyroid supplementation, a large number of my patients with this disorder eventually experienced a dramatic reduction of this condition or total disappearance.

The remainder showed slight or no improvement, indicating the possibility that their psoriasis had one or more other causes. These are some alternative modalities which have worked: a gluten-free diet, avoiding food allergens such as corn, citrus fruits, nuts, milk, acid beverages (coffee and soft drinks), and acid-containing pineapple and tomatoes.

S.S. Bleehen, M.D., Professor of Dermatology at the Royal Hallamshire Hospital in Sheffield, England, demonstrated that the omega-3 oil in 5½ ounces of mackerel, salmon, or sardines taken daily significantly improved this disorder's itching, redness, and scaling.[2] Dr. Bleehan fed the patients ten omega-3 capsules daily for twelve weeks. Similar results have been demonstrated by other researchers with the same regimen.

Still another effective regimen is 4 to 8 tablespoons of lecithin daily, as shown by an experiment with 254 psoriasis patients. Most of them recovered within five months.

It is sensible insurance for a healthy and youthful-appearing skin to have one's thyroid function checked and, if needed, supplemented. Otherwise, as illustrated by case studies in this chapter, a poor complexion can contribute to many emotional problems, an added burden that none of us needs.

9

MIND AND EMOTIONS: THE
THYROID CONNECTION

*E*xhaustion and lack of endurance are not the only handicaps of many untreated hypothyroids grimly trying to
compete in the real world. To these must be added emotional problems, of which these individuals are sometimes
not even aware.

The late Roy G. Hoskins, M.D., an eminent endocrinologist,
found that even in seemingly mild cases of myxedema, there is
an underlying irritability and hostility, in addition to mental and
physical sluggishness.[1] In another common type of hypothyroidism, Dr. Hoskins noted a chip-on-the-shoulder attitude, an abnormal responsiveness to petty annoyances, but not necessarily
the usual overweight or sluggishness. A state of general fatigue
exists, along with "general poor health and, particularly, lack

of endurance often designated chronic nervous exhaustion—and inability to endure physical or mental strain."

Dr. Hoskins referred to findings of endocrinologist H. F. Stoll, who discovered the following characteristics in "chronic hypothyroid invalidism": irritability, lying, suspiciousness, delusions, retarded ability to think, inability to concentrate, introversion, and failing memory. Even mild to moderate stress can tilt the delicate balance of the low-thyroid person and cause acute anxiety or depression. Such events as marriage, birth of a first child, a financial reversal, and new job responsibilities can bring on greater energy depletion, headaches, temper tantrums, diarrhea, or constipation, according to Dr. Stoll.

A study of twenty untreated hypothyroids by Dr. Martha Schon of the Neuropsychiatric Service at Memorial Hospital in New York City revealed such emotional traits as fatigue, nervousness, irritability, contrariness, and temper explosions, which made it easy to mistake them for neurotics. She noted a major difference, however. Genuine neurotics blame others or circumstances for their problems. Low-thyroid persons will generally accept responsibility for their emotional conduct.[2]

Dr. Schon found that with thyroid supplementation, almost all physical and emotional symptoms lessened or disappeared. Patients developed a sense of well-being and integration of personality. Apparently subclinical hypothyroidism can remain latent for years and not show itself in emotional or mental symptoms until after severe stress. A number of my patients have had this experience. Dr. Schon made the same discovery, observing that mental pressures with which patients could not cope brought on hypothyroidism.

Postpartum depression (the "blues" experienced by some women after delivery of a baby) may be attributable to a low-thyroid condition. That hypothyroidism can cause mild to severe neuroses and psychoses is not a new discovery.

Let us remember that Sigmund Freud, the father of psychoanalysis, predicted that some day a biologic or physiologic therapy would prove more effective in coping with emotional illness than psychotherapy. Carl Jung agreed.[3]

In the 1920s, Dr. Karl Mayer, a German scientist, demonstrated the power of thyroid extract to act as a biochemical psychiatrist on a patient no livelier than a block of ice—and equally silent—and normalize him.

More recently, successful use of thyroid hormone and vitamin therapy on psychiatric "rejects"—patients virtually unimproved with psychoanalysis—convinced Dr. Nathan Masor that conventional psychiatry needed biochemical backing.

Edward R. Pinckney, M.D., and Cathey Pinckney, authors of *The Fallacy of Freud and Psychoanalysis*, agree that unless the physical requirements for thyroid hormone are satisfied, psychiatric techniques will not help.

According to the Pinckneys,

> All too often, thyroid disease will manifest itself through nothing but behavioral symptoms. Neurotic actions may be the sole result of too little or too much thyroid, and the taking of a few inexpensive pills each day can produce instant normality in someone who seems to have a mental illness. Compare this type of treatment with years and years of costly lying on a couch, trying to uncover some infantile sexual frustration.
>
> But thyroid disease is not the only illness that indicates neurotic behavior. Patients with lung cancer repeatedly show marked hostility reaction. Infectious diseases, pelvic inflammations, and even enlarged arteries have produced the very symptoms the psychoanalysts claim are due to unresolved sexual problems that began in childhood. What is contradictory to the Freudian doctrine is the fact that once an organic diagnosis is made and treated, there is an immediate disappearance of all neurotic behavior.[4]

An investigator at the University of North Carolina, Dr. P. C. Whybrow, studied a group of patients with severe mental disturbances who seemed excellent candidates for typical psychiatric treatment.[5] One of them was a woman whose son had been killed in a head-on car collision many years before and who constantly said that it would have been better if she had been the one killed. She had recurring dreams of reclaiming him from his grave by digging him up with her bare hands. All day long she heard her son calling to her. Considering herself a heavy burden for her family, she often entertained thoughts of suicide.

Another woman, plagued with insomnia, experienced vivid, horrifying dreams when she did sleep—the death of her son and the mutilation of other family members. "I'm losing my mind," she insisted to family and doctors.

Both serious cases were quickly cleared up and the patients returned to normal behavior after thyroid treatment, thanks to enlightened psychiatrists.

Dr. Whybrow also found that hypothyroidism often manifests itself in two mental symptoms that are severe handicaps in daily living: poor recent memory and difficulty in concentrating. A Georgetown University study discovered these very symptoms in more than half of 109 cases of hypothyroidism.[6]

The most extreme form of hypothyroidism, myxedema, which is four to five times more common in women than in men, exaggerates mental shortcomings. Thinking, remembering, and reacting occur in slow motion, if at all. A need to concentrate often puts the person to sleep. As one recovered patient told me, "In myxedema, thinking results in nonthinking. Mental effort is next to impossible. One is just a supervegetable."

Dr. Masor reports that in even less extreme hypothyroidism, thinking is slow and memory impaired, often compounding emotional conditions such as listlessness, restlessness, irritability, a paranoid tendency, easy fatigue, and miscellaneous body pains.[7] The fact that these symptoms melt away with appropriate daily thyroid therapy indicates that, in most cases, they are probably due to hypothyroidism.

In addition to supplementation with thyroid hormone, the diet should supply all essential nutrients. Lack of any B vitamins—particularly thiamine (B_1) and cyanocobalamin (B_{12})—can slow thinking and cause memory lapses and irritability, as studies of semistarved prisoners of war have revealed. On the other hand, supplying subjects in starvation experiments with missing B-complex vitamins, with an accent on B_1 and B_{12}, brought about enhanced thinking and remembering, among other positive results.

In a double-blind experiment with matched-ability children, Dr. Ruth Flinn Herrell added just 2 mg of vitamin B_1 to the daily diet of one group and a placebo to that of the second group. At the end of the study, the first group's mental and physical abilities had risen from 7 to 87 percent. Those of the other group remained almost the same.[8]

An article in the *British Medical Journal* by Dr. J. MacDonald Holmes, which cited various experiments, revealed that a deficiency of vitamin B_{12} brought on devastating mental and emotional symptoms, such as difficulty in thinking and remembering, confusion, mood disorders, agitated depression, paranoia, delusions, visual and auditory hallucinations, maniacal behavior, and epilepsy.[9]

Along with good nutrition, aerobic exercise encourages brain and memory function, says Professor Robert Rivera, a memory expert and speech teacher at Valley College in Van Nuys, California. Professor Rivera has found that more efficient blood and oxygen circulation to the brain can cause a significant increase in a person's I.Q.—as much as thirty points.

You may be able to validate Professor Rivera's findings by trying these simple exercises. First, you inhale for eight counts, hold your breath for twelve counts, then exhale for ten counts. He recommends repeating this exercise ten times. (Warning! If you feel dizzy, stop exercising at once!)

Second, you practice sitting up erectly at work and improve posture by standing and flattening yourself against a wall, then stretching. If the experiment is successful, you should observe a new sense of vigor, well-being, and clarity of thinking.

The importance of oxygen to brain function is underscored by the fact that the gray matter, where thinking is done, uses one-quarter of our oxygen intake. Arterial blood of the brain must have an oxygen saturation of 90 percent for efficient thinking, according to Dr. Masor. If it is reduced to 85 percent, the ability for fine concentration and fine muscular coordination decreases. Reduce it to 74 percent, and faulty judgment results.[10] Such oxygen deprivation may also lead to emotional instability. Further oxygen reduction causes the nervous system to be depressed. Complete oxygen starvation for more than four minutes will often contribute to irreversible brain damage.

Hypothyroidism can cause oxygen deprivation in the brain in numerous ways: by impeding blood circulation (slowing the delivery of oxygen and nutrients); by slowing the rate of oxidation (burning) of food (glucose) to nourish brain cells; by depressing production of blood cells; by contributing to athero-sclerosis (narrowing of arteries); and by limiting the amount of blood that reaches the brain. Dr. Masor points out that narrowing of vital brain arterioles by even one-sixteenth of their caliber can limit oxygen supply and bring about mental and emotional disturbances.

How hypothyroidism depresses blood cell production (and can actually contribute to a form of anemia) has been covered in detail in chapter 5. How subnormal thyroid function encourages atherosclerosis will be explained in later chapters on heart and artery diseases.

Over and above contributing to disturbances of thought and memory processes, hypothyroidism may cause severe emotional changes, which, unfortunately, may be misdiagnosed as psychiatric disorders and treated unnecessarily with powerful drugs (some of them habit forming) and hospitalization. One of its most serious, persistent, and widespread consequences is depression, the subject of the next chapter.

10

A NEW LOOK AT DEPRESSION

*D*epressed persons are more likely to get relief from thyroid supplementation than from warmed-over psychotherapy.

New evidence that thyroid insufficiency is at the root of much depression and fatigue was announced by Mark Gold, M.D., and his associates at a conference on affective illness at Friends Hospital in Philadelphia.[1] In examining 350 inpatients and 44 outpatients at Fair Oaks Hospital, Summit, New Jersey, Dr. Gold found a "significant incidence of low-level hypothyroidism," convincing him that depression is often the first sign of low-level thyroid failure which may not be detected by the usual thyroid function tests. Traditional blood tests for thyroid function in depressed patients revealed only 10 percent hypothyroids. Ninety percent of the depressed who were clinically hypothyroid showed normal thyroid blood tests.

Dr. Gold discovered that, when untreated, hypothyroidism became increasingly severe in a very short time. Early diagnosis and treatment led to a desirable reduction in depression. It is imperative to evaluate all psychiatric patients for hypothyroidism, Dr. Gold feels, because new data show that if thyroid function is reduced by 10 percent, brain thyroid function is diminished by a corresponding amount. A slowdown of the thyroid, even if we remain normal, will cause some changes in the brain. It doesn't surprise Dr. Gold that hypothyroids appear to be psychiatric patients.

He also explained that more than 10 percent of patients who visit psychiatrists with depression have a condition called asymptomatic autoimmune thyroditis, an ailment in which the immune system attacks the thyroid gland tissue, causing inflammation and underfunction of the organ. This disorder, often called Hashimoto's Autoimmune Thyroiditis (HAIT), is discussed in greater detail in a separate chapter.

However, most cases of thyroid-induced depression are caused by simple hypothyroidism. A letter to me from a patient who had suffered from depression of unsuspected origin for decades expresses the anguish that many such persons have in common.

My depression started when I was sixteen. The doctor ordered a basal metabolism test, which turned out to be a little low. He prescribed one grain of thyroid. I took it for a year and felt better.

Then I discontinued thyroid; I don't remember why. When I was thirty-five, the depression came back, along with low energy, but I never sought help. I didn't realize what was wrong.

I'm married and have three children but never seem to have enough energy to do anything except take care of the children. In my late forties, I lost interest in everything, just dragging around, feeling low and blue. I was little more than a vegetable. I couldn't have cared less if I woke up the next day.

Finally, a doctor diagnosed me as having depression. I had a series of shock treatments and several mood-elevating drugs.

Then, when my doctor relocated, I couldn't find another doctor to help me. I struggled along with periods of mild depression and very low energy.

About five years ago, I heard Dr. Broda Barnes on a radio talk show, discussing hypothyroidism and his test. Later, I asked my new doctor for a thyroid function test, which proved negative. He refused to prescribe thyroid.

All my life, I had noticed that I ran a subnormal temperature but hadn't thought much about it. One day I took my early-morning temperature and found it low. My cousin, who was visiting, had some thyroid pills, and I started taking a small dose. Almost immediately my depression lifted and my energy rose, too.

Then I heard Dr. Barnes on the air again, this time as your guest, and I decided to see you. I'm so glad I did. As you know, my basal temperature was low and you gave me thyroid. Many, many thanks for seeing through my problems, for realizing I was not a mental patient who needed more shock treatments, mood-elevating drugs, or psychoanalysis. I feel great now!

Within a month, her fifteen-year-long depression was eliminated. It saddened me that this well-meaning person could not get simple, safe, low-cost thyroid to help her and instead was subjected to two series of arduous, expensive, and unnecessary shock treatments, which could do nothing to compensate for her shortage of thyroid hormones.

I wish I could say that this is a rare case. However, many of my patients are over age fifty and, as children, teenagers, or even adults, had had thyroid supplementation which was cut off when they or their doctors moved. During the 1950s, blood tests came into vogue and were not always positive for hypothyroidism. Patients were told that they no longer needed thyroid, and most of them suffered decades of unnecessary depression, anxiety, and physical discomfort and limitation.

In fairness to the doctors of the 1950s and 1960s, the Barnes Basal Temperature Test was not then widely known, although Dr. Barnes's landmark paper on this test had already been published in the *Journal of the American Medical Association*. Today, however, there is little excuse for being unaware of it and its validity.

Despite the Basal Temperature Test's accuracy in revealing

hypothyroidism, there is a minute percentage of cases which are too subtle to be detectable by this method. Not long ago, a patient in her early thirties, whom I'll call Phyllis, took the Barnes test and registered 97.8 degrees the first day and 97.7 the second day. She tried again on the third day and showed a temperature of 97.7. This averaged out to less than a tenth of a point below normal. Yet this woman had a serious problem with depression. She admitted that frequently, in the electronic assembly department which she supervises, she almost burst into tears at the slightest frustration, something she couldn't afford to do without reducing her stature and jeopardizing her position, which she had worked hard for fifteen years to attain.

I asked all the right questions. Had she gone through severe stresses—the death of a spouse, relative, or close friend, a revolutionary change on the job, the breakup of a love affair?

"No, doctor. Nothing like that," she responded.

"Anything seem radically wrong physically?" I asked.

"No. I'm a little more tired than usual. That's all."

"Are you always depressed, or is it intermittent?"

"I do have good days and weeks, sometimes months. But it's worse this winter than last."

I darted a glance at the calendar (sometimes you need a calendar to determine the season, because winters in northern California are quite mild) and realized that Phyllis had given me the clue I needed. She was definitely hypothyroid, despite her body temperature reading. Her deepest depression was in the winter season, when temperatures were 10 to 15 degrees cooler than in fall or summer. Colder weather makes it necessary for the thyroid to step up the burning of fuel. This slight change accented her hypothyroidism, mild as it was.

I explained the problem to Phyllis, who agreed to take a grain of thyroid daily. She never regretted it. Within three weeks, her depression began to recede, and two months later she said, "It's hard for me to remember not feeling okay. My energy level is great. It's wonderful to be a human being again."

Like Phyllis's case, Benton's had certain mystifying aspects at first. A certified public accountant who owned his own firm, Benton plunged into deep depression near the middle of April— the end of income tax season. That was understandable, because of the extreme stress he was under at tax deadline time.

However, it was now the end of May, and the depression had grown worse. Certainly a person in good health would have recovered already.

Benton's basal temperature was just a shade under the normal 97.8. A complete medical history and physical examination done at that time were inconclusive. Because of his symptoms, however, I decided to start him on a half-grain of desiccated thyroid. Even this small amount of natural thyroid medication worked wonders.

Thyroid hormone has been studied intensively in depressed patients. In one double-blind controlled study, just 25 mcg of thyroid daily enhanced the antidepressant action of the drug imipramine by 50 percent. Forty mcg was even more effective with imipramine.[2]

Of course, not all depression is caused by hypothyroidism.[3] Poor nutrition is another major unsuspected cause. In such cases, dietary counseling and nutritional supplements banish depression almost miraculously.

An unsuspected cause of depression in women is the taking of oral contraceptive pills. When a patient is depressed and on the Pill, I have her change to another form of contraception as soon as possible and treat her immediately for B-complex deficiency, particularly vitamin B_6, known to be depleted in chronic users of oral contraceptives. If there is, in fact, a B-complex deficiency, a B-complex vitamin including at least 50 mg of vitamins B_6 usually helps to dispel depression.

Sometimes when the lack of B complex is caused by the use of birth control pills, severe depression follows childbirth (postpartum depression). This condition usually responds to B-complex vitamins.

The trace mineral lithium is often thought to be an excellent treatment for depression. Actually, it may worsen depression, because it interferes with thyroid function. On the basis of a thorough study, P. L. Rabin and D. C. Evans of Vanderbilt University School of Medicine verify this fact in the *Journal of Clinical Psychiatry*: ". . . goiter formation and hypothyroidism are not infrequent following lithium therapy. . . ."[4]

Unfortunately, hypothyroidism is still not widely enough recognized as a major cause of depression. It would be a mistake, however, to consider subnormal thyroid function and nutritional deficiencies as the *only* causes.

11

MEDICAL LOOK-ALIKES:
HYPOGLYCEMIA AND
HYPOTHYROIDISM

nother heavyweight contributor to depression is hypoglycemia (low blood sugar), an insidious disorder with many emotional and physical symptoms, the best known of which is deep fatigue.[1]

In a survey of 600 hypoglycemia patients, Dr. Stephen Gyland found that depression ranked fifth among their complaints and was experienced by 77 percent of his subjects.

It is understandable why hypoglycemia causes a long list of emotional ailments in addition to depression: forgetfulness, insomnia, anxiety, confusion, antisocial behavior, crying jags, lack of concentration, and assorted phobias. When our blood sugar is too low, our brains are deprived of glucose, the only fuel they can use. This starvation brings on the symptoms which are misdiagnosed as neuroses.

Hypoglycemia results mainly from how the body handles—or mishandles—sugar, rather than from the amount of sugar in the blood at a given time. When a normal person takes in a simple refined carbohydrate, such as table sugar, the blood level of sugar rises. Then the hormone insulin, secreted by the pancreas, soon brings down blood sugar to the fasting level.

When the hypoglycemic ingests sugar, however, the pancreas suffers shock and overreacts, discharging so much insulin into the blood that sugar is removed too rapidly, creating a glucose deficit. Secondary results from prolonged hyperinsulinism are an off-balance nervous system, overstimulated adrenal glands often stressed in the process of elevating blood sugar level, and an eventual shortage of blood sugar–elevating hormones—adrenal, glucagon, and a pituitary gland hormone.

From the standpoint of symptoms, hypoglycemia is like hypothyroidism. Dr. Broda Barnes felt that these disorders are almost as closely related as Siamese twins, and his reasons make good sense.

He told me how he happened to stumble onto this connection. A legal secretary, prior to being treated by Dr. Barnes, passed out in her office, apparently from a heart attack, and was rushed to a hospital's intensive care unit. Three days of comprehensive, sophisticated tests revealed nothing organically wrong. She had other blackouts, more siren-screaming races to intensive care, more tests, more medical costs, and still no diagnosis firm enough to support a therapy program. Then she found a physician who understood the biochemical basis for hypoglycemia and put her on a high-protein, low-carbohydrate diet, which brought about some improvement. However, she was not completely satisfied. She was referred to Dr. Barnes, who observed that she showed many symptoms of hypothyroidism, including a subnormal basal temperature.

With natural thyroid therapy, she recovered rapidly and never again experienced a blackout. As Dr. Barnes put it, "The light suddenly dawned. If she were hypothyroid and hypoglycemic, might not the two ailments occur together in many individuals?"

He explained his theory in the following terms: "A sluggish liver results from subnormal thyroid activity. During periods of stress, the liver can't produce enough sugar from protein. Then hypoglycemia occurs. Thyroid therapy stimulates the liver to normal function, and hypoglycemia usually disappears."

Dr. Barnes cited three bits of evidence of sluggish liver in hypothyroidism. For more than one hundred years, researchers have noted that myxedema patients (those with extremely low thyroid function) have a yellowish skin color, caused by too much carotene in the blood. A liver low in thyroid hormone has difficulty converting carotene to vitamin A, which is colorless. Thyroid therapy stimulates liver function, and the yellowish skin color vanishes.

Another piece of evidence is that blood cholesterol is usually high in hypothyroidism. Thyroid supplementation lowers cholesterol, because the liver is once again working normally, turning excess cholesterol into bile salts, which are discharged in the bile.

The third piece of evidence is that the sluggish liver of the hypothyroid stores glucose more slowly than a normal organ. Therefore, the blood level of sugar may register high during a fasting glucose tolerance test. The patient may also spill glucose in the urine and for these reasons will probably be labeled a "prediabetic."

"When such an individual is put on thyroid therapy, the liver begins to function properly and the glucose tolerance test is normal," said Dr. Barnes. "Many so-called prediabetics are really hypothyroids. This accounts for the fact that so few of them ever become diabetics."

Blood sugar levels are also closely associated with correct functioning of the adrenals, two ductless glands which perch on top of the kidneys and produce the hormone adrenalin. Most of us are familiar with one essential function of the adrenals: triggering the discharge of liver glucose (stored as glycogen) into the bloodstream to give us instant energy in the face of danger. These key glands also secrete and release other essential hormones. The major ones are cortisol (hydrocortisone) and cortisone, both glucocorticoids related to liver sugar.

A study included in perhaps the most prestigious textbook on the thyroid gland, *The Thyroid*, edited by Sidney C. Werner, M.D., and Sidney H. Ingbar, M.D., gives a clue as to how hypothyroidism influences at least one important function of the adrenal glands related to blood sugar.

One of cortisol's most significant functions is stimulating the liver's production of glycogen. An experiment cited in *The Thyroid* shows that hypothyroids secrete cortisol at a reduced rate. This means that liver sugar is produced more slowly. Treatment with thyroid hormone normalizes cortisol metabolism.

The Werner-Ingbar book states that hypothyroidism in animals sometimes causes adrenal atrophy (wasting away), which could undermine every function of this gland. The findings in human beings have not been so conclusive. What is well established, however, is that the thyroid gland is closely associated with blood sugar levels, although all the reasons for this are not as yet known.

Dr. Barnes added a footnote in regard to hypothyroidism and hypoglycemia. In more than four decades as a medical doctor, he treated more than 5,000 patients for the symptoms of subnormal thyroid function and did not see one case of hypoglycemia develop. He admitted, however, that only in the last two decades had this disorder become well enough known for him and other medical doctors to be alert to it.

Patients who went to Dr. Barnes with hypoglycemia usually responded to thyroid therapy with no change in diet. My experience in this regard varies slightly. In many instances, my patients have overcome low blood sugar with thyroid hormones. However, I have also had excellent response from diet.

My dietary approach to this disorder is purposely uncomplicated. First, I explain to patients that a simple carbohydrate wastes no time going through the digestive process and into the bloodstream—foods such as sugar, corn syrup, and glucose, for example. Complex unrefined carbohydrates—legumes, nuts, seeds, vegetables, whole grains, whole-grain cereals—are slower, followed by proteins and then fats, the slowest.

A mixed diet—some complex carbohydrates, protein, and a little fat—assures gradual release of sugar into the bloodstream. The pancreas is protected from sugar shock. Ample protein from meat, fish, poultry, eggs, or dairy products and low-carbohydrate vegetables and fruits make an ideal diet for the hypoglycemic. Most fruits and vegetables can be included, although I usually eliminate those in the 20 percent carbohydrate bracket: bananas, sweet cherries, fresh figs, grape juice, and prunes, as well as kidney, lima and navy beans, corn, and hominy. Fruits and vegetables to be eaten sparingly are the following in the 15 percent carbohydrate group: apples, apricots, blueberries, sour cherries, grapes, loganberries, pears, pineapple, plums, and raspberries, as well as artichokes, parsnips, and peas.

Some authorities on hypoglycemia recommend from five to seven small meals daily, rather than the traditional three. By mixing food groups, I find that most patients can manage hypoglycemia well with three meals, but I suggest that they experiment. If more small meals work for them, I urge them to follow such a routine.

So much for low blood sugar. Next we will deal with high blood sugar.

12

DIABETES—A PREVENTABLE DISEASE

A little knowledge about diabetes, a blood sugar disorder that plagues almost 11 million Americans, will go a long way to prevent it and—for those already diabetic—to lessen this ailment's health-destroying effects, reduce dependency on insulin, and dramatically decrease the chances of sometimes fatal diabetic complications.

Telltale symptoms of diabetes are excessive thirst, frequent and copious urination, constant hunger, extreme systemic acidity, rapid weight loss, severe itching, fatigue, weakness, and, above all, high sugar level in the blood and urine.

Elevated blood sugar is due to a breakdown of the body's energy use system. Glucose, a simple sugar derived from food, is our major fuel for heat and energy. Although blood circulation carries glucose to all of our body cells, it cannot penetrate the cell walls unless it is attached to molecules of the pancreatic hormone insulin. In an insulin shortage, much blood sugar accumulates and circulates helplessly, finally passing into the kidneys for excretion in the urine.

On its way into our stomachs, the food we eat triggers the release of insulin into the bloodstream. Most blood sugar is used for energy. However, some enters the liver to be changed into glycogen and is stored there and in the muscles for use according to the body's needs. If we overeat, the excess calories are converted by our bodies into fat deposits.

Insulin is secreted by the pancreas, a yellowish glandular organ lying horizontally under the stomach. This hormone is formed in a part of the pancreas called the islets of Langerhans, which contain the all-important alpha and beta cells. Alpha cells secrete a hormone called glucagon, which, when called upon, raises the blood sugar level by activating the conversion of stored glycogen into glucose. The beta cells secrete the hormone insulin, which lowers blood sugar level. The outputs of the alpha and beta cells are supposed to be in balance. In the diabetic, however, insulin is often in short supply, for reasons which will be discussed later.

In addition to these secretions, the pancreas excretes proteolytic enzymes, molecules which help create the proper pH (acid-base) environment in the digestive system for these proteolytic enzymes to function. They break down proteins into body-usable amino acids.

Many theories explain how diabetes develops. Perhaps the most accepted one is that repeated and heavy intake of sugar causes the body's energy system to become defective. Sugar entering the bloodstream signals the beta cells to secrete more insulin, keeping them in production until the glucose level drops to normal. Repeated assaults by large amounts of sugar force the pancreas to work overtime in producing insulin. Eventually, it becomes exhausted and production slumps.

In some instances, however, insulin shortage may not be the problem. Experiments by Dr. Walter Mertz, former chief of the U.S. Department of Agriculture's Vitamin and Mineral Research Division, indicate that a shortage of chromium can bring on diabetes.[1]

To escort glucose through cell walls, insulin needs the close cooperation of infinitesimal amounts of chromium as a catalyst. Most maturity-onset diabetes (also known as Type 2 diabetes) results from a diet of chromium-poor processed foods and could probably be prevented by use of chromium-rich foods such as brewer's yeast, beef liver, chicken, various meats, and whole grains.

Some scientists state that diabetes is caused by the islets of Langerhans's release of pro-insulin, rather than biologically usable insulin. For unexplained reasons, this "not quite" form of the hormone never goes through its final chemical changes.

Research at the University of Texas Southwestern Medical School suggests that diabetes is a hormone disorder brought about by a shortage of insulin and an excess of blood sugar–raising glucagon.

Authorities agree that genes predispose us toward diabetes, that children born of at least one diabetic parent are more likely to be diabetic than those from nondiabetic parents. They may be diabetes prone because the pancreas does not function properly or because their cell receptors do not take up glucose efficiently.

While admitting the importance of the inheritance factor, other authorities indicate that innumerable environmental factors, including food selection, preparation, consumption, and repetition, as well as stresses, are probably even more important. One group within this school of thought holds that heredity is given more weight than it deserves, because researchers gather their statistics without considering that poor diet and other negative environmental conditions passed down from generation to generation are also a key part of physical ailments which appear to be strictly hereditary.

It is now well known that one of the adrenal gland hormones, epinephrine, released into the bloodstream in fight-or-flight situations, increases free fatty acids in the blood and turns off the release of insulin. Unresolved and continued stress can therefore upset the balance of pancreas hormones and bring on diabetes.

Another kind of stress, obesity, invites diabetes. At a conference on diabetes mellitus and obesity, Dr. W. John H. Butterfield, Professor of Medicine at Guys Hospital in London, revealed an amazing similarity in how the body handles carbohydrates in diabetes and in gross overweight.[2]

Dr. Butterfield described his experiment on comparative cell glucose uptake of three groups of test subjects: juvenile diabetics, maturity-onset diabetics, and normal controls.

Juvenile diabetics absorbed no sugar in their cells, a strong indication that they were short on internally secreted insulin. Glucose uptake of older diabetic patients and obese normal subjects was similar. Lean controls took up more sugar than plump ones.

Obese subjects handled carbohydrates almost like diabetics, said Dr. Butterfield. As obesity progresses, less and less insulin reaches the insulin-responsive muscles, so less and less glucose uptake occurs there, making it necessary for more and more insulin to be formed. When obesity increases to certain proportions, the pancreas can't keep up production of insulin to meet demand, and hyperglycemia results. Reversible-obesity diabetes, then, adds up to a breakdown of the body's insulin-glucose economy.

Another significant insight of Dr. Butterfield's about the proneness of obese people to diabetes is that body fat competes with muscle for insulin, and fat wins. Then carbohydrates are changed into more fat.

Both obese and lean diabetics usually reduce blood fats and the need for insulin on a high-fiber diet. This is the conclusion reached by James Anderson, M.D., of the University of Kentucky, a long-time researcher in high-fiber diets—those containing large amounts of raw foods, fruits, vegetables, whole-grain breads, bran, nuts, and seeds. The most marked improvement was in obese patients who lost the greatest amount of weight. Excellent high-fiber foods are spinach, prunes, corn, fresh peas, blackberries, sweet potatoes, apples, whole-wheat bread, potatoes, broccoli, almonds, raisins, zucchini, plums, and kidney beans.

Associate Professor Somasundaram Addanki of the Ohio State University College of Medicine agrees with the need for a high-fiber diet in managing *and* preventing diabetes. However, he goes farther.[3] Ninety percent of diabetes-prone individuals can avoid this disorder by not eating "the typical high-fat, high-sugar, and low-fiber diet consumed in Western countries," he writes in the journal *Preventive Medicine.*[4]

Professor Addanki speaks from personal experience as well as in-depth research on this subject. A diabetic who married a diabetic, he says that he and his wife did not develop diabetes until they left their native India and started eating American foods. He does not agree that heredity is a primary factor. Only 8 percent of cases can be attributed to heredity, as comparative studies in Africa and Japan indicate. These findings relieved Addanki about the future of his children.

Further data that the typical American diet exerts the most powerful influence on the development of diabetes emerge from a comparison of Japanese living in Japan and others who moved to Hawaii. After eating Western food in Hawaii, they invariably developed diabetes in greater numbers.

A biochemist and nutritionist, Addanki explains why the poor American diet turns healthy individuals into diabetics. Fatty, sugary, low-fiber foods stimulate certain intestinal bacteria to produce excessive estrogen, a female hormone. It is also probable that an enzyme in fatty tissues unites with testosterone, the male hormone, to synthesize more estrogen. Estrogen desensitizes skeletal muscles to insulin action. As more weight is added, more estrogen is produced, more insulin is required to be effective, and there is greater stress on the pancreas, the insulin producer, which wears out too soon.

The excess estrogen theory explains why obese adult men are often impotent, while women frequently experience a more powerful sexual drive. In a United Press International story explaining his theory, Professor Addanki admitted to six years of "diabetic impotence" before a change of diet brought him control over his disease. He advises all fat people to give up sugar, white flour, and fatty foods if they want to avoid the risk of developing diabetes.

Another authority who has evidence that exhaustion of the pancreas underlies the development of diabetes is William H. Philpott, M.D. A prominent clinical ecologist, he has a different explanation as to how this happens, and he elaborates it in an illuminating book, *Victory over Diabetes*, written with Dwight K. Kalita, Ph.D.[5] He observes that the pancreas secretes a substance called somastatin, which acts as a balancing mechanism between the organ's other hormones, glucagon (blood sugar raising) and insulin (blood sugar lowering).

"Obviously, a proper harmony must exist between these various functions of the pancreas to avoid diabetes," he writes. "If we were to stop at this point with our examination of the pancreas, we might conclude, as has been done by many physicians, that diabetes is a simple matter of controlling high blood sugar levels by the daily injection of insulin.

"However, as we have already seen, although high blood sugar levels may indeed be controlled by the use of insulin, the associated killing complications of diabetes are not easily dealt with. There is, in fact, medical evidence . . . that daily injections of insulin may, in part, actually be responsible for some of the many severe cardiovascular and cerebrovascular complications associated with this disease." (Complications of this disorder will be dealt with in detail in a later chapter.)

Dr. Philpott explains that pancreas-made insulin travels through the bloodstream to the liver, where at least half of it is used. The rest of the body needs only a small amount.

Insulin injected under the skin of the arm, leg, or buttocks travels the entire peripheral circulatory system before reaching the liver, and much more insulin than is needed in the vascular system remains there. Compounding this problem is the fact that unless sufficient insulin is injected to satisfy the liver's requirements, a serious condition, ketoacidosis, will develop. Dr. Philpott feels that, under these conditions, hyperinsulinism is almost unavoidable and contributes to severe complications of diabetes.

Why should a natural substance such as insulin create problems? Dr. Philpott answers in the following terms: ". . . Dr. R. W. Stout, of Hammersmith Hospital in London, actually showed that when laboratory rats were given insulin intravenously, the insulin stimulated the synthesis of cholesterol in blood vessel walls.

"Other investigators have shown that when too much insulin is present in the blood, all kinds of *metabolic debris* can be found, including certain chemicals that are deposited on the insides of blood vessels that have been partly occluded [closed], as in arteriosclerosis."

No part of the body, including the pancreas, is necessarily

exempt from this condition. Over and above injected insulin, other outside factors can undermine the pancreas, including chemicals in the environment and foods to which we may be allergic or hypersensitive.

The first organ to be influenced by exposure to ingested foods and chemicals, the pancreas has the key task of turning these substances into forms usable by the body and also of protecting the body from negative reaction to them. Food allergens and harmful chemicals cause the pancreas to be overstimulated and overworked, and thus weaken it.

"All addictions, of course, whether they are foods of any kind, chemicals, tobacco, and/or alcohol, eventually lead to pancreatic insufficiency of varying degrees," Dr. Philpott explains, "but what is important to realize is that most affected in pancreatic insufficiency of these types are the bicarbonate and enzyme productions of the organ. . . ."

Let's look at what happens in pancreatic insufficiency. Added to a lessening ability to secrete insulin and glucagon, the pancreas produces inadequate amounts of pancreatic enzymes and bicarbonate, which threatens the proper functioning of the entire organ.

Unless the pancreas can make sufficient proteolytic enzymes to secrete into the intestines, proteins cannot be properly broken down into amino acids for body use. This leads to a deficiency of amino acids and a disastrous chain reaction. Proteolytic enzymes are made from amino acids. In a deficiency of amino acids, these enzymes will soon be deficient.

"With an amino acid deficiency, there is more than just a reduced enzyme production from the pancreas . . . . Insulin is composed of fifty-one amino acids. When these all-important building blocks of hormones are in short supply, the quality and quantity of insulin production actually begin to diminish. This, of course, can lead to a deficiency of insulin with the resulting effect of high blood sugar or diabetes," writes Dr. Philpott.

Subnormal function of the pancreas also causes diminished production of lipase, an enzyme essential to proper metabolism of fats. This causes a rise in free fatty acids in the bloodstream, which is encouragement for arteriosclerosis.

Still another complication from a deficient pancreas and its reduced production of proteolytic enzymes is that proteins are not properly digested into amino acids and large particles in the bloodstream lodge in the tissues. The body's immune system is immediately activated and it attacks these particles as undesirable aliens, causing inflammation and injury in the arteries or wherever else they lodge.

Dr. Philpott warns that cooking foods above 118 degrees Fahrenheit destroys digestive enzymes, putting an added burden on the pancreas, salivary glands, stomach, and intestines to come "to the rescue and furnish digestive enzymes (protease for the proteins, lipase for fats, and amylase for carbohydrates) to break down these substances.

"To do this repeatedly, the body must rob . . . enzymes from other glands, muscles, nerves, and the blood to help in its demanding digestive process. Eventually, the glands—and this includes the pancreas—develop deficiencies of enzymes, because they have been forced to work harder, due to the low level of enzymes in cooked food."

An experiment in the University of Minnesota's Department of Anatomy showed that rats fed an 80 percent cooked food diet for 155 days had an increase of pancreatic weight by 20 to 30 percent "with a corresponding decrease in digestive enzyme secretions. And what is true of animals is also true of man," writes Dr. Philpott.

Although the pancreas can manufacture enzymes, we must not overdraw on our enzyme potential.

". . . The more we use our enzyme potential, the faster it is going to run out," he maintains. "When you eat food that is raw, the enzymes contained in the food immediately start breaking down the food ingested."

In other words, if you eat as much raw food as possible, you put less burden on your pancreas and extend its healthy life.

When pancreas function is diminished, production of bicarbonate is also reduced. This is a vital secretion, needed to increase the alkalinity of the small intestine.

"In pancreatic deficiencies, acute metabolic acidosis after the meal occurs," writes Dr. Philpott, "since the pancreatic bicarbonate, now undersupplied, has not neutralized acid from the stomach as it empties into the duodenum plus the small intestine.

"This reduction of proper bicarbonate levels in the pancreas results in a chain reaction whereby the pancreatic proteolytic enzymes, which are also secreted into the small intestine, and which need an alkaline medium in which to function best, are destroyed."

There is a wealth of additional helpful information in Dr. Philpott's *Victory over Diabetes*, which is a book that every diabetic should have for ready reference.

Another stress on the pancreas not mentioned by Dr. Philpott is subnormal body temperature caused by hypothyroidism, particularly myxedema, and by less extreme subnormal thyroid function. This may be the reason why so many diabetics are also hypothyroid.

Some years ago, C. D. Eaton, M.D., of Detroit, published a revealing report, "Co-Existence of Hypothyroidism with Diabetes Mellitus," in the *Journal of the Michigan Medical Society*.[6] In studying hundreds of his diabetic patients, he found symptoms of hypothyroidism and diabetes to be similar—all but the carbohydrate metabolism disturbance in the latter. Symptoms in common were low energy, weakness, constipation, itching, sleepiness, high levels of blood fat, muscle pains, high susceptibility to infection, poor wound healing, early atherosclerosis, and gangrene. He discovered that hypothyroidism was far more frequent in diabetics than in nondiabetics.

Dr. Eaton observed that insulin controlled the blood sugar level in diabetics but did nothing to correct the other symptoms. Administration of small doses of natural thyroid did, however, as I will explain in a later chapter.

To summarize and accentuate the key points in this chapter, here are the principal ways to prevent diabetes or to lessen its effects and the chances of diabetic complications:

1. Refrain from eating refined sugar and other refined carbohydrates. (Remember that processed food products often contain hidden sugars. Read labels carefully.)

2. Make sure your diet includes some chromium-rich foods—brewer's yeast, beef liver, chicken, meat, and whole grains—because without chromium insulin cannot carry nutrients through the walls of your trillions of cells.

3. Try to avoid unnecessary stress, and make practical adjustments to that which is unavoidable. Stress slows down insulin production.

4. Exercise regularly.

5. Eat a high-fiber diet for reasons of general health but particularly to reduce chances of developing diabetes or of lessening the need for insulin.

6. Avoid becoming obese. Overweight individuals are prime targets for diabetes. (The next chapter deals with weight loss.)

7. Keep your pancreas healthy, not only by avoiding assaults of refined sugar which overwork this organ, but also by avoiding chemicals, tobacco, and alcohol, and by eating more raw vegetables for their live enzymes. A steady diet of cooked foods can deplete the existing bank of digestive enzymes and harm the pancreas.

8. Be certain that your body temperature is normal and that you are not hypothyroid, a condition which places stress on the pancreas.

9. Remember that insulin can control blood sugar levels but does nothing to prevent complications of diabetes. Thyroid hormone can help in this regard.

13

OVERWEIGHT: HOW TO BE
A GOOD LOSER!

Whoever first called the struggle to shed unwanted weight the Battle of the Bulge was guilty of a serious understatement. It seems more like the Hundred Years' War!

I am constantly besieged by patients whose best efforts at losing weight have been none too good. It is not surprising that they lose their fighting hearts. Many of them have been on every diet touted by best-selling books: high carbohydrate–low fat; high fiber; low carbohydrate–high protein; juices; fasts; and other regimes conceived by the profit-motivated human mind.

Some patients lose weight, but not for long. Sooner or later—usually sooner—they slip back into old eating habits, and the fat comes back bigger and better than ever. As one of those fortunate fellows who carry no more fat than a racing grey-

99

hound. I am going to give you a plan that keeps me slim and helps my patients reduce. My system doesn't promise as quick returns as best-seller regimes, but it does work. It starts with the underlying principles of encouraging good health and proper thyroid function, which are basic to efficient weight loss.

Most overweight individuals are undernourished and suffering from subclinical malnutrition. This condition doesn't always lead to immediate catastrophic illness, but it will lead to biochemical imbalance that may cause health problems and preclude weight loss. It is important to avoid incomplete and unbalanced diets. Temporary shedding of a few pounds is not worth the loss of good health.

We are all different and therefore require different quantities of the same essential nutrients to stay healthy. No matter how complete your diet appears, you can't get from it all the essential nutrients in proper amounts. You must therefore take nutritional supplements to maintain optimal health. You must be realistic about your food supply. On its trip from the ground to your gullet, your food may lose as much as 50 percent of some essential nutrients, even before it is processed.

In order to be in good health and to lose weight, you must have normal thyroid function—or appropriate supplementation—to realize full values from your food. Even if your diet contains all essential micronutrients in proper amounts, you may not be getting full nutritional benefit from it.

Food must be broken down and absorbed through the gastrointestinal mucosa. This process is often impaired in hypothyroidism. Next, food must be processed by pancreatic enzymes and converted by the liver in order to become biochemically active. Assimilation is often faulty in hypothyroid patients. Then the digested food must be transported by the circulatory system to the sites of use at the cellular level and successfully enter the cells to provide nutritional fuel. Lack of certain nutrients retards the process.

After all this, wastes have to be efficiently eliminated from cells and carried by the circulatory system for detoxification by the kidneys and liver and thrown off by the bowels, urinary system, skin, and lungs—all of which function below par in hypothyroid individuals.

In hypothyroidism, a decreased rate of oxygen use and a

diminished rate of heat production translate into a decrease in metabolism and an inability to lose weight, no matter how hard we try. Administration of thyroid hormone restores both oxygen consumption and metabolic functioning to the hypothyroid individual.

Now comes a key fact. All dieters are familiar with the "sticking point"—the point at which the bathroom scale stubbornly refuses to go lower. In the hypothyroid, this is attributable to a worsening of the hypothyroidism, in which the body sets its thermostat lower.

Hypothyroidism does not make you fat. Dr. Barnes always pointed out that upwards of 40 percent of his hypothyroid patients were actually underweight. However, if you are overweight and hypothyroid, you will probably need to be taking thyroid hormone to facilitate the usefulness of any diet you are on.

Your doctor has probably told you that taking thyroid hormone to lose weight is an unnecessary placebo if you don't have low thyroid blood tests. Unfortunately, this is not the case. It is possible to be hypothyroid even with an adequate thyroid hormone output because of biochemical differences in the receptor sites in our cells, and this condition will show up on the basal temperature test.

What can you do to lose weight? Follow the rules listed below.

1. Make sure your thyroid gland is functioning normally so that you can rule out hypothyroidism, a handicap to weight loss. Start with the Barnes Basal Temperature Test.

2. Eat frequent small meals from the five major food groups.

3. Increase your vegetable intake for all of its nutritional contributions, particularly live enzymes which help the digestion and absorption process, and added dietary bulk to speed up elimination.

4. Avoid refined carbohydrates, including sugar, white flour, and white rice.

5. Avoid foods containing preservatives and artificial additives (coloring, flavoring, stabilizing, and foaming agents).

6. Don't add salt to foods. Avoid restaurants which salt their menu items. Avoid sodium-containing additives such as MSG.

7. Avoid overcooked foods. Use leftover cooking liquids in soups and gravies.

8. Minimize your use of animal or saturated fats. Use only lean cuts of meat, trim off fat, and remove fat-laden skin from chicken.

9. Don't use heated vegetable oils. Don't fry foods in oil. Heating vegetable oils and fats makes them as harmful to the body as animal fats and robs your system of essential fatty acids.

10. Get a computerized nutritional evaluation. This will pinpoint your dietary deficiencies. Better yet, have a consultation with a physician who specializes in preventive health maintenance.

11. Improve your diet by taking nutritional supplements.

12. Add bulk to your diet with fiber.

13. Check on evening primrose oil, a supplement sold at all nutrition centers and helpful in weight reduction programs. Two capsules after each meal (or three times a day) is the recommended amount for adults.

14. Avoid diet beverages, dark teas (of the nonherbal variety), coffee, and more than 4 to 6 ounces of fruit or vegetable juices at one sitting or more than one piece of raw fruit at a single meal.

15. Never starve yourself.

16. Get professional psychological counseling if you have been overweight for more than a year. Many individuals and families working to lose weight often unconsciously sabotage their own programs for a variety of hidden reasons. A professional counselor can often unearth these problems. It is also difficult for some dieters to adjust to the success of their programs, to becoming more attractive and more socially acceptable. Such conflicts can be brought to light by counseling and, after a few brief sessions, eliminated.

17. Remember, strictly vegetarian diets are notoriously deficient in micronutrients such as vitamin B_{12} and others; this has been mentioned in previous chapters. Such shortcomings must be corrected by dietary changes and nutritional supplementation.

18. Exercise aerobically (unless you are seriously ill or your doctor has advised against it). This is an essential part of any weight control program. The best exercise that most of us can enjoy and participate in is brisk walking for fifteen to twenty minutes, three or four times a week.

19. Recognize that you are responsible for the success or failure of your weight control program. You will notice that I did not include any rigid menus in this chapter for the simple reason that most of them don't work. We tend to revert to our old, established eating habits, no matter what diet we're on, because of ethnic likes and dislikes, mistrust of the new, and inertia. More important than a set of menus is an awareness of nutritional principles on which you can build your own best diet based on your food likes and dislikes. If you eat small meals from all the essential food groups and eliminate junky, refined, and convenience foods from your diet, you will almost always lose weight.

20. Don't expect perfection in following your diet. This can lead to depression if you slip. Remember, two steps forward and one step backward is better than the reverse. Strive to the best of your ability for moderation. Allow yourself to binge on rare occasions, if you consciously control when those occasions occur. If you can't do this, please reread number 16 and pay careful attention to number 21.

21. If you're following all of the previous suggestions and are still struggling to lose weight, you are probably suffering from food allergies, which often cause serious food addictions and weight gain. Food allergy and sensitivity were purposely not discussed in detail, because they fall outside the scope of this book. However, my own clinical experience indicates that most minor food sensitivities and allergies are resolved by correcting hypothyroidism and nutritional imbalances.

22. See a clinical ecologist—a physician who specializes in treating food allergy programs—and start a food rotation diet. If there is no clinical ecologist in your area, read a book such as *Dr. Mandell's 5 Day Allergy Relief System*, which offers a step-by-step program for testing foods by means of an "elimination diet." Once aware of the foods to which you are sensitive,

you can rotate them, eating none of the offending ones any more than once every four days.

23. Check with your doctor to make sure you don't have *Candida albicans*, a yeast infection that tends to contribute to weight gain. If you have it, follow treatment for it.

24. Relax and enjoy your program. With time and persistence, you will take off or keep off excess weight which can contribute to a host of ailments, among them cardiovascular disorders, which are the subject of the next chapter.

14

HOW TO PREVENT A
HEART ATTACK—YOUR OWN!

*H*idden in the throats of unsuspecting millions is the reason for many—if not most—heart attacks: a subnormal thyroid gland.

Unfortunately, many medical doctors still do not recognize this fact and instead continue to advocate avoidance of many wholesome, nourishing, cholesterol-containing foods for the purpose of diminishing cardiovascular ailments. It is difficult to understand how they can overlook a mountain of evidence that hypothyroidism is a major silent assassin—a mountain whose base was formed in England more than a century ago.

It all began with a case mentioned earlier—Dr. William M. Ord's severely atherosclerotic female patient with the grossly enlarged, fibrous, nonworking thyroid gland; mucin-logged,

105

swollen tissues; and a tight-skinned, masklike face. Reports of similar cases by other contemporary doctors made the medical community aware that this new ailment was widespread and required special study. In 1883 the London Clinical Society formed a task force, including elite Harley Street physicians, for this purpose. In the course of five years, the medical researchers identified and investigated one hundred cases of myxedema.

Results of experiments, observations of patients, and examinations of autopsies, reported in a hefty 300-page volume, revealed unequivocally that myxedema was caused by decreased function of the thyroid gland. Atherosclerosis, commonly found in these cases, received no more attention than other symptoms, inasmuch as cardiovascular ailments were a rarity then. Epidemics of contagious diseases finished off most people before they could live long enough to develop cardiovascular disease.

Then, in 1890, Viennese pathologists discovered that thyroid deficiency helps bring on heart attacks, thanks to the wisdom and foresight which Austrian Empress Maria Theresa had demonstrated some one hundred years earlier. The Empress had passed a national law making it mandatory that the body of each patient who had died in a hospital go through the autopsy procedure. This law actually turned Austrian hospitals into laboratories of learning so that, in a real sense, Maria Theresa accelerated medical progress for the world.

Unfortunately, knowledge of heart attack prevention seemed of little value in the 1890s, because heart attacks were still uncommon. An idea had been born before its time—a solution for which there was no problem.

Yet for the sake of science, researchers pursued further experiments. They found that after the thyroid was removed from test animals, they always developed atherosclerosis and mucinlogged tissues. Next, Professor Kocher of Berne, Switzerland, a surgeon in a known goiter belt, found that after lifesaving thyroidectomy in 101 human beings, the same thing happened. If he had not operated on them, however, their massive goiters would have compressed the windpipe and caused suffocation.

Professor Kocher's surgery proved to be only a delaying action, because the patients quickly developed atherosclerosis and other symptoms identical to those in Dr. Ord's classic case and soon died. To assure continued thyroid hormone production and save lives, Professor Kocher then developed a surgical technique for removing only the part of the thyroid gland threatening the windpipe.

During the same period, Professor T. Billroth, Vienna's most eminent surgeon, noted for perfecting the stomach ulcer operation still in use, totally removed gigantic goiters and, like Kocher, lost the lives he was trying to save.

Over and over, Austrian pathologists observed and reported that thyroidectomy invariably brought on exaggerated hardening of the arteries. Despite articles on the findings of Drs. Kocher and Billroth in the world's medical journals, surgeons in some enlightened nations persisted in their practice of total thyroid removal until the 1950s.

Intrigued by the devastating results of thyroidectomy, Dr. Billroth assigned his most brilliant student, von Eilsberg, to make further investigations of arterial changes in animals— sheep and goats—after removal of the thyroid gland. In 1895 von Eilsberg reported that thyroidectomy brought on all the symptoms of myxedema, including gross degeneration of arteries throughout the body. It is of great significance that the coronary arteries, which supply the heart with blood, nourishment, and oxygen, were among those that underwent degeneration. Several years later, Drs. E.P. Pick and F. Pineless, also of Vienna, confirmed these findings but, in using fresh thyroid extract on subjects, were able to prevent premature damage to the arteries.

Supplementation with thyroid only appeared to be new at that time. Chinese doctors two thousand years before Christ rejuvenated aging patients with failing faculties by means of an animal thyroid soup, with the result that patients felt younger, had more energy, and often regained ability to think and remember. Many centuries later, during Queen Victoria's reign, London's most prominent Harley Street doctors took a cue from the Chinese and served elderly and failing patients special sandwiches the main ingredient of which was raw animal thyroid gland.

Many patients were squeamish about eating raw thyroid gland, so doctors looked for alternatives. One effort that failed was transplanting thyroid glands from the newly dead or from animals into hypothyroid patients. The body rejected this foreign tissue. Finally, after long and arduous experimentation, G. R. Murray, a British medical doctor, concocted a glycerine extract of fresh thyroid tissue, injecting the juice into patients. Although it achieved desired results, Dr. Murray found that his preparation rapidly oxidized and molded. Then he struck upon the idea of removing fat from the fresh animal glands and drying them. This process preserved the active thyroid principle.

Now he needed a patient to try his desiccated thyroid. A middle-aged woman with acute myxedema, not many heartbeats from death, volunteered. She never regretted her decision, because her symptoms disappeared, and she remained in excellent health for nineteen years, when she died of natural causes at age seventy-two. Several times she stopped taking thyroid supplements and, in each instance, her former symptoms returned until she renewed her thyroid regime.

Although Dr. Murray's natural desiccated thyroid formula is still used—it has been improved upon through the years—much research on its importance in the prevention and cure of cardiovascular ailments has been forgotten. The result is millions of premature deaths. Revealing research reports on thyroid therapy now gather dust in the clamor for some new miracle cure for cardiovascular ailments, some new solution to an already solved problem.

To paraphrase someone wiser than I am, those who don't know medical history and fail to familiarize themselves with it are doomed to repeat it. But when will they become enlightened? How many years or decades from now? How many unnecessary deaths from now?

Today, for better or for worse, physicians are married to the dubious theory that a diet low in cholesterol and saturated fat will reduce serum cholesterol levels and the hazards of serious cardiovascular ailments. More than a decade ago, results of a ten-year, $150 million study of cholesterol by the National Institutes of Health (NIH) were announced. The major conclusions were: (1) that there is a direct link between the level of blood serum cholesterol and heart disease; (2) that lowering cholesterol significantly reduces the incidence of heart disease; and (3) that in instances of marked elevation of cholesterol, use of the drug cholestyramine can significantly reduce coronary heart disease.

The fanfare that accompanied the NIH announcement was so loud that it drowned out many facts relevant to the case. Basil Rifkind, director of the study, stated that the NIH research strongly indicated that the more we lower dietary cholesterol and fat, the more we reduce the risk of heart attacks.

But Rockefeller University's Dr. Edward Ahrens, who has conducted cholesterol research for over forty years, believes just the opposite. More concerned with factuality than diplomacy, he told *Time* magazine: "Since this was basically a drug study, we can conclude nothing about diet; such extrapolation is unwarranted, unscientific, and wishful thinking."[1]

Few Americans are afflicted with severe familial hypercholesterolemia—superhigh levels of blood cholesterol (just one in five hundred suffers from even a moderate form of this disease, says the same issue of *Time*)—so Dr. Ahrens offers a second objection to the study: the antimeat, butter, and egg propaganda accompanying the NIH announcement. He says that denying everyone red meat, eggs, and dairy products, when only a minute fraction of the population is afflicted with hypercholesterolemia, is reducing the joy of life unnecessarily.

Dr. John Story, Purdue University cardiologist, scoffs at what he calls "cholesterolphobia." In the same issue of *Time*, he indicates that we should not treat everyone with diet, just as we wouldn't give insulin to everyone for fear of their developing diabetes.

Dr. Michael F. Oliver, president of the British Cardiac Society and Duke of Edinburgh Professor of Cardiology, Edinburgh University, expressed a similar thought in *Modern Medicine*.[2] He feels that persons with very high cholesterol levels—265 mg/dl or greater—should be identified and assisted in lowering blood cholesterol. "This does not mean that the entire population should undergo a reduction in cholesterol levels," he states.

Quoted in the same issue, George V. Mann, M.D., associate professor of medicine and biochemistry at Vanderbilt University's School of Medicine, agrees that patients should be carefully screened for cholesterol levels, and those with a cholesterol level below 240 mg/dl should be "reassured that no specific treatment should be undertaken."

Dr. Mann, however, frowns on giving patients with high cholesterol levels the drug cholestyramine used in the NIH research project, since he feels that the drug presents problems. It is unpleasant to take, and 68 percent of subjects who took it in the NIH test experienced side effects, usually in the gastrointestinal tract. Professor Oliver admits to being disturbed about twenty-one cases of gastrointestinal cancer and eight deaths from this drug, as well as mouth and pharynx cancers.

In a letter to the authors during this period, Edward R. Pinckney, M.D., coauthor with Cathey Pinckney of *The Cholesterol Controversy*, called attention to the hazard of using cholestyramine. Certainly there were fewer deaths in the group of men whose blood cholesterol was reduced with cholestyramine in relation to test subjects who did not take the drug: 37 out of 1,906, compared with 47 out of 1,900. There were 73 percent more gastrointestinal cancers, and 800 percent more deaths from these cancers, in the group that took the drug. (Previous animal studies also showed that cholestyramine promotes colon cancer when a cancer-inducing agent is given with the drug.) And rather than decrease the incidence of gallstones, as lowering cholesterol in this way had been reported to do, cholestyramine increased gallstones by 45 percent; 44 percent more of the men taking the drug had to have gallstone-related surgery than did those not taking the drug. Other trends in the study included an increase in bile duct diseases and heartburn, as well as more suicides, homicides, and accidents in those participants taking the drug. One must ask if such risks are worth the admittedly slim benefits that cholestyramine delivers.

Other pertinent questions are equally troublesome. Why was $150 million spent on cholesterol research involving a drug whose negative effects outweigh the positive? And how did medical science ever get sidetracked with recommending avoidance of dietary cholesterol and saturated fat, a practice which fails to address the basic problem?

It all began in 1913 with the Russian physiologist N. Anitschkov, who drew an erroneous conclusion from one of the faultiest experiments ever designed by a scientist. To gain information of use to human beings, the experimenter usually selects a member of the animal kingdom whose physiological processes closely resemble those of human beings.

Anitschkov's history-changing work revolved around rabbits fed huge doses of cholesterol. Rabbits are vegetarians. No self-respecting rabbits would ever eat cholesterol-containing foods. Their livers are not equipped to handle them chemically. As a result of this unnatural diet, the cholesterol content of their blood skyrocketed by several hundred percent and, in the end, these high concentrations of cholesterol proved toxic to them. This severe biochemical stress caused some atherosclerosis and the appearance of cholesterol in arterial lesions. To Anitschkov's credit, he realized that his research results did not necessarily apply to human beings, and he never suggested a low-cholesterol diet to control atherosclerosis.

Many decades later, in 1964, an explanation of the rabbit findings emerged from Anitschkov's laboratory through one of his proteges, L. V. Malysheva, who, in a published paper, reported that huge doses of cholesterol suppressed rabbit thyroid function as thoroughly as surgical removal of the thyroid gland.[3]

However subnormal thyroid function comes about, the result is the same: the development of atherosclerosis. Malysheva explained that deteriorated arteries in the rabbits were due to low thyroid function, not to cholesterol itself.

Researchers in Anitschkov's lab, Malysheva included, rejected the cholesterol theory, and American physicians embraced it.

Another biochemist, I. B. Friedland, a student of Anitschkov's, did much research on cholesterol and fats and in 1933 published a comprehensive report, representing five years of study. He made a significant discovery. When he fed rabbits large amounts of cholesterol, as Anitschkov had done, he was able to prevent the development of high levels of blood cholesterol and atherosclerosis by administering thyroid hormone to them. He concluded that thyroid hormone controls blood fat and cholesterol levels and recommended thyroid therapy in human beings with elevated fats in the blood serum.[4]

Dr. Barnes once told me that "if the Friedland recommendation had been followed, cardiovascular diseases would have been conquered decades ago and much time and many lives would have been saved."

In the cholesterol controversy, a key question is whether this fatty substance plays a major role in the deterioration of arteries. More than 125 years ago, Rudolph Virchow, professor of pathology and the father of what was then a new science, performed many autopsies and concluded that cholesterol has only a minor influence. In a paper published in Berlin, he revealed that degeneration of the blood vessels' connective tissue had started before cholesterol appeared in the lesions. Next, drops of fat accumulated there and then, finally, came cholesterol. Virchow considered cholesterol a belated sign of fatty degeneration.[5]

Another research finding that deflated the cholesterol balloon was that of a German physician, H. Zondek, during World War I.[6] With Germany isolated from the rest of the world and supplies of protein foods running low, military personnel as well as civilians were, of necessity, eating mainly grains and vegetables—a low-cholesterol, low-fat diet.

Dr. Zondek, who was in charge of a ward of cardiac patients, made the astute observation that these soldiers had all the symptoms of myxedema, the most dominant of which was heart failure. The usual treatment for heart disorders at that time was digitalis, which had already failed to help his other patients, many of whom were bedridden. Inasmuch as they had swollen tissues, no energy, shortness of breath, and enlarged hearts, he decided to try thyroid therapy. Much to his surprise and delight, his patients were soon able to return to military duty or civilian life. He gave the name "myxedema heart" to their former ailment.

Soon after the war, Dr. Zondek wrote *Diseases of the Endocrine Glands*, a book translated into English in 1944, featuring illustrations of electrocardiograms of some of his patients. Individuals with "myxedema heart" showed low voltage, because of weak heartbeats. After thyroid therapy, when the heart contracted with more power, the voltage on the EKG returned to normal. A low voltage reading on the EKG reveals the status of the thyroid gland more accurately than many common blood tests for thyroid function, as many doctors have discovered.

Have we been unduly alarmed about intake of cholesterol in relation to blood serum levels of this compound? Numerous studies in various nations indicate that we have.

The much-publicized fourteen-year Framingham study of thousands of individuals, aimed at revealing the major risk factors for heart attack, failed to zero in on dietary cholesterol as the enemy within, despite the prestudy assertion by Dr. William B. Kannel, the project's director, that the blood test for cholesterol levels was perhaps the most useful method for determining present or impending heart disease. Results of the study changed his opinion.[7] Half the people who died of heart attacks failed to show the high cholesterol levels he believed warned of impending danger.

As a matter of fact, Dr. Kannel saw "no discernable association between the amount of cholesterol in the diet and the level of cholesterol in the blood." Regardless of how much or how little animal fat is in the diet, some people will have low blood cholesterol levels, while others will have moderate levels, and others high levels, he stated.

Not long ago, the University of California School of Medicine fed 1,934 men and women anywhere from zero to fourteen eggs each week. Although one large egg contains about 250 mg of cholesterol, researchers were surprised to find no statistically significant relationship between number of eggs consumed and the blood serum cholesterol level.

Some years earlier, experimenters at the University of California at Los Angeles under Dr. Roslyn Alfin-Slater found no increase in cholesterol levels on normal diets when egg intake was increased.[8]

"We, like everyone else, had been convinced that when you eat cholesterol, you get cholesterol," she told the *Los Angeles Times*. "But when we stopped to think that all the studies in the past never tested the normal diet in relation to egg eating . . . we decided to see what happened to blood cholesterol levels on normal diets when egg intake was increased. Our finding surprised us . . . ."

The research of Professor A. H. Ismail at Purdue University confirmed the results of the UCLA group.[9]

Eggs are not really saboteurs of health. Researchers at Massachusetts Institute of Technology found that by eating two eggs per day, subjects benefited from the 5 grams of lecithin in the yolks.[10] They learned that within twenty-one days, such a regime increased the brain's plasma choline content by 500 percent, enhancing the synthesis of acetylcholine, a key neurotransmitter of the brain. Results of this study indicate that lecithin can be helpful in restoring short-term memory loss.

Does a high–polyunsaturated-fat diet actually prevent or cure cardiovascular ailments? A six-year study in England is typical of research undertaken to establish the facts.[11] Four hundred elderly men were divided into two groups. Half of them were fed a diet high in polyunsaturated fats—no less than 3 ounces of polyunsaturated oil daily, plus polyunsaturated margarine. Whole milk, butter, cheese, egg yolks, and saturated cooking fats were forbidden. The other half stayed on their usual diet, which contained six times as much saturated fat as polyunsaturated fat.

At first, cholesterol levels came down in the first group, a common occurrence with this sort of diet. Then, after the initial year, they began to rise. Following conclusion of the study, the cholesterol levels of the first group were about the same as when they started. Blood cholesterol of the saturated-fat eaters stayed virtually the same, too. However, the death rate from cardiovascular disease was slightly higher in the group which ate polyunsaturates—twenty-seven patients to twenty-five. Results of a study conducted in Oslo, Norway, under similar conditions, were almost the same.

If the low-cholesterol diet is so effective, how can one account for the results of the Roseto, Pennsylvania, study, reported in the *Journal of the American Medical Association*, and studies of Somali camel herdsmen, the Masai tribe of Tanzania, and natives of the Cook Islands?[12]

Citizens of Roseto eat a diet that sounds like a shortcut to suicide to low-cholesterol advocates—all of the "no-no's": eggs, fatty meat, foods fried in lard, and other high-cholesterol delicacies such as prosciutto ham, rimmed by half an inch to an inch of saturated fat, and peppers fried in lard. But their blood cholesterol levels ranged from 136 to 500, averaging 224, comparable with that of participants in the Framingham study, about average for the nation. Shouldn't such an outrageous diet cause an abnormally high death rate from heart ailments? Let's look at the facts. After an eleven-year study, there were hardly any heart attacks in men under age fifty-five. In men over age sixty-five who showed symptoms of heart disease, the rate of survival was high.

Somali camel herdsmen drink an average of five quarts of high-fat camel milk daily. Shouldn't their blood cholesterol levels rocket out of sight? Actually, the highest blood serum cholesterol reading among them was 153. The Masai tribe lives almost entirely on meat and milk (whose fat content is almost twice that of ours) and shows a cholesterol level around 125 and negligible heart disease. Those over age sixty-five autopsied after accidental death revealed only negligible signs of atherosclerosis. Comparisons have been made between two groups of Cook Islands Polynesians, one of which eats twelve times as much saturated fat as the other. Heart attacks were almost nonexistent in both groups.[13]

Because some authorities claim that low-cholesterol diets work, and others claim the opposite and have statistics to back them, Drs. Stewart Wolf of the University of Texas and John Bruhn of the University of Oklahoma Medical School analyzed more than one hundred articles from all over the world to isolate a dietary common denominator which might be considered a risk factor. They could find no consistent pattern about a certain kind of fat or a particular cholesterol level which seemed to cause heart disease.[14]

Another landmark study reveals some fascinating information about diet and heart disease, and that will be the subject of the next chapter.

15

BE KIND TO YOUR ARTERIES!

*O*ne of the prime arguments of those who favor the low-cholesterol diet is that heart attacks in Europe decreased drastically during World War II because of the scarcity of high-cholesterol foods.

Dr. Broda Barnes investigated this matter in depth, spending many summers in Graz, Austria, examining some of the world's most complete and definitive autopsy records.

"It is true that cholesterol-containing foods were scarce in Europe during World War II," he told me. "And, yes, heart attacks did decrease, but the interpretation of these facts led many investigators to the wrong conclusion. They failed to probe deeply enough. Instead of checking records of autopsies, they only counted the number of persons who had died of heart attacks."

117

So, in order to learn the truth for the protection of the living, Dr. Barnes went to the dead, checking 70,000 autopsies recorded between 1930 and 1970.

Heart attacks had dropped sharply in the war years between 1939 and 1945. But he discovered unexpected evidence that astonished him. *The low-fat diet had not protected arteries from atherosclerosis!* Autopsies revealed that the number of individuals under age fifty with atherosclerosis had doubled between 1939 and 1954. Further, the degree of injury to the arteries of these persons was approximately twice as great on a scale of zero to four. Not only had the low-cholesterol diet failed to guard the arteries, but atherosclerosis had increased fourfold.

Why?

"We found that tuberculosis had risen far faster than heart attacks as the cause of death," said Dr. Barnes. "Tuberculosis victims rarely live beyond forty years—not quite long enough to have heart attacks.

"In most instances, those who died of tuberculosis showed extreme damage to coronary arteries. It is clear that if the adult patients had not died of tuberculosis, they would have been cut down by a heart attack in a short time. Wartime conditions had substituted tuberculosis for heart attacks as the major cause of death. Low-cholesterol diets had had nothing to do with protecting the people from heart attacks.

"A few years later, conditions were reversed," said Dr. Barnes. "The antibiotics for tuberculosis had become available, and deaths from heart attacks started to rise. The autopsies told us why: the adult dying from a heart attack had healing tuberculosis in his or her lungs. The antibiotics had stopped immediate death from tuberculosis, giving the advanced arterial damage a chance to become the killer."[1]

Dr. Barnes is not the only researcher who has found that the low-fat diet often fails to prevent heart attacks and that a high-fat diet does not necessarily bring on heart attacks. One of the most comprehensive projects, the Tecumseh study conducted by Allen B. Nichols, M.D., and his colleagues at the University of Michigan School of Medicine, reported similar findings and additional insight into causes for high serum cholesterol and triglycerides, a blood fat believed to contribute to cardiovascular ailments. The researchers checked almost the entire adult population of Tecumseh, Michigan, to determine the effect diet and overweight might have on blood cholesterol and triglyceride levels. The influence of one hundred different food items—high or low in fats and sugar—on 4,057 persons was tabulated.

An article in the *Journal of the American Medical Association* (October 26, 1976) reported these findings: There was no significant relationship between how frequently fat, sugar, starch, alcohol, and tea were consumed and the blood serum level of fats. Serum cholesterol and triglyceride concentrations were significantly higher in markedly overweight men and women. High fat levels in the bloodstream have long been associated with increased risk of heart disease and other health problems.

Dr. Nichols warns that these findings do not mean that diet and blood fat levels are not at all related, only that obesity more obviously raises serum cholesterol and triglyceride levels than any particular dietary regime.

"Other factors besides fat intake determine cholesterol levels among the general public," he says. "From this study's findings, one may infer that weight reduction should be the initial course for control of hyperlipidemia in the general population."[2]

Other studies indicate that more is involved in elevated cholesterol levels than intake of fats. Several researchers have found, for instance, that low thyroid function encourages high blood cholesterol. Experiments by the physiologist L. M. Hurxthal in the early 1930s revealed that blood cholesterol levels were high in hypothyroids and low in hyperthyroids.[3]

In their 1940 book, *The Biochemistry of Disease*, Bodansky and Bodansky went a step further, stating that the rise in cholesterol in hypothyroidism is just a part of the total pattern of increased blood fats. They claimed a close relationship between appropriate thyroid supplementation and a decline in these symptoms.

The relationship between low thyroid function and high serum cholesterol level found by three researchers, E. F. Gildea, C. B. Mann, and J. P. Peters, indicates that a serum cholesterol level below 275 mg percent practically excludes the diagnosis of hypothyroidism. Gildea discovered that two grains of thyroid would reduce cholesterol and triglyceride levels.

Bodansky and Bodansky make the interesting point that hypothyroidism can be diagnosed by high blood cholesterol, and effectiveness of treatment can be determined by the decline in blood serum level of cholesterol. A give-and-take relationship apparently exists between the decrease in basal metabolism in thyroid deficiency and the rise in blood cholesterol. *"On the average, the rise in cholesterol is approximately four times as great as the drop in metabolism."*[4] (Emphasis added.)

It remains a mystery to me why modern medicine fails to make use of this information. Perhaps it is because, during the mid-1930s, physicians started patients on too high dosages of thyroid and brought on heart attacks and, in several instances, death. The customary treatment for heart failure in that period was digitalis, administered in large dosages to saturate the patient, then in reduced dosages to maintenance level. No procedure could have been more wrong for thyroid. Large to massive dosages were tried—anywhere from four to thirty grains daily—causing the heart to race beyond its ability. From this flagrant misuse, thyroid developed a bad name, one it is still having difficulty overcoming. It is perhaps for this reason that a prime way to lower critical blood fats, including cholesterol, is often denied to patients who need it.

Like the word *thyroid*, the word *cholesterol* usually triggers a negative reaction—with little justification. Cholesterol is much denounced and disparaged in medical circles, and a great deal of information and misinformation has been spread about this waxy, gray-yellow, fatlike alcohol which does not readily dissolve in water or blood. If we and the rest of the animal kingdom had no cholesterol, we would be part of the vegetable kingdom. (Vegetables contain no cholesterol.) Without a steady supply of this substance, we probably would not be around to complain about it. Cholesterol is so vital to our lives that we have a built-in mechanism in the liver and in each body cell to manufacture it. Ideally, when cholesterol intake is high, the liver and the cells gear down production. When intake is low, they increase production.

If you take in a great deal of dietary cholesterol, your body, if in proper balance, will get rid of the excess. The amount of cholesterol you eat, therefore, doesn't automatically have a real relationship to its level in your blood serum. If you literally stuff yourself on cholesterol-rich foods, the small intestine provides the built-in protection of limiting absorption. Excess cholesterol does not make it through the intestinal wall and into the bloodstream. It simply exits from the body through the bowel.

Contrary to the opinion of some, cholesterol can be synthesized from carbohydrates and proteins, as well as from fats. Therefore, no matter what kind of diet you eat, your body will have plenty of raw material to be made into cholesterol. If eaters of eggs, milk products, and meat happen to have a slightly higher blood cholesterol level than vegetarians, the reason may be simple, says one observer. When animal fats are digested, they are not soluble in water or blood serum. Therefore, intestinal tract cells must synthesize cholesterol to unite with them so that they can be transported through the bloodstream to be metabolized or stored. It is this synthesized cholesterol—not dietary cholesterol—that may raise the blood serum level of animal-fat eaters.[5] Vegetable fats are more soluble in water and thus require less cholesterol to be produced in the intestinal tract to promote their utilization.

Why do we need cholesterol, anyway? For many reasons.

It is a *must* for the creation of a new life. When the sperm cells of a man join the egg of a woman to create a new human being, they bring along their own supply of cholesterol. In a short time the mother-to-be's blood serum level of cholesterol rises by about 50 percent, the liberal amount necessary to supply the cholesterol needed by the fetus's trillions of cells until birth. Dr. Broda Barnes made the wry comment that if cholesterol were harmful to arteries, as so many have stated, "the fetus would have a heart attack before the baby saw the light of day."

The newborn baby comes fully equipped with the right enzymes to make possible the production of cholesterol in each cell, a necessity for the growth of tissue and for development of the brain. As adults, we no longer can synthesize cholesterol in the brain for a very good reason: we don't need to. Cholesterol already there and in the spinal cord—about 23 percent of the total in the body—is used and reused. Some authorities believe that brain cholesterol serves as part of the insulation for myriad nerve fibers there and as a nonconducting separator to prevent short-circuiting.

Cholesterol has other uses. It helps make fats soluble to be burned as fuel for muscles and connective tissue, the supporting members for various organs. About 10 percent of body cholesterol is in the skin, where it has a well-known use. Through a chemical reaction to sunlight, skin cholesterol produces vitamin D, which makes possible the assimilation of calcium and phosphorus essential to forming and sustaining strong bones and teeth. It also helps the growth of new skin to replace that which is scratched, cut, or burned.

You may not be aware of the contribution cholesterol makes to your body in emergencies: it serves as the basic building blocks for hormones produced by the adrenal glands. Without cholesterol, you couldn't survive stress-filled situations.

Despite cholesterol's all-important role in the body, it is still regarded by many as the enemy within. But does eating high-cholesterol foods really elevate our serum cholesterol? Not necessarily. Individuals from families with a pronounced record of early heart disease have been shown to develop elevated cholesterol levels from a high-cholesterol diet. Other than that, the evidence that food intake causes this condition is inconclusive at best. Then what causes high blood cholesterol levels?

Heredity is probably a major contributing factor. Our anxiety and stress levels are also causes. Students before critical exams, athletes prior to key games, military men and women before combat (fliers, particularly), and accountants at tax time all have elevated cholesterol. High blood pressure, obesity, smoking, high blood uric acid levels, little or no exercise, and being male have all been associated with increased cholesterol levels.

One of the most dramatic and promising ways of reducing elevated cholesterol is, unfortunately, not as well known as it should be. It involves increasing the ratio of high-density lipoproteins (HDL) to low-density lipoproteins (LDL). If you have more HDL than LDL, your chances of escaping a heart attack are far more favorable.

Earlier we mentioned that fats and water don't mix well—usually not at all. The way that fats (including cholesterol) can be transported in the watery medium of the bloodstream is by becoming attached to lipoproteins, a combination of fat and protein. The best information today holds that LDL carries fats and cholesterol to the cells, including those in the arteries, and deposits them there. HDL units are like mini–dump trucks that haul off excess cholesterol (some think they even remove cholesterol from cells) and carry it to the liver for elimination from the body.

There are five effective ways of increasing the ratio of HDL to LDL: (1) refrain from smoking; (2) exercise vigorously (check with your doctor first); (3) slash your intake of calories (become or stay fairly lean); (4) substitute some unsaturated fats (for instance, those in fish and fowl) for saturated; (5) eat certain foods and food supplements, such as cold-water fish, brewer's yeast, garlic, and lecithin.[6]

Instant results are not guaranteed. The program must be pursued for a period, particularly if you are middle-aged or older.

Now, finally, through the HDL theory, scientists are beginning to understand what they have known for many years; that regular and vigorous exercise helps to prevent cardiovascular disease. A team of researchers led by Josef Patsch at Baylor College of Medicine found that jogging actually clears fats from the blood. Markedly higher levels of HDL were discovered in physically active individuals. How does this come about, according to the Patsch theory?

Within several hours after a meal, fat particles in the bloodstream (chylomicrons) encounter a blood enzyme which digests part of their cores. The remains are carried to the liver for digestion. Surfaces of the fat particles are then released by a blood enzyme and unite with other blood chemicals to become HDL.

Patsch does not understand exactly how exercise increases HDL. However, his research indicates that vigorous exercise must be continued regularly to keep HDL levels high. Such exercise must be pursued for at least several months to increase HDL to a pronounced degree, and it declines rapidly if one becomes inactive. In other words, quick-fix exercise is not going to help much. You have to exercise vigorously for a lifetime to extend your lifespan and improve your health. Eliminating high-fat and cholesterol-rich foods to lower blood fats and cholesterol will not do the trick. Such an approach does not take into consideration that health and illness are functions of many factors, not just a single unproven one.

Let's take a close look at how and why cholesterol affects the body.

Arteries are lifelines for channeling blood from the heart to living cells in constant need of nourishment and oxygen for burning their fuel. They must be kept clear, or trouble results.

A cross-section of human blood vessels reveals three layers of tissue. The innermost is an ingenious, smooth, and slippery lining which permits near-frictionless flow of blood. Enclosing the inner layer is a circle of muscle fibers which permits the blood vessels to expand and contract as the heart expands and contracts. On the outside is the third layer, coarse and stout connective tissue to reinforce the blood vessels or the arteries.

Blockages occur where there has been wear and tear on the artery wall. An irregular area is presumably the starting point for a buildup of cholesterol which, in time, can slow or stop the blood flow.

Some scientists speculate that arterial degeneration starts in the wall of the artery. Nature will not overlook such a defect, so she attempts to cope with it. Fibrin, a blood component essential to clotting, seals the stress point and begins a buildup on it. Pathologist Rudolph Virchow noted that this occurs long before cholesterol becomes involved. In performing autopsies, he discovered that arterial deterioration started long before blood fat began to cling to the fibrin, and that this was followed by the accumulation of cholesterol. He also discovered that a person's circulation almost shut itself off before cholesterol attached itself to the plaque on the artery walls.

Numerous pathologists have since come to the same conclusion: cholesterol buildup in the wall of arteries occurs only after arterial degeneration is far advanced. It seems strange, then, that cholesterol is singled out when arterial plaque is composed not only of cholesterol but also of fibrin, calcium, triglycerides, ceroids, and sometimes blood platelets.

Although numerous studies done long ago showed the thyroid connection in the degeneration of arteries, a striking study in more recent times demonstrates the value of thyroid therapy to the hearts and arteries of hypothyroid patients.

In a monograph, *Thyroid Function and Its Possible Role in Vascular Degeneration,* Dr. William B. Kountz reviewed earlier experiments linking low thyroid and deteriorating arteries and studied 288 hypothyroid patients with elevated blood cholesterol—his own and those at the infirmary of Washington University, St. Louis. These included (1) businessmen averaging fifty-five years of age; (2) infirmary outpatients whose ages averaged sixty-one and (3) infirmary inpatients averaging sixty-seven years of age.[7]

Few in the first group had atherosclerosis. Many in the second group were found to have moderate cardiovascular degeneration. Everyone in the third group showed evidence of advanced blood vessel disease.

Dr. Kountz administered thyroid to some in each group and kept others as controls. After five years of observation, he compared those on thyroid therapy with controls on the basis of number of deaths from heart attacks and strokes.

In the first group—the youngest men—no one on thyroid therapy died, compared with 15 percent of the controls. Effects of thyroid treatment were most marked in the older men. Only 3 percent of the second group died, compared with 19 percent of the controls. In the third group, the fatality rate was half as high among those on thyroid as among the controls.

While assuring proper thyroid gland function or adequate supplementation seems the most basic approach to protecting or regaining a healthy cardiovascular system, sometimes other measures help, too, such as proper intake of vitamins, particularly vitamins C, B_6, and E.

An article in *Lancet* stated that 1,000 mg of vitamin C daily lowered cholesterol levels of healthy individuals and that long-term shortage of this vitamin contributed to arterial diseases which invite heart attacks and strokes.

In a revealing publication of the Linus Pauling Heart Foundation, *How Vitamin C Prevents Heart Attack and Stroke,* Matthias Rath, M.D., who completed significant research with the late Dr. Linus Pauling, states:

"Heart attack and stroke are essentially unknown in most animals producing vitamin C in their own bodies. In human beings dependent on dietary vitamin C and frequently having a low intake of this vitamin, heart disease is a leading cause of death and disability.

". . . Vitamin C stimulates the production of collagen molecules, which play the same role in the human body that iron reinforcement plays in a skyscraper building.

"Heart disease is a form of prescurvy . . . Heart attack and stroke are a direct result of low vitamin C intake over the years."[8]

Rabbit experiments conducted by Dr. Anthony J. Verlangieri, while at Rutgers University, prior to joining the University of Mississippi, revealed that lack of vitamin C in the daily diet brought about the loss of certain chemical compounds in the artery linings, creating roughness and irregularities where harmful plaques could readily form. High blood levels of vitamin C increased the amount of these chemicals, helping assure that artery linings stay smooth.[9]

In an article in the *Journal of the American Geriatric Society*, Dr. M. L. Riccitelli of the Yale School of Medicine reported various experiments over twenty-two years which paralleled Dr. Verlangieri's findings.[10]

Several investigators have discovered that vitamin C–deprived animals developed atherosclerotic lesions like those in human beings and were cured by administration of vitamin C over long periods of time. Vitamin C not only reduced blood cholesterol levels but seemed to prevent cholesterol accumulation on artery linings.

Research done by Constance Spittle Leslie, M.D., a pathologist at Pinderfields Hospital in Wakefield, Yorkshire, England, convinced her that atherosclerosis is a deficiency disease similar to beriberi, scurvy, rickets, and pellagra, caused by poor diet and reversible by corrective nutrition. Many of her findings have been published by the prestigious medical journal *Lancet*.

Dr. Leslie conducted an important experiment on herself. Noting that her cholesterol count dropped sharply when she ingested what are considered by some to be large doses of vitamin C, she reduced her cholesterol count from 230 to 140 by taking more liberal amounts of vitamin C. She then brought her cholesterol levels right up by restricting her vitamin C intake.[11]

Another vitamin, too, seems to influence cholesterol levels

and atherosclerosis, vitamin B_6. Dr. Roger Williams cites a Russian experiment which revealed low blood plasma levels of vitamin B_6 in co-enzyme form in thirty-one of forty-eight patients with atherosclerosis and high cholesterol counts, and he theorizes that vitamin B_6 contributes to body production of lecithin, a dissolver of cholesterol.[12] On the basis of this and other experiments, Dr. Williams advises that daily intake of sufficient vitamin B_6 is one of the best guarantees against harm from fat and cholesterol combined with proteins.

Although many claims of early experimenters with vitamin E relative to cardiovascular ailments have not been substantiated, more recently this vitamin has been found to monitor and regulate magnesium and manganese penetration into heart cells, to enhance microcirculation, and to reduce arterial deterioration in the legs.

One theory of how arteries deteriorate is that they are attacked at their weak points by free radicals, highly active atoms or molecules. Any irregular site invites deposits of fats, cholesterol, and calcium. Vitamin E is a known killer of free radicals and, as such, protects the integrity of arteries. Vitamin E also normalizes clotting time of blood, minimizing or eliminating the chance of clots that can block arteries and take lives.

Additionally, vitamin E has a proven track record in managing intermittent claudication, leg pain caused by obstructed circulation. Probably the most impressive performance relative to this condition was revealed in a seven-year study by Sweden's Knut Haeger, M.D., a vascular surgeon.[13]

Those who suffer from intermittent claudication can walk only a short distance before the pain becomes unbearable. Once they stop walking, the pain slowly recedes. Dr. Haeger found that as little as 300 to 400 IU a day of vitamin E and daily walking brought about two results within several months: the ability of patients to walk longer distances before experiencing pain and increased blood circulation to the lower leg.

His 220 age-matched subjects (including some diabetics) had limited flow of blood to the feet. Such patients are subject to gangrene, a decaying of the flesh which follows choking off of the blood supply. The subjects were divided into two groups. Half received 300 IU of vitamin E daily; the other half were given placebos. During the seven-year period, only one of the patients on vitamin E had to have a leg amputated because of gangrene, compared with eleven on the placebo.

Dr. Haeger's experiment and those cited earlier offer convincing evidence that vitamins are valuable in efforts to manage vascular disorders.

It is customary to think of artery ailments in terms of extremes—gangrene, deadly heart attacks, and strokes. Yet there is a whole range of illnesses in various parts of the body which arise from imperfect arteries—conditions which can be prevented and, in many instances, reversed, if the proper measures are taken. That is the subject of the next chapter.

16

DRAMATIC TREATMENT FOR CIRCULATORY PROBLEMS

So far as circulatory ailments are concerned, headlines and millions of words are devoted to strokes and heart attacks, but little helpful information is offered about the prevention of less extreme yet still disabling complaints arising from chronic arterial disease.

The major disorders of this kind are neuropathies (nerve deterioration which often limits leg, arm, or eye function), kidney failure, detached retina, blindness, and—perhaps most frightening—gangrene. These often painful and handicapping conditions can limit the lifespan of anyone, particularly diabetics and the elderly. The good news is that something tangible can be done about these ailments.

As matters now stand, almost 98 percent of some eleven million diabetics in the United States will suffer one or more of these complaints, the nightmarish complications of diabetes. Unfortunately, most of them do not know that with preventive health maintenance they can very likely be spared these health catastrophes.

A specific example will illustrate this point. At a party a number of years ago, I heard a woman say, "My eyesight is beginning to fail as a result of my diabetes, and my doctor tells me he can't do a thing about it." The dismal prospect offered this woman by her physician was just to wait around to go blind.

Turning abruptly, I said to her, "I just overheard your last remark. I'm a medical doctor and I may be able to help you."

I made an appointment for her to visit my office five days later, after she had taken her armpit temperature on two consecutive days.

Sure enough, she was hypothyroid. I put her on a grain of thyroid and, after a month, when her temperature had failed to move upward, increased it to two grains.

Within nine weeks, she was feeling better than she had since the age of twenty-five and, even more satisfying to her, her eyesight remained 20/40 without glasses. Even after five years her eyes still test 20/40. Not long ago when I saw her, she gave me an undeserved compliment.

"Doctor, I owe my eyesight to you."

"Thanks for the compliment," I responded. "I helped, but you actually owe your eyesight to Broda Barnes, a medical doctor who made the discovery concerning diabetic complications that I used in your case and in others."

As far as I am concerned, Dr. Barnes is worthy of a Nobel prize in medicine for many solid reasons, one of the most important of which is his discovery that thyroid supplementation in diabetics who are hypothyroids can stop diabetic complications and, in some instances, even reverse them. I know this is true from my own practice and from that of others who follow Dr. Barnes's methods.

In my opinion, Dr. Barnes's contribution is the most noteworthy breakthrough for diabetics since the discovery of insulin. It all began in 1965, when he suddenly realized that twelve diabetic patients whom he had treated for fifteen years showed no signs of diabetic complications.

Then came additional surprises.

His new diabetic patients with atherosclerosis, very high blood cholesterol levels, nerve deterioration, and impaired eye or leg movement experienced what modern medicine thought impossible: an arresting of these conditions and, sometimes, reversals and complete cures. Over the next fifteen years, forty-three diabetic patients who came to him were put on thyroid supplementation, and none manifested the slightest sign of typical diabetic complications.

A clear picture began to emerge. Dr. Barnes went to the medical literature and soon learned that several other medical doctors had independently discovered what he had and had published papers on the subject in important medical journals. These illuminating, lifesaving articles had been overlooked or ignored by most physicians and eventually forgotten.

Dr. Barnes was appalled. In the years between the publication of these articles and 1965, hundreds of thousands—even millions—of diabetics had unnecessarily gone through pain, disability, depression, and early death.

Among significant studies yellowing in medical libraries was the 1930 research of Dr. Elliott P. Joslin, founder of Boston's Joslin Clinic. Before Drs. Banting and Best had extracted a safe and effective preparation of insulin in 1921, diabetics usually lived only four years after their illnesses were diagnosed. Now their life spans were extended. Instead of dying in a coma, diabetics were living seven years longer and then dying of different causes, among them heart attacks. Insulin was unable to prevent these devastating complications.

One of the few persons to understand the basic reason for complications of diabetics, Dr. Joslin published his findings in the best medical journals and predicted that some day atherosclerosis would be conquered and that subsequently the diabetic would live a normal life span.

Most diabetologists snubbed his findings and the heretical notion that insulin wasn't the final solution. They maintained that all physicians had to do was diagnose diabetes early enough and treat it vigorously enough.

"So they diagnosed it early and treated it vigorously, and, judging from their results, not early or vigorously enough," according to Dr. Barnes. Because of the longer life of diabetics, more complications of this ailment had time to appear. Foremost among them was hardening of the arteries.

"I find articles and books making the nonsensical statement that diabetes aggravates or accelerates hardening of the arteries," Dr. Barnes said. "No way! Hypothyroidism is perhaps the leading cause of this condition."

In Dr. Barnes's nearly half a century as a general practitioner, none of his five thousand patients (either with a normal thyroid gland or on thyroid hormone) showed a sign of diabetic complications. Further, only five of his patients developed diabetes in this period. The national average is 200 per 5,000 individuals— *forty times higher*.

On two occasions, Dr. Barnes told me something that I have subsequently observed in my practice; namely, that the same kinds of complications observed in the diabetic also appear in the low-thyroid patient and that, when thyroid is administered, some of these complications, particularly neuropathies, disappear.

All diabetic and hypothyroid complications arise from the same basic cause: clogged arteries which prevent the blood from bringing in food and oxygen and carrying off wastes.

Let's look at all the complications, starting with kidney failure. Kidney function is lost. Toxic wastes cannot be eliminated in the urine and accumulate in the bloodstream. Unless dialysis comes to the rescue, the patient dies of uremia.

A less common but even more devastating result of diabetic arteriosclerosis is gangrene. Gangrene occurs mainly in the legs, because their circulation is less efficient. The blood has to be forced against gravity back to the heart. In the fingers or arms, blood flows to the heart more easily.

Gangrene became much more prevalent after the discovery of insulin. Before this time, people generally did not live long enough to develop it. As critical as this condition is—and as difficult to treat—some patients have been spared the agony of developing it, thanks to Dr. Barnes's methods.

A new patient was brought to Dr. Barnes for treatment, a gray-haired sixty-year-old man who was paralyzed on one side from a recent stroke. As Walter lay on the examination table, a remote part of his anatomy caught Dr. Barnes's attention— the big toe of the right foot. It looked abnormally red and misshapen, like a moderate-size, rotten, mashed tomato. The paralysis and stroke suddenly became less important. Walter had gangrene! His poor circulation had been worsened because of his paralyzed side.

"Many a knife-happy surgeon would have lopped off that big toe," Dr. Barnes informed me, "but that wouldn't have stopped the gangrene. It keeps climbing to the ankles, then the thigh. Then it usually goes to the other side and starts all over. The knife fights a delaying action—at the end of the toe, then at the ankle, at the knee, and finally at the thigh. The surgeon's knife operates the patient into disability and then, often, into death."

Dr. Barnes had an alternative. Gangrene and the stroke already told him that the patient had circulatory problems, perhaps of low-thyroid origin. Learning that Walter had lived most of his life in the state of Indiana, a part of the great United States goiter belt, he had additional evidence of possible hypothyroidism. The underarm temperature test showed a subnormal reading of 96 degrees, just the confirmation Dr. Barnes needed. He administered one-half grain of desiccated thyroid per day and kept a close watch on the patient. Things happened fast. Within a week, the rotten, mashed tomato appearance of Walter's right big toe began changing. A month later, the toe was completely healed.

Remarkable recoveries from diabetic complications such as this encouraged Dr. Barnes to share his discoveries with other doctors. But a giant roadblock kept the mass of the medical community from even trying his method: the lack of controlled double-blind studies to prove his findings on a completely objective level.

"Rarely can a physician in private practice conduct controlled experiments," Dr. Barnes readily admitted, "but he sometimes makes pertinent observations that deserve the attention of clinical investigators with facilities to give them further evaluation." Deserving attention and getting it were two different things.

Dr. Barnes also had fascinating experiences in reversing neuropathies, which run the gamut from annoying to devastating. If atherosclerosis damages a nerve to the eye muscle, the patient may lose his or her ability to move the eye from side to side. Deterioration of nerves in the leg could make walking difficult or impossible.

One case which Dr. Barnes described in an interview is an example of positive accomplishments which are possible with the thyroid treatment of neuropathies. A patient was referred to him by an Arizona doctor. Muscles between the man's left knee and thigh had become atrophied and weak. In excruciating pain, the patient had to take painkillers day and night. He could hobble around for short distances but only with a cane.

The man was frustrated and depressed that his pain limited his daily activities and brought him agony. After verifying that this patient was hypothyroid, Dr. Barnes explained that he was going to put him on a small daily dosage of thyroid. Skeptical but willing to try anything, the patient agreed to take the thyroid but insisted on staying in a Fort Collins, Colorado, motel near Dr. Barnes's offices in the event that thyroid did not agree with him. (He had heard some of the ancient thyroid scare stories.)

Within one week, he was able to cut down on the painkiller. His general health improvement encouraged him to go back to Arizona and continue thyroid supplementation. Within a month, he could walk painlessly without the cane and threw it away. Two years later—the last information Dr. Barnes had on the patient—his leg was completely normal.

Although some doctors still say that neuropathies in the eyes, which contribute to blindness, are caused by diabetes, this is not true. Atherosclerosis is the cause—deterioration of the tiny arteries of the eyes.

Although most doctors who have used thyroid hormone have been able to treat diabetics to prevent disabling neuropathies and blindness, perhaps the most dramatic and revealing work has been done by Drs. Michael Walczak of Studio City, California, Murray Israel of New York City, and I. R. Ross of Maryland, all members of the Vascular Research Foundation.[1]

Their findings add a ray of hope to the otherwise ominous information of the National Society for the Prevention of Blindness, which projects that some 50 percent of persons who have diabetes for at least twenty years will develop retinopathy (deterioration of the retina of the eye), while 95 percent of those who have diabetes for thirty years will probably develop this disease.

Drs. Walczak, Israel, and Ross treat impending blindness (diabetic retinopathy) with oral thyroid hormone extract and heavy intakes of vitamin B complex, vitamin C, and the natural enzyme varidase. Diuretics are also given to remove excess body fluid. Forty out of forty-five patients—twenty-five of whom were legally blind—were measurably improved after thirteen months on the above regime. Two did not improve, and three became worse. Such startling results came in the wake of a Harvard School of Public Health announcement that no cure exists for the progressively disabling complications of diabetes.

One of the most dramatic changes came in a patient who had been totally blind in one eye prior to taking part in the research project. Vision in his other eye was diminishing so fast—20/200—that he became almost a vegetable and sat around in a deep depression. Elevated cholesterol and blood pressure as well as irregularities of metabolism made him seem a prime candidate for failure in the project.

However, after five months on the Walczak-Israel-Ross regime, his blood pressure went down markedly, and his cholesterol reading plummeted from 294 to 215. Best of all, his vision improved to 20/60, and he became encouraged, recharged with optimism, more energetic, healthier, and able to work again.

One of Dr. Walczak's patients experienced an equally exciting transformation, a forty-seven-year-old woman who was weak and had pain, cold extremities, albumin in the urine, advanced diabetic retinopathy, and was in a pregangrenous state. She came into the experiment with little hope, inasmuch as all other known treatment for retinopathy had done her no good. She was in such poor shape that Dr. Walczak wondered if she would live long enough to go blind.

On the thyroid-vitamins-enzyme-diuretic regime, she soon reported less pain, greater warmth in her extremities, more strength and endurance, and no albumin in her urine. Rather than risk subjectivity, Dr. Walczak sent her to an impartial ophthalmologist for comparative measurement of her vision. In the words of this doctor, her progress was "almost unbelievable."

Still another of Dr. Walczak's cases, a sixty-six-year-old woman, had such deteriorating eyesight that she could see only foggy outlines of objects. A year after she joined the experiment, she could distinguish different flowers in pots 20 feet away. Then, five months later, came an incredible improvement. For the first time in years, she could read the newspaper. The independent and impartial ophthalmologist who tested her eyes found that her right eye had improved to 20/25 and the left to 20/40. Improvement continued.

Dr. Walczak believes that, effective as this form of treatment is even in what appear to be almost impossible cases, it is even better when used preventively, in the early stages of retinopathy, when the disease has not as yet begun to hamper vision. Eleven of twelve patients with retinal deterioration showed definite and encouraging improvement on this regime in one experiment.[2] While conservative physicians may want to wait for the results of double-blind studies before adopting this regime, every week, month, or year that passes may be critical to those with retinopathies and other complications of diabetes. There is no time for fence-sitting. Millions desperately need helpful treatment such as this. There is little time to waste with these patients before beginning thyroid therapy. It is time for those with sight and foresight to help those who are about to lose their sight and possibly their lives.

Unquestionably, much can be done to prevent arterial deterioration, as well as other diseases, including cancer, which is the one most feared by the most people. This is the subject of the next chapter.

17

GUARD YOURSELF
AGAINST CANCER

That tiny thyroid gland—less than an ounce in weight—can bring you pounds of prevention against cancer, a disease that picks its victims indiscriminately.

Interesting evidence links hypothyroidism and cancer. A survey by Dr. J. G. C. Spencer of Frenahay Hospital in Bristol, England, revealed a higher-than-average cancer rate in the goiter belts of fifteen nations on four continents.[1]

Subnormal thyroid function appears to invite cancer. This has been shown clinically in numerous animal experiments. Malignant tissue from rats grafted onto other rats took hold readily in those animals whose thyroid glands had been removed, but rarely in those with normal thyroid function.

Findings with thousands of laboratory rats as well as with

human beings by Dr. Bernard Eskin, Director of Endocrinology in the Department of Obstetrics and Gynecology at the Medical College of Philadelphia, indicate that a deficiency of iodine, one of the thyroid gland's major nutritional components, encourages breast cancer.[2] Dr. Eskin discovered that the highest incidence of breast cancer and deaths from it are in the goiter belts of Poland, Switzerland, Austria, and the United States. The iodine-impoverished Great Lakes region of the coast-to-coast goiter belt shows the highest death rate from breast cancer in the United States. Conversely, iodine-rich Japan and Iceland have the world's lowest rates of goiter and deaths from breast cancer. In fact, the breast cancer death rate in Japan, where iodine-rich seafood and seaweed are on the daily menu, is one-fifth that of the United States.

As stated earlier, sufficient dietary iodine does not always assure proper thyroid gland function. However, normal function of this gland—or supplementation with thyroid extract—seems to deter cancer.

Studies show that hypothyroids and hyperthyroids appear to be more cancer prone than the general population. Several years ago, there were the makings of a bitter controversy in this area. One faction named hypothyroidism a major cause. Other factions disagreed violently.

A German medical journal (*Klinical-Wochenshr.*) several years ago ran an article admitting that there is a keen difference of opinion among experts.[3] According to the authors, one group feels that a shortage of circulating thyroid hormones makes the skin of the breasts hypersensitive to prolactin (the pituitary gland hormone that promotes milk production) and estrogen. This could contribute to cancerous growths. But they also say that thyroid hormone replacement is associated with the risk of breast cancer. Other evidence disputes this stand, and the American Thyroid Association favors hypothyroid patients' continuing thyroid therapy, if such therapy is indicated.

As far as hyperthyroidism is concerned, the authors state that excess thyroid hormones in the blood seemed to slow the growth of inoperable breast cancer. This is disputed, too, they say, and refer to other findings which relate hyperthyroidism to the development of breast cancer in premenopausal women.

A subsequent report in the journal *Cancer* concluded that "a proportion of breast cancer patients are mildly hypothyroid . . . ."[4] A year later, the *Journal of the American Medical Association* presented research by a team of eleven authorities, who conducted a case-control study to establish, once and for all, whether or not thyroid hormone therapy increases the risk of breast cancer.[5] The team compared 659 women with breast cancer and 1,719 control subjects and found no evidence that thyroid supplements increased the risk of breast cancer, even when thyroid supplements had been taken for more than fifteen years.

Thyroid replacement in hypothyroidism has been said to reverse cancer in some instances. One such case was presented in the journal *Neurology*.[6] A hypothyroid patient with a large tumor of the pituitary gland was given thyroid hormone. The tumor rapidly disappeared. Another case of a slightly different nature appeared in the *Southern Medical Journal*.[7] A woman with primary hypothyroidism was found to have a large pituitary tumor and, concurrently, the cessation of menstruation and an excessive flow of milk. Nine months after thyroid therapy was started, there was clinical and radiologic evidence that the tumor had regressed, along with the other symptoms.

These cases and the remarkable findings of John A. Myers, M.D., F.R.S.H., indicate that alternatives should be carefully examined before women patients are rushed into surgery, particularly for removal of the ovaries.[8]

Dr. Myers's success in treating serious female conditions by nonsurgical methods has opened new vistas for all physicians and their patients. It is Dr. Myers's opinion that, although cancer is a formidable enemy, we should not let cancer phobia run away with rational decision making. The primitive fear of the unknown and the potent drive for survival sometimes stampede us into undesirable treatment alternatives. An atmosphere heavy with fear impels the surgeon who removes a cancerous breast to perform surgery on a normal, though susceptible, second breast. Occasionally, patients request this as a security measure. Likewise, when a cancerous uterus is removed, sometimes a sound ovary is cut out, too, for fear that cancer will develop there. On occasion, both ovaries are taken out.

Preventive surgery of the ovaries is easier to rationalize in women beyond menopause, as Dr. Myers indicates. The ovaries produce the hormones estrogen and progesterone, as well as ova. The first two can be replaced. So why not part with the ovaries? For a very good reason. The ovaries make another important and little-known contribution to survival and well-being, as Dr. Myers learned while reviewing a paper on atherosclerosis by Joseph Stambul, M.D., Chief Cardiologist, Department of Medicine, Southern Division of the Albert Einstein Medical Center.

Dr. Stambul stated that atherosclerosis in the coronary artery is six times more prevalent in men than in women, a key reason why women live longer than men. The obvious explanation—and a gross simplification—is that women produce estrogen. However, he also said that another hormonelike substance is synthesized by the ovaries—protein-bound iodine, or diiodotyrosine—which keeps cholesterol in solution in the blood, rather than allowing it to accumulate in the lining of arteries.

Long before he learned of Dr. Stambul's thesis, Dr. Myers claims that he had used diiodotyrosine to soften the breasts of nursing women, particularly hypothyroid women. He states correctly that cysts and abscesses can develop in breasts which become caked in nursing mothers and offers an example of a patient who had a hardened and painful left breast. He administered 200 grams of diiodotyrosine and, within two days, brought the breast back to good health. In another similar case, the mother's breasts were so painful and hard that they yielded too little milk to satisfy the baby. Over a period of several hours, the mother was given 10 grams of diiodotyrosine to dissolve under her tongue. Almost immediately her breasts softened, the pain ceased, and milk began spurting from her nipples. That was the end of her nursing problems.

Still another female ailment was solved by the same method. A forty-five-year-old woman had a large abscess on her left breast and a cyst four millimeters long on her left ovary. The knowledgeable gynecologist who made the diagnosis recommended surgery for both conditions. Deeply upset, the woman appealed to Dr. Myers for treatment without surgery. Over a two-day period, he gave her some 50 grams of powdered diiodotyrosine to dissolve under her tongue, in addition to intravenous magnesium, B complex, and vitamin C. Response came quickly and both conditions healed rapidly. Inasmuch as her breasts were still quite hard, heavy, and doughy, Dr. Myers continued the treatment. Within a matter of days, her breasts softened and regained the normal feeling of fluidity.

These are not isolated cases. Dr. Myers has had the same results in innumerable similar cases. He also tells of subduing persistent vaginal infections—trichomonas and yeast infections as well as nonspecific leukorrhea, which had resisted various treatments—in patients, most of whom were hypothyroid. Dr. Myers treated these patients with thyroid hormone and intra-vaginal iodine. Their hypothyroid conditions cleared up and so did their infections. Within minutes after the vaginal treatment with iodine, several of the women with hardened breasts felt and saw a softening. Women with cysts had them disappear in time.

Such measures help ward off conditions which, in some instances, may be forerunners of cancer. Dr. Myers has validated the Stambul findings concerning the ovaries and the importance of their secretions in numerous cases, including the following:

Several weeks after her ovaries were surgically removed, a forty-six-year-old-woman found goiters swelling her throat. The woman, a Navy nurse, had had a total hysterectomy in the Navy Hospital in Bethesda, Maryland. While recovering from her operation, she was found to have developed nodules on her thyroid gland. Alerted to the possibility of cancer, she was told to have the nodules removed. Rather than endure more surgery, she asked Dr. Myers to treat her. He did so with estrogen, iodine, vitamins, and minerals. The thyroid nodules began shrinking slowly. After two years, they disappeared. Two years later when she was examined by Navy doctors at Corpus Christi, Texas, and they reviewed her medical record from Bethesda, they refused to believe that she had ever had thyroid nodules.

Aside from Dr. Stambul's and his own observations relative to the protective, life-extending power of the ovaries, Dr. Myers cites the dog experiments of Perkin and Brown of Lahey Clinic, Boston. After the thyroid gland of a male dog has been surgically removed, his protein-bound iodine plummets to one-tenth its normal level. After the same operation, a female dog's protein-bound iodine remains the same until the ovary is removed. Then it drops to the same level as that of the male.

Over and above being protected from cardiovascular problems

by ovarian secretions, women are also protected against cystic fibrosis as well as cancer of the breast and ovaries. Dr. Myers states that iodine, tyrosine, vitamins, amino acids, and trace minerals will guard a woman against numerous ailments, and that she should not give up her ovaries in panic at any point in her life, unless they have been proved to be cancerous. Then it is foolish to resist.

18

THYROIDITIS: A GROWING MENACE

*O*ne of the great mysteries which would require a medical Perry Mason to solve is an inflammatory condition known as Hashimoto's Autoimmune Thyroiditis (HAIT). In this autoimmune illness, the body produces antibodies which attack the thyroid gland as if it were a threatening invader such as bacteria, viruses, or fungi (yeast). Why? We don't know conclusively. However, there are clues as well as a workable means of coping with this disorder. More about that later.

HAIT appears to be hereditary, because often not only a parent has it, but also one or more of the children. Unfortunately, it is not suspected in children and, therefore, they may go on suffering untreated. In my practice, it is not uncommon for me to treat an entire family.

Way back in the year 1935, Hashimoto's Autoimmune Thyroiditis was almost too rare to be a statistic, occurring in probably 6 individuals in 100,000. Today approximately 2 out of 100 are afflicted with HAIT, according to an article in *Medical Clinics of America*. More recent estimates boost that figure to about 3 percent of the population—as it is among my patients.

Inasmuch as HAIT is a diagnosis which is often not suspected and, therefore, not treated, we decided to devote a full chapter to it. We particularly alert women to this condition, because statistics show that 95 percent of patients turn out to be women.

Do these figures agree with my medical findings? No. Among my patients, almost an equal number of men have HAIT. However, because it is a condition not generally suspected in men, HAIT often is a diagnosis that should be made but isn't.

In different stages of this serious illness, a person can manifest symptoms of either under- or overactive thyroid function (hypo- or hyperthyroidism).

What are HAIT'S classic symptoms?

1. Deep fatigue, often written off as chronic fatigue syndrome. Such patients go to sleep exhausted and wake up even more so. Their endurance is often low to nonexistent. Usually performing their day-to-day activities is beyond them.

2. Depression. Patients' exhaustion and inability to function normally bring on feelings of futility. In any acute onset of depression—especially in adult women—thyroiditis should be suspected and ruled out by proper testing for antibodies to the thyroid. Thyroiditis is frequently a common cause of postpartum depression.

3. Memory loss, characterized by severe problems with recent memory and ability to concentrate, is often a disaster for working adults and students.

4. Nervousness ranges from mild anxiety to full-blown panic attacks—some of which are true psychiatric emergencies. These are puzzling to HAIT patients and, often, to their physicians who, in desperation, usually recommend psychotherapy

or prescribe powerful tranquilizers. Most patients with psychiatric symptoms brought on by thyroiditis tell me, "I have no reason I know of to feel this way. Something's wrong physically, yet all my medical exams are normal." (However, at this point, they haven't had autoimmune antibodies to their thyroid gland checked.)

5. Allergies, food and environmental.
6. Heartbeat irregularity and palpitations.
7. Muscle and joint pains.
8. Sleep disturbances and insomnia.
9. Reduced sex drive.
10. Menstrual problems.
11. Suicidal tendencies.
12. Digestive disorders.
13. Headaches and ear pain.
14. Lumps in the throat.
15. Difficulty swallowing.

Many new patients who come to me with HAIT are baffled. Recently a woman patient told me:

"I don't understand any of it, mainly the depression. I have a husband who loves me, a good position, and caring relatives and friends. Something's wrong physically, but no one's able to figure out what it is."

A few of my new patients have admitted becoming so desperate that they have voluntarily signed into a psychiatric hospital because they feared harming themselves. Unfortunately, the typical treatment for patients with chronic depression in whom thyroiditis goes undiagnosed is a powerful antidepressant, which, quite frequently, makes them worse.

Inasmuch as exhaustion, depression, and other psychological problems are the most common complaints of HAIT patients, they often eat to feel better and gain weight that's difficult to lose. Inability to curb their intake of food and added weight make them even more depressed.

HAIT is often a missed diagnosis because the routine thyroid hormone blood levels test used to rule out thyroid disease is frequently normal, and no additional testing is then performed. If you suspect HAIT is your condition, share that suspicion with your doctor and ask him or her to order a specialized blood test known as an antithyroid antibody panel consisting of anti-thyroglobulin and antimicrosomal antibodies. These tests can be performed by any physician or authorized by him at a clinical laboratory. They will corroborate a presumptive diagnosis of HAIT.

Often the signs of thyroiditis are contradictory. Usually any elevation of antithyroid antibodies is significant. Yet, in severe cases, there may be a reading of low antithyroid antibodies and, in a mild case, markedly elevated antibodies.

My policy is to treat patients medically for thyroiditis even when they have just a small elevation of antithyroid antibodies, if they also present symptoms of this disorder. I emphasize this point, because many doctors become interested in this condition only if the antibody level is sky high.

D.M., a forty-seven-year-old woman, is just one example of the hundreds of patients I've treated for HAIT over the years. She came to me complaining of a two-year history of chronic fatigue and severe depression, alternating with bouts of anxiety and heart palpitations.

During this trying period, she had been hospitalized for six months in a psychiatric unit and treated with lithium, a major antidepressant, and had had numerous rounds of shock therapy. In the year that I first saw her, her weight had ballooned up by 50 pounds with no real change in her food intake.

Noting that her thyroid levels were normal, but that she had an elevation of antithyroid antibodies, I treated her with thyroid medication, starting with a quarter grain of Armour desiccated thyroid, increasing that dosage by a quarter grain every several weeks.

Within ninety days, all of the major symptoms were under control, and she was on the road to recovery. Along with this treatment, I upgraded her diet with liberal amounts of vitamins, minerals, and essential fatty acids—particularly GLA, EPA, vitamin B complex, and vitamin C. Within months, she had lost all of her excess weight and felt as if she had been reborn.

Although thyroiditis can affect any age group, most patients are in the age range from thirteen to forty years. If either parent of a patient is diagnosed with HAIT, I urge him or her to have other bloodline family members checked for antithyroid antibodies elevation, if they are suffering from symptoms mentioned above—particularly if no other medical cause has been detected.

Many of my patients ask if they have to stay on thyroid supplementation indefinitely. My answer is, "A person with diagnosed HAIT doesn't have to remain on prescription thyroid forever when careful attention is paid to eating a well-balanced diet of natural foods and taking proper supplements."

I have been able to wean many of my HAIT patients from a thyroid supplement in a relatively short time—within three to six months—by bolstering their immune systems nutritionally.

What causes HAIT? I have no evidence from published research. However, my clinical experience leads me to believe that HAIT is caused, in part, by viral infections such as chronic Epstein-Barr virus or systemic candidiasis that may trigger the body's autoimmune response to the thyroid.

Supernutrition with accent on whole grains and fresh vegetables often strengthens the immune system enough for it to control these microorganisms, resulting in a sharp decrease in the body's autoimmune response to the thyroid.

When this favorable result is realized—this particular treatment is almost always successful—my patients are slowly withdrawn from their thyroid medication and can then rely on and be treated by their optimum nutrition.

19

EVENING PRIMROSE OIL: WONDER-WORKER

*T*he more I read, the more excited I grow.

Twenty-two published reports covering clinical and double-blind studies of evening primrose oil had convinced me that this is the most remarkable all-purpose food supplement to burst onto the horizon in a generation.

And the more I read, the more I realized that evening primrose oil and thyroid hormone prevent and relieve an almost identical list of disorders: arthritis; cardiovascular ailments; premenstrual syndrome; skin problems such as acne, eczema, and ichthyosis; infection and inflammation; diabetic complications; and certain other degenerative diseases which encourage faster aging.

Why do evening primrose oil and thyroid hormone seem to work effectively on many of the same disorders? Research needs to be done to offer a conclusive answer, although certain facts already seem clear. Prostaglandins (PGs), whose precursors are contained in the essential fatty acids (EFAs) in evening primrose oil, are present in infinitesimal amounts in every human cell and, though short lived, exert a strong influence on every bodily function. Thyroid hormone, too, is carried through the bloodstream to every cell, where it governs life processes.

PGs, like thyroid hormone, are involved in blood circulation, in metabolism, in growth and reproduction, and in proper functioning of the immune system. Individuals deficient in PGs catch every communicable disease. So do hypothyroids.

Aside from comparisons with thyroid hormone, evening primrose oil has an incredibly promising life of its own. It is important—even fundamental—for us to know exactly what it is and what it can do for us.

Evening primrose oil, which sounds like a beauty product that might be found in a woman's boudoir, is actually something that should be on her vitamin shelf as well as that of everyone in the household. It contains an essential fatty acid, a vitamin-like compound that can't be made in the human body. (That is what "essential" means in this context.) The World Health Organization suggests that adults should take in at least 3 percent of their total calories as EFAs; the figure is 5 percent for children and lactating women.

EFAs perform many functions; their chief roles are as integral parts of every membrane in the body and as the precursors of prostaglandins, key short-term regulators which help control all bodily organs.

Unless enough EFAs are supplied, physical abnormalities develop. These include defects in heart function and in circulation; subnormal complexion with acne and eczema; poor immune function; failure of wounds to heal; reproductive shortcomings or failure, particularly in men; inflammatory ailments and arthritis; infiltration of fat and fibrosis of the liver; failure of the brain to develop normally; imbalance of body water; and atrophy of exocrine (ducted) glands.

Can't we get enough EFAs from the usual sources of polyunsaturates? Not always. Not all polyunsaturates are biologically active. Vegetable oils are rich in linoleic acid, an essential raw material for prostaglandins, but coconut, olive, and palm oil are not. Vegetable oils processed for cooking fats and margarines often lose their EFA activity and can even become anti–EFA factors. Human milk has a high content of linoleic acid; other foods have negligible amounts.

On its way to becoming PGs, linoleic acid must go through conversion to gamma-linoleic acid (GLA), then to dihomo-gamma-linoleic acid (DGLA).

Only breastfeeding infants can get GLA, DGLA, and certain PGs directly; the rest of us must obtain them through the metabolism of ingested linoleic acid. Females are far better at converting this acid into GLA than males, so the latter require a larger intake.

A biochemical obstacle course blocks persons following a typical Western lifestyle from forming GLA from linoleic acid: a diet heavy in saturated fats and cholesterol, processed vegetable oil, and alcohol.[1] These impediments grow more daunting when added to the aging process and slower metabolism, virus infections, degenerative diseases, radiation, and zinc deficiency.

Only nursing infants were privileged to get prostaglandin precursors and some PGs directly until recent scientific experiments revealed the remarkable biochemical values of evening primrose oil, which contains 8 to 9 percent GLA and more than 70 percent of cis-linoleic acid, the EFA–active form.[2]

Where has evening primrose oil been all our lives? It has been around for centuries, but was not fully appreciated until recently. For hundreds of years, Native Americans pressed the oil from seeds of the evening primrose, a lovely yellow Eastern Seaboard wildflower that blooms and dies in a single evening. They cured skin problems and wounds by applying this oil, and took it orally for asthma. Early colonizers of America shipped evening primrose oil plants back to England, where the flower achieved such healing successes that it was called the King's cure-all.

From 1965 to 1981, Agricultural Holdings Ltd., a British seed company, conducted an extensive botanical search and found more than one thousand varieties of evening primrose, from which it developed plants with the richest yield of consistently high-quality oil.

The critical role of evening primrose oil in promoting the formation of prostaglandins has excited the scientific community. Now there is a ready source of PG precursor to help realize the unlimited possibilities of prostaglandins to keep us healthy.

The explosion of publications about prostaglandins has reached unimaginable proportions: hundreds of papers in some months—far more than most physicians can read and still carry on a medical practice.

Like evening primrose oil, prostaglandins are not new. They were known more than fifty years ago and given their peculiar name because they were first discovered in semen in the prostate gland. In the 1960s—long after it was too late to put PGs through a legal name change—it was found that they are synthesized in almost every body cell. A decade after that, scientists learned that aspirin kills pain by blocking the production of two forms of PG.

By providing precursors of PGs, evening primrose oil has been discovered to be clinically valuable in a wide range of medical problems, including arthritis, cardiovascular ailments, premenstrual syndrome, breast pain, obesity, hyperactivity, diabetes, brittle nails, hair loss, skin diseases, and allergies.[3] It was shown to be effective in controlling adjuvant arthritis in rats and rheumatoid arthritis in some human patients.[4]

Evening primrose oil also appears to lower the risk of heart attacks in animals and human beings. Its high content of EFAs keeps blood platelets from sticking together and forming clots, and helps lower blood cholesterol and blood pressure.

Evening primrose oil has also earned high marks in a disorder that plagues many women, premenstrual syndrome (PMS). Its symptoms include fluid retention, swollen ankles, painful breasts, pelvic congestion, abdominal bloating, headaches, and mood disorders such as depression, irritability, weeping, and, in some cases, uncontrollable rage.

In two experiments in Great Britain, evening primrose oil showed promise in preventing symptoms of PMS. At one of the world's largest PMS clinics, St. Thomas Hospital in London, M. G. Brush, M.D., administered evening primrose oil to seventy women who had failed to get relief from one or two other attempted treatments. Taking two capsules three times daily, 67 percent of the women were completely relieved of PMS symptoms. Twenty-two percent gained partial relief. A surprising total of 89 percent of treatment-resistant women experienced partial to total relief.[5]

At the Universities of Wales and Dundee, one hundred women took part in a placebo-controlled double-blind crossover study with evening primrose oil to treat breast pain. (Many of the subjects experienced worse pain premenstrually.) A majority of the women experienced significant pain relief.[6]

In an area of concern to both women and men, evening primrose oil showed ability to help obese subjects lose weight. Among individuals more than 10 percent above ideal weight who took this supplement, 50 percent lost weight without a change of diet. Subjects who were within 10 percent of ideal body weight showed no weight change on evening primrose oil. Those who lost weight claimed they noted a reduced appetite without any effort on their part.[7]

Evening primrose oil has proved somewhat helpful in cases of alcohol addiction and much more so in lessening the harmful effects of alcohol. GLA, DGLA, and PGE1, a critical prostaglandin, are depleted in alcoholics. Conversion of linoleic acid to GLA is blocked by alcohol, causing a functional lack of EFA, even though intake of linoleic acid seems to be sufficient. DGLA is rapidly used up, and the process of replenishment from linoleic acid is shut down.[8] After appreciable drinking, levels of the prostaglandin PGE1 drop down and bring on depression. In turn, depression predisposes the person to further drinking and to alcoholism—especially for women, according to a scientific report. Evening primrose oil can help relieve the depression and discourage additional drinking. In one experiment, it prevented severe postalcohol depression, tachyarrythmias (too-rapid heart action), and hangovers.[9]

Aside from seriously depleting GLA, DGLA, and PGE1, alcoholism causes liver damage and kidney defects. Evening primrose oil has been shown to break the enzyme block caused by alcohol and to protect both liver and kidneys.

Rarely a disorder of adults, hyperactivity is a serious problem for children, their parents, and their teachers. Sometimes these "perpetual motion" children who are often classroom disturbers can be helped by the Feingold diet, which eliminates foods with additives and junk foods.

Food additives appear to offer weak resistance to the conversion of EFAs to PGs. One new theory holds that hyperactivity may be caused by subnormal intake of EFAs. (Thirst, common in this ailment, is a revealing symptom of EFA deficiency in animals.) Boys outnumber girls in hyperactivity by three to one. Inasmuch as boys have trouble converting EFA to PGs, they require about three times as much EFA as girls.

Preliminary studies of hyperactive children by clinicians in the United States, Canada, South Africa, and the United Kingdom indicate that approximately two-thirds of the subjects improve after ingestion of evening primrose oil. A peculiarity noted in these experiments is that certain children responded better to the oil if it was rubbed into their skin. Researchers believe that this is true because some individuals have poor intestinal tract absorption. Dosages used were two to three capsules each morning and evening and, after six to eight weeks, one in the morning and one in the evening.[10]

In another disorder, diabetes, evening primrose oil helps in two ways, one immediate, the other long range. Experiments demonstrated that diabetic animals cannot readily convert linoleic acid to GLA. Presumably, the same thing happens in human beings. EFA supplementation often raises levels of linoleic acid, GLA, DGLA, and certain prostaglandins in diabetics.

An EFA–rich regime also helps control long-term complications of diabetes. A five-year study of 102 diabetics at Erasmus University in Rotterdam used matched groups of patients, one on a normal diet, the other on a linoleic acid–enriched diet (13 percent of the calories). At the study's end, 62 percent of males and 55 percent of females on the normal diet developed retinopathy (deterioration of arteries in the retina that often impairs sight). Only 27 percent of males and 32 percent of females on the linoleic acid–enriched diet developed retinopathy.[11]

Essential fatty acids play a crucial role in the health and beauty of skin, hair, and nails. When individuals are deficient in EFAs, or if EFAs cannot be translated into GLA (as is the case in zinc deficiency), skin lesions similar to those in eczema and ichthyosis (fish skin) develop, along with hair loss and brittle, cracking nails. Experiments have established that children with eczema have low levels of EFAs; it has also been shown that depriving children of EFAs leads to eczema.[12] Infants on mother's milk get preformed GLA, so the problem in forming this compound from linoleic acid is eliminated. The only other way to get preformed GLA is from evening primrose oil. Three capsules contain roughly the same amount of GLA as a day's supply of human milk. Marginal effectiveness of EFA in improving eczema may mean that the principal problem lies not in the amount of linoleic acid available but in the amount convertible to GLA.

A double-blind, placebo-controlled experiment at the University of Bristol in England showed that evening primrose oil brought about a modest but significant improvement in eczema of adults and children.[13] In a related condition, brittle and cracking nails, nails were dramatically improved by evening primrose oil; this was demonstrated in an experiment at Hairmyres Hospital in East Kilbride, Scotland. Dr. Allan Campbell, a prominent researcher, concludes that poor nails are a newly discovered symptom of EFA deficiency.[14]

With regard to a severe skin ailment, atopic eczema, a double-blind controlled cross-over study of different doses of evening primrose oil on ninety-nine patients revealed significant clinical improvements in high dosages with no side effects, according to a study reported in *Lancet*.[15]

Atopic eczema is one of numerous, often dissimilar, diseases linked biochemically to one another—among them, allergies, asthma, and hay fever—that are endured by some forty million Americans. Several studies on atopic disorders show three prominent features: (1) they run in families; (2) atopics are deficient in certain essential blood ingredients, including elements for synthesizing prostaglandins; and (3) their immune systems have deficiencies that reduce their effectiveness in dealing with threatening invaders.

Every minute of the day and night we are exposed to bacteria and viruses and to foreign substances in the air we breathe, the food we eat, and the water we drink. Some of them are harmless; others are harmful. Our immune systems must distinguish which is which and neutralize or destroy harmful invaders. T suppressor lymphocyte cells are the immune system's "field generals"; they issue orders as to which invaders to attack.

The best present scientific information holds that in atopic persons, the T suppressor cells are defective. The field generals are not competent to command. They are indiscriminate. Immune system soldiers under them blindly obey orders and attack harmless substances—foods such as eggs and milk proteins, as well as pollens, molds, and animal dander—along with the real enemies.

This senseless warfare manifests itself in allergies, asthma, eczema, and sometimes in headaches, when the brain is the battle area. Much current data indicates that prostaglandins control the T suppressor cells. A PG shortage in numbers and in specific types is believed to cause abnormal and harmful immune response. The protectors turn on the protected. It is no wonder that atopics are far more susceptible to infection and inflammation than normal individuals. The solution? Providing sufficient evening primrose oil.

Many authorities feel that a malfunctioning immune system, which makes a person susceptible to illness, also causes premature aging. Experiments show that animal aging is related to loss of ability to convert linoleic acid into GLA, which could account for cardiovascular and immune system abnormalities and degeneration. Studies are under way to determine if bypassing the body's need to translate linoleic acid into GLA by supplying evening primrose oil is a deterrent to aging. Time and research may soon provide the answer.

Unfortunately, some individuals are conditioned, even programmed, to feel and act old—physically and mentally—just by the large number of birthdays they have experienced.

20

ALZHEIMER'S DISEASE:
SENILITY OR SOMETHING ELSE?

"*D*r. Langer, I guess I have Alzheimer's disease," sighed the tense, attractive, middle-aged woman across the desk from me. Aside from being slightly overweight, a condition almost hidden by her smart, tailored beige suit, Antoinette, a new patient, looked nothing like Alzheimer's disease victims I had seen.

"What makes you think so?" I asked.

"I'm so forgetful. I sometimes forget where I parked my car at the supermarket—or even that I have a car. It's so hard for me to think that I almost have to push thoughts around in my brain by strength of will."

Previously, she had recited a lengthy list of other symptoms— overwhelming fatigue, cold hands and feet, constipation, frequent depression, weight gain, and dryness of skin, among the majors.

"I'm not a betting man," I replied. "However, if I were, I would bet that you have a condition that can be reversed within weeks—a few months at the most. You have many key symptoms of hypothyroidism."

Relief seemed to melt away her tension, and she leaned forward for more assurance. She got it from me. "I sometimes can't find *my* car in the supermarket parking lot."

We both laughed, then I told her how to take the Barnes Basal Temperature Test and prescribed appropriate blood tests for thyroid hormone and thyroid-stimulating hormone.

Antoinette's armpit temperature turned out to be just 96.8—a good degree under normal for the resting state. Her blood tests showed low readings of thyroid hormones T_4 and T_3—and a high reading of the pituitary gland's thyroid-stimulating hormone, the latter a strong indication that her thyroid function was sluggish.

After a few weeks on one-quarter grain of Armour desiccated thyroid, she improved dramatically—far quicker than I had hoped, although her basal temperature was still subnormal.

"I'm beginning to remember again—and *think*," she bubbled. "It's almost unbelievable that a tiny bit of thyroid can help this much."

"That's just the beginning," I promised. "Your physical symptoms will soon improve, too."

They did, and she did! One more happy patient was on the verge of graduating to nonpatient status!

Antoinette's case was anything but rare. Dozens of my new patients with faulty memory and difficulty in thinking immediately assume the worst. So much has been publicized about Alzheimer's disease and senility that the first thing that patients think is that they're losing their minds. Then the power of negative thinking takes over and symptoms become even worse, because people think the worst.

Such reactions are not always the fault of patients. Some doctors are to blame. Often when a retired person—even a former professional—tells a physician that his memory is failing and that he sometimes is in a confused state, the doctor will write off the condition to senility or Alzheimer's disease and dismiss the patient without treatment.

Even sadder is the fact that such senior citizens are sometimes institutionalized as if they have untreatable mental ailments or senile dementia when, with a careful physical examination, they will often be found to be suffering from insufficient thyroid hormones, nutritional deficiencies, or a combination—one condition influencing or even worsening the other.

Numerous studies reveal that new cases of mental or emotional disturbances are far more numerous in people older than age sixty-five than in younger individuals. However, it is a serious error to accept that advancing age means losing memory, ability to reason, and sanity. Less than 5 percent of senior citizens are institutionalized for such psychiatric disorders.

Too little thyroid hormone, the physical and mental consequences of poor nutrition, and nonchallenging or nonstimulating people or environments—particularly prevalent for sedentary retirees—make them feel they are growing old and senile.

Queen Victoria began studying Hindustani, one of the world's most difficult languages, after she was seventy-five years old. Frank Lloyd Wright created some of his greatest architectural designs after age seventy-five. Michelangelo was painting masterpieces after age eighty. Pablo Picasso turned out works of art when he was well into his nineties. Benjamin Franklin was eighty-four years old when he wrote his moving appeal to Congress for the abolition of slavery.

Mark Twain and Jules Verne did some of their best writing after age seventy. Italian playwright Luigi Pirandello never wrote a play until age fifty, and then became prolific and famous in this activity. He won the Nobel Prize for literature after he celebrated his seventy-fifth birthday.

Daniel Defoe, who authored *Robinson Crusoe*, didn't think himself too old to continue his work. He wrote thirty books after the age of sixty-seven.

Significant accomplishments by superseniors are not limited to the mental area. Georges Adan, of France, made a convincing statement for the belief that we improve with age. At the age of twenty-five, Georges rowed a boat across the English channel in seven hours and forty-five minutes. When he celebrated his seventieth birthday, he rowed a similar boat across the same channel in six hours and twenty-four minutes. King Gustav V of Sweden played five sets of tennis to celebrate his eighty-fifth birthday.

Naturally, all of us can't realize such astonishing achievements at an advanced age. However, these accomplishments show us how well people can do when they continue to think and act young and retain their interest in themselves, others, events, career, and/or hobbies.

Memory loss, difficulty in thinking, disorientation, and confusion are sometimes caused by brain deterioration but, in most instances, they are brought on by correctable conditions. Narrowed blood vessels and arteries can do this—as can pathological nerve conditions such as tangled nerve fibers in Alzheimer's disease.

Clinical studies by Dr. Dean Ornish demonstrate that arteries can be flushed out with a diet accenting fresh vegetables and fruit. Chelation, too, can "Roto-Root" out blockages and help to restore normal blood circulation.

When a person suffers low thyroid function, blood carrying fuel and oxygen to the brain does not reach its destination with vigor and thrust, because the heart pumps languidly. Further, digestion and assimilation are slowed down by hypothyroidism, making it difficult to get maximum nutritional values from food.

Certainly Alzheimer's disease is a reality—a grim reality—and how the intake of aluminum, a nonnutrient mineral, affects the thyroid gland is not conclusively documented. However, there is evidence that aluminum is found accumulated in the brain of Alzheimer's disease victims, along with tangled nerve fibers—neurofibrils—minute nerve conductors within brain cells. In contrast, neither aluminum nor tangled neurofibrils are found in the brains of individuals who do not have Alzheimer's disease.

There are pros and cons on the subject. Some scientists ask if aluminum is a cause or an effect of Alzheimer's disease. Others say aluminum *is* a cause and that we shouldn't wait for complete documentation before taking it out of our bodies.

High blood levels of aluminum were discovered in many of four hundred psychiatric patients suffering senile symptoms, including memory loss, reports the Brain Bio Center in Princeton, New Jersey.[1]

How does aluminum enter us in the first place? Some is absorbed through the intestines and some through the skin from toiletry products. Due to its tiny ions, aluminum can slip through the blood-brain barrier with ease. Its ions are less than half the size of those in essential minerals like calcium, magnesium, potassium, and sodium.[2]

If aluminum is truly a Trojan horse, how does it commit brain sabotage? Researchers Timothy L. MacDonald, W. Griffith Humphreys, and R. Bruce Martin at the University of Virginia in Charlottesville, may have found the answer.[3] They believe it acts against the microtubules which support cell structure. These microtubules form what biochemists call "spindles." Cells can't divide without sound spindles. When cell replication is blocked in nerves, it is conceivable that tangled fibers are the result.

Microtubules are always in process—being assembled and taken apart—using a raw material named "tubulin," a composite of amino acids and the mineral magnesium. The researchers discovered that magnesium and aluminum compete to be incorporated in tubulin and that aluminum is taken into tubulin ten times faster than magnesium. Aluminum is not as strong as magnesium for microtubule raw material. So cells made with aluminum, amino acid, and tubulin collapse more readily.

Aluminum invades us through food, beverages, medications, and cosmetics. It is in breads and pastries, baking powder, baking powder biscuits, cheese, cheese sauces, pickles, salad dressings, salt and other condiments (added to keep them free running), white flour, fruit juices in aluminum cans, cookware and aluminum foils for wrapping and cooking foods, and municipal water supplies in the form of alum.

It is present in medicines and antacids, antidiarrhea products, antiperspirants and deodorants, some cosmetics, feminine hygiene products (including douches), some hemorrhoid preparations, lipstick, skin creams, lotions, and toothpastes.

Although not in my area of treatment, removal of aluminum through chelation is known to help some Alzheimer's patients in early or middle stages of this condition. Several of my physician friends and acquaintances have achieved positive results through chelation. Richard Casdorph, M.D., of Long Beach, California, has noted improvement of Alzheimer's disease through lowering blood concentrations of aluminum by means of the chelating agent EDTA.[4]

Foods and supplements said to block absorption of aluminum are vitamin C and calcium, magnesium, manganese, and zinc. In a six-month research project, 50 percent of Alzheimer's disease patients fed large amounts of lecithin improved in certain mental functions—remembering and thinking—and in their ability to take care of their personal needs.

M.I.T.'s Richard Wurtman, M.D., discovered that there is 90 percent less of the neurotransmitter acetylcholine (made from lecithin)—essential for chemical contact between cells—in the brains of Alzheimer's disease patients than in those of individuals who do not have this disease.[5] This is an essential chemical for assuring contact between cells.

Much of what is considered senility in elderly patients is actually pseudosenility brought on by a multitude of conditions: physical illness, medications, glandular disorders—including low or high thyroid activity—nutritional deficiencies, and even prolonged stress.

Various diseases can invite symptoms that look like senility: anemia—insufficient red blood corpuscles to deliver enough oxygen to the brain; liver disease—improper handling of blood sugar, often due to hypothyroidism; hypoglycemia—low blood sugar that brings on many mental manifestations; and even urinary infections, resulting in body and brain toxicity.

Tranquilizers and sleeping pills used regularly cause side effects that ape symptoms of senility. A major job of the liver and kidneys is to remove toxins from the body. With age and nutritional abuse, these organs slow down their functions and toxins stay in the body longer, sometimes affecting the brain.

Deficiencies of proper nutrients created through eating a lot of junk food and processed food which has lost most of its vitamins, minerals, and enzymes account for many symptoms of senility, which people are too quick to attribute to Alzheimer's disease.

Fortunately, when these nutritional insults are eliminated—or at least minimized—and B-complex vitamins and vitamin C are added in generous doses, many such symptoms will disappear. However, as biochemists indicate, nutrients limited to the

RDA aren't going to undo what many years, decades, or even a lifetime of deprivation have brought about.

It is no coincidence that most of the nutrients for reversing pseudosenility are those mentioned in chapter 3, Care and Feeding of the Thyroid, and are essential for supporting the health and full-strength function of the thyroid gland.

Four of the B vitamins are especially important to reversing symptoms of senility: B_1, niacin (B_3), pantothenic acid (B_5), and B_{12}. Many studies have shown that depriving test subjects of vitamin B_1 brings on neurological and psychiatric symptoms that ape those of senility: memory as retentive as a sieve, jitteryness and shakes—especially common in alcoholics who have far outstripped their supply of vitamin B_1—and quick-trigger irritability and outbursts of temper.

Our nervous systems could not survive daily living, let alone the stresses of the day, without ample pantothenic acid.

Niacin deprivation can invite a host of pseudosenility symptoms: anxiety, confusion, depression, disorientation, and undependable memory. Abram Hoffer, M.D., of Victoria, B.C., Canada, with Sir Humphrey Osmond, created the first effective nutritional treatment for schizophrenia with niacin and vitamin C, and advocates its use for the above-mentioned symptoms.[6]

Not only does this B vitamin niacin provide biochemical support for the nervous system and brain, it also is essential for a critically important reason. It keeps red blood cells from clumping into units too large to slide through the tiny capillaries of the brain. Such clumping means that oxygen carried by the red blood cells is choked off from brain cells, which consequently die. An oxygen-starved brain shows all manifestations of senility.

Mental and emotional symptoms of vitamin B_{12} deficiency are low mental energy, difficulty in concentrating, agitation, and hallucinations.

Antioxidants such as vitamins A, C, E, beta-carotene, glutathione peroxidase, superoxide dismutase (S.O.D.), and selenium are needed to keep free radicals from disabling or damaging brain cells. And one of the little known causes of pseudosenility is a deficiency of the mineral zinc. Numerous studies show that zinc deficiency can bring on confusion and memory loss, plus diminished ability to taste and smell—necessary senses for a good appetite and taking in essential nutrients.

Magnesium, choline, and lecithin are also key nutrients for fending off or correcting symptoms of pseudosenility, often misdiagnosed as Alzheimer's disease.

Inasmuch as thyroid hormones help keep every one of your body's trillions of cells using food and oxygen efficiently, you must be sure that your thyroid gland is functioning properly or—if it isn't—that it is properly supplemented.

Another important, little-known, and, therefore, unsuspected cause of symptoms resembling those of senility is sustained stress. Glucocorticoids, steroid hormones released by the adrenal glands, may cause damage to brain cells, especially those of the hippocampus, state researchers at the Salk Institute for Biological Studies (San Diego).[7] This is the part of the brain where memories are made and kept. And stress damage can make it impossible to store new memories and recall old ones.

During periods of stress, these glucocorticoids block glucose (blood sugar) from entering many kinds of cells—including those of the brain—conserving available fuel for physical action such as muscle movement in running or defending oneself. Cut off from glucose, the only fuel they can use, brain cells become damaged or die.

Another study that confirms the Salk findings was conducted by researchers at Washington University in St. Louis. Nineteen adults were administered either glucocorticoids or a placebo for four consecutive days.

Volunteers receiving the stress hormone showed a marked loss of memory, compared with the placebo takers. After a week off the stress hormone, the volunteers' memory returned fully.

A study by Dr. Mark Rosenthal, assistant professor of medicine at the University of New Mexico, and Dr. Clare Jeanne Sanchez, assistant professor of medicine at the University of South Carolina,[8] discloses that hypothyroidism can cause a host of symptoms similar to those of Alzheimer's disease: disorientation, irritability, loss of sound judgment, memory failure, and mental slowness. Hypothyroidism is a "great masquerader," says Dr. Rosenthal.

"We know that those who act senile or demented should be

screened for hypothyroidism," echoes Dr. Sanchez. "We recommend that all elderly people who come to their doctors for whatever reason should get a . . . screening for hypothyroidism. If hypothyroidism goes too far, it can cause permanent brain damage."

In any stay-young program, it is essential to have a normally working thyroid gland—or proper supplementation—because thyroid hormone is a MUST for the good health and longevity of every body and brain cell, every tissue, and every organ and gland.

21

THE GREAT CONTROVERSY:
SYNTHETIC VERSUS NATURAL

*I*t was a quiet war.

On one side stood the vast army of traditional medical doctors, schooled to prescribe synthetic thyroid formulas for hypothyroidism. On the other side stood a small number of holistically oriented doctors, influenced by the great success of Dr. Barnes in treating hypothyroidism with Armour natural desiccated thyroid. Traditional doctors had a crushing advantage: an army of hundreds of thousands versus tens of thousands. It was David versus Goliath all over again. Clearly, the vast army felt secure that levothyroxine, the generic name for thyroid brands such as Euthyrox, Levothyroid, Levoxyl, and Synthroid with thyroxine (T_4), was superior to natural forms of thyroid that contain both thyroxine (T_4) and triiodothyronine (T_3).

Then, just before the twentieth century gave way to the energy-charged twenty-first century, an article in the *New England Journal of Medicine* sent a shock through the medical community.[1] Research by Lithuanian endocrinologists at Kaunas Medical University and others at the School of Medicine at the University of North Carolina at Chapel Hill revealed that T_4 hormone alone is not nearly as beneficial in treating hypothyroidism as is a combination of T_4 with T_3. Suddenly, the thirty-year-old practice of using only T_4 to treat underactive thyroid was called into question.

The theory of the synthetic T_4 treatment that prevailed since the 1970s held that part of the T_4 is converted to sufficient T_3. One book on the topic states, "When taken on a daily basis, thyroxine as T_4 allows for a steady and continuous production of T_3 in bodily organs."[2] This is only partially true. When the adrenal system is weak or exhausted from various physical, emotional, or mental stresses—even the mildest adrenal insufficiency—it must be strengthened before or during thyroid treatment for the treatment to be effective.

Earlier in this book, I made a statement about adrenal exhaustion that bears repeating: "Adrenal exhaustion is a condition that may preclude substantive improvement of your symptoms. Your own nutritionally oriented physician may be able to help strengthen your adrenals by placing you on a small amount of hydrocortisone (5 milligrams four times a day, after meals and before bedtime). This regimen has been clinically tested for twenty-five years by William McKendries Jeffries, M.D., and I urge you to have your doctor read his book *The Safe Uses of Cortisone*, which documents why and how to use cortisone to help restore you to peak health."

Michael Schachter, M.D., F.A.C.M., in an on-line article titled "The Diagnosis and Treatment of Hypothyroidism," underscored the need for strengthening weak adrenal function to avoid feeling worse and experiencing symptoms typical of an overactive thyroid gland: a too-rapid heartbeat, palpitations, and increased sweating.[3] Symptoms that indicate a weak adrenal system, he states, include allergies, asthma, breathing difficulties, acne, eczema, psoriasis, lupus, flaky dry skin, arthritic pains, and wide emotional swings.

Previously, low production of T_4 was believed to be the major cause of hypothyroidism. Dr. Schachter feels it is rather due in large part to an inability to convert the less active T_4 into the active T_3. A weight-loss or low-protein diet may not provide enough of the amino acid tyrosine or enough iodine for the thyroid gland to synthesize T_4. Dr. Schachter also mentions the need for sufficient cortisol, iron, zinc, copper, and selenium in order to convert T_4 into T_3. (More about selenium in chapter 22.)

In the research published in the *New England Journal of Medicine* mentioned earlier, a combination of T_4 and T_3 proved far superior to just T_4 alone. Thirty-three patients were studied for two five-week periods. These patients all suffered from hypothyroidism caused by autoimmune thyroid disease, in which the immune system attacks the thyroid gland, or by surgical removal of the gland to treat cancer.

In one five-week trial, patients were administered their regular dose of T_4 only. For the next five weeks, they were given T_4 and T_3. Twenty of the thirty-three patients reported more energy, better ability to concentrate, and feeling better overall on the combination of T_4 and T_3. Patients on a combination of both hormones performed better on standard neuropsychological tests, and their emotional health improved.

In some physiological readings, such as pulse, blood pressure, cholesterol, and reflexes, the differences between the T_4 alone and a T_4/T_3 combination were small. However, the researchers observed that "treatment with thyroxine plus triiodothyronine improved the quality of life of most patients." Patients who don't feel improved on the T_4 synthetic might well improve on a combination of T_4 and T_3. I have found this to be true in my own practice as well; most hypothyroid and thyroiditis patients originally prescribed only synthetic T_4 respond well to Armour natural desiccated thyroid, which contains both naturally occurring T_4 and T_3.

Despite this, most doctors object to natural thyroid because, they say, hormones in animal thyroid cannot be uniformly standardized, as synthetics can. Further, they claim that natural products contain a somewhat higher amount of T_3 in relation to T_4 than standard synthetic T_4/T_3 combinations. In the medical practices of Dr. Barnes and myself, natural thyroid worked well in almost all cases. Rarely have I had to use synthetic formulas containing T_3 and T_4. (In fairness, however, I must admit that on rare occasions, when a patient was either sensitive to the natural hormone preparation or was a vegetarian who objected to taking animal-derived natural thyroid, I have successfully used synthetic hormones.)

One fact in favor of natural thyroid overlooked by most doctors and researchers is that it also contains the thyroid hormone T_2. We can assume that because T_2 occurs in nature, there must be a need for it even if we do not yet know what it is. This has proved true for so-called "vestigial" organs once thought to be useless, such the appendix, the tonsils, and even the spleen. As Dr. Barnes once told me, drug companies making synthetics arbitrarily decide on a single ingredient as the key corrective factor, ignoring other seemingly less important accompanying factors, as is the case in synthetic T_4. If synthetics are intended to be substitutes for natural products, why not imitate nature faithfully in every aspect?

On the on-line About.com Guide to Thyroid Disease, Mary Shomon writes:

> For years, patients have been told that all they need is levothyroxine treatment to get them into "normal TSH (thyroid-stimulating hormone) range," and thyroid treatment is considered complete. Time and again, people who still suffered with symptoms—including fatigue, depression, cognitive problems, and more—were told that once their thyroid range was normal, these problems were no longer related to the thyroid. Instead, they were now depression, stress, PMS, or "simply in your head." Patients who had done well on Armour, then switched to Synthroid, for example, and complained of not feeling well, were told they were "getting old."[4]

Ever since research demonstrated that the T_4/T_3 combination is more effective than T_4 alone, however, the thousands of medical doctors once branded as "mavericks" have been proved right by no less a mainstream authority than the *New England Journal of Medicine.*

22

SELENIUM DEFICIENCY AND HYPOTHYROIDISM

*M*uch has been written about the trace mineral selenium as a part of the enzyme and antioxidant glutathione peroxidase that protects cell membranes and DNA and helps to prevent cancer, heart disease, and premature aging. Recent research discloses that selenium is also a key part of an enzyme that converts thyroxin (T_4) into triiodothyronine (T_3), the major hormone that makes cell metabolism of nutrients possible. This explains why selenium-deficient individuals usually turn out to be hypothyroid.

To correct selenium deficiencies, it's best to supplement with selenium yeast; selenium in this form is far more body available than it is in its inorganic form. Biochemist Richard Passwater, Ph.D., writes that 150 micrograms daily of selenium yeast raises the blood levels of selenium of healthy adults. The safe range of intake of selenium is 50 to 200 micrograms daily.[1] Dr. Passwater also reports that vitamin C increases the absorption of organic selenium-containing yeasts. (I recommend that my patients take at least 500 milligrams of vitamin C three times daily.)

However, there's more to the story as to how selenium intake relates to thyroid function. Deficiency of the hormone T_4 is often associated with dietary iodine inadequacy, commonly worsened by goitrogens in water and food.

In a letter to the *Journal of Orthomolecular Medicine*, Harold D. Foster, Ph.D., a biochemist at the University of British Columbia, Victoria, B.C., Canada, writes:

> Depressed serum T_4 levels, however, are not necessarily accompanied by below normal serum T_3 . . . When severe iodine inadequacy is present, serum T_3 tends to remain stable or even rise as T_4 levels drop . . . . This relationship occurs because T_3 contains less iodine, weight for weight, then does T_4 . . . . It is more metabolically active, and, hence, is produced by the thyroid when iodine is scarce . . . . Only in extreme iodine deficiency, when there is inadequate iodine even to produce T_3, does its level decline. However, the T_4 to T_3 conversion requires the catalytic selenoenzyme iodothyroninedeiodinase. As a consequence, T_4 and T_3 deficiencies together are commonest in individuals living in environments depleted in both iodine and selenium. In contrast, depressed T_3, without unusually low serum T_4, is characteristic of populations in regions where diets contain adequate iodine but lack selenium. Furthermore, animal studies suggest that, just as excess iodine consumption results in lowered serum T_4 levels, an elevated intake of selenium may depress serum T_3.[2]

In addition to its role in thyroid function, selenium, like iodine, also appears to protect against breast cancer and various other types of cancer. In his book *Healing Nutrients*, Patrick Quillin, Ph.D., writes that researchers determined soil levels of selenium throughout the United States. Next, they studied distribution of cancer cases across the United States. When they laid the selenium map over that of the cancer map, they found an astonishing correlation. States most deficient in soil and water selenium showed the highest incidence of cancer. South Dakota, richest in soil selenium, reported the least cancer cases. Ohio, poorest in soil selenium, reported the highest incidence of cancer—a frightening 200 percent above that in South Dakota.[3]

Women have special considerations to make before taking selenium, particularly those women who are considering becoming pregnant. "A decline in serum T_4 is likely to be most significant during pregnancy, since this hormone is of major importance to the developing fetal brain," writes Dr. Foster. "Shortages are known to result in mental retardation and even in neurological cretinism." However, pregnant women—or those likely to become so—should not be given selenium supplements unless they know for certain that their iodine intake is adequate. Therefore, it's advisable to treat premenopausal hypothyroid patients whose hypothyroidism is not due to excess dietary iodine or selenium with desiccated thyroid tablets.

23

A NEW LOOK AT IODINE

We examined the role of iodine deficiency in hypothyroidism in chapter 2. Iodine deficiency has also been long known to reduce the capacity to learn and remember. Now, we find that an iodine deficiency can undermine the desire to succeed, as a study conducted in India demonstrates.[1] Banarasi D. Tiwari and associates at the Sanjay Gandhi Post Graduate Institute of Medical Sciences in Lucknow, India, compared one hundred boys, aged nine to fifteen years old, from two villages in eastern India. Iodine was deficient in the soil and water of one village: consequently, fifty boys from that area had goiters, indicative of low thyroid function. Iodine was adequate in the soil and water of the other village, so fifty boys from there showed no symptoms of low thyroid function.

All the boys attended school. Testing revealed that boys from the iodine-deficient area were slower learners than those from the iodine-sufficient area (with one exception: in recall of verbally relayed information). Boys with goiters improved less after practice drills than did the others. Researchers concluded that they had probably suffered nerve damage in earlier development that affected their ability to learn and retain information. Invariably the older goitrous children's performances were inferior to those of the younger children, suggesting that their impairment was cumulative. Most surprising was the finding that childhood iodine deficiency not only impaired the boys' ability to learn, but their motivation to learn as well.

"These abnormalities may prevent millions of children from achieving their full potential, even if learning opportunities are available," Tawari told *Science News*.

The goiter belts we mention in chapter 2 are no longer as important a health issue in the United States and in other developed nations as they once were, for two reasons: first, because food now comes from all parts of the world, and second, because many people eat heavily salted (and iodized) processed foods. In fact, some authorities now oppose supplementing with iodine, because many people—especially children and youths— eat so many fast foods seasoned heavily with iodized salt: French fries, potato chips, potato skins, hamburgers, and other junk foods. Even sugary processed products contain hidden sodium.

In a report titled "Minerals: Iodine" that appeared on Health World Online, Elson Haas, M.D., states that a gram of salt (1/28th of an ounce) contains roughly 76 micrograms of iodine. The average person uses three grams of salt daily that contain 228 micrograms of iodine, far exceeding the RDA of 150 micrograms.[2] Despite this, the incidence of goiters is again rising. Can factors other than iodine be involved?

Dr. Haas writes, "There is no significant danger of toxicity of iodine from the natural diet, though some care must be taken when supplementing iodine or using it in drug therapy." A regular excessive intake of iodine—too much iodized salt or too many kelp tablets—may produce iodine toxicity and reduce thyroxine production and thyroid function.

In addition to the threat of iodine toxicity, one must be aware of the danger of insufficient iodine intake which still exists for certain population groups, including dieters on superlow caloric intake, anorexics and bulemics, and individuals on low-sodium diets so prevalent among heart disease patients. Numerous studies show that the low-sodium diet does little to prevent heart disease. Assuring enough potassium to balance the sodium intake is far more important.

Only infinitesimal amounts of iodine are needed daily for the following age groups: 35 micrograms for newborns to six months; 45 micrograms for those six months to a year old; 60 micrograms for one- to three-year-olds; 60 micrograms for those four to six years of age; 80 micrograms for seven- to ten-year-olds, and 110 to 150 micrograms for those age eleven and older. Pregnant women require 125 micrograms, and lactating women 150 micrograms.

Nursing women—any individuals, for that matter—can usually fulfill their iodine quota by eating ocean fish such as cod, haddock, halibut, or sea bass twice weekly. The supplement cod liver oil contains a lot of iodine. Kelp, a brown seaweed, is the supplement richest in iodine.

I'm often asked during public appearances, "If sufficient iodine intake can help to prevent mental retardation, can it also reverse learning disabilities and elevate IQ caused by such a deficiency?" In the few such efforts that I've witnessed, iodine supplementation contributed to small gains, but not enough to warrant recommending it for this purpose. Apparently, the neurological damage was too great. All the more reason to prevent such damage in the first place!

For more than a generation, it has been known that a pregnant woman's extreme hypothyroidism can cause her infant to be mentally retarded—a condition called cretinism. Deficiency of thyroid hormone during the fetal stage or early life may cause the infant's thyroid gland to be a fraction of normal size. It may even be missing. Typically, the cretin baby has thick, sallow, and wrinkled skin, thickened lips, an enlarged tongue, an open mouth that drools, a broad face, and a flat nose. Cretins are dull, unresponsive to stimulus, and apathetic. Large at birth, they fail to grow normally and become dwarfs in adulthood, if they live that long.

Although reversal of this condition is impossible, improvement is possible. Dr. Broda Barnes told us about several such cases referred to him. Early thyroid supplementation normalized growth and improved the mental ability to some extent. "Total reversal can't happen in such cases, except by divine intervention," Dr. Barnes told us. Fortunately, the odds of this happening today are quite long. However long the odds are, they don't comfort the woman to whom it happens.

In our book *Super Smarts*, Jim Scheer and I stress the importance of couples—not just women—preparing for pregnancy with proper food, supplements, and exercise, because they don't always know when conception will take place, and the condition of the man's sperm is an often underrated factor.[3]

In his classic book *Nutrition and Physical Degeneration*, Dr. Weston Price, a Cleveland dentist who circled the world observing, interviewing, and photographing natives of primitive cultures, compared—no, contrasted—the superhealthy cultures in isolated areas of their lands who thrive on native food with those hooked on the fractional foods of modern civilization.[4] His comparison showed refined sugar, flour, and other processed food to cause rampant tooth decay and every one of our degenerative diseases, including chronic conditions that date back to the womb.

For instance, even though they knew nothing about iodine and the thyroid gland, Eskimos of the Arctic Circle prepared women for pregnancy with iodine-rich fish eggs. Fathers consumed milt, the sperm-containing fluid of salmon, to assure them the highest degree of fertility. During pregnancy and nursing as well, women followed a highly nutritious diet to assure the baby a sound body and brain.

One of Dr. Price's most fascinating discoveries was a tribe in the South Pacific that—with no understanding of the biochemistry involved—provided an iodine- and nutrient-rich diet for pregnant women. Dr. Price was shown a species of spider crab that the islanders fed mothers-to-be "so that their children will be physically excellent and mentally bright."

A young woman of the tribe is required to tell her chief as soon as she knows she's pregnant. The chief then arranges a feast to celebrate the "new person" who will soon join the colony. During the feast, the chief has one or two young men bring the pregnant woman special seafood to give her and her fetus the most nourishing fare to assure the baby a strong body and a good mind.

Newer information supports the need for all women intending to become pregnant not only to get sufficient iodine, but to be tested for hypothyroidism as well. An article in the *New England Journal of Medicine* warned that untreated hypothyroidism during pregnancy could cause baby to have a substantially lower IQ, diminished motor skills, and attention deficit disorder, as well as problems in mastering language and reading.[5] Researchers found that women with underactive thyroid function during pregnancy are almost four times more prone to have babies with lower IQ scores. Nineteen percent of children born to thyroid-deficient mothers had IQ scores of 85 or lower, compared with only 5 percent of infants born to mothers with normal thyroid function. An IQ level this low can seriously impair a child's chances for an education and success in life.

James E. Haddow, M.D., who led the study, wrote: "The children whose scores are in this range may face lifelong developmental challenges. It might be possible to prevent these problems through early diagnosis and treatment of thyroid disease in their mothers."

The researchers reported that the mothers found to be hypothyroid had been in this state for five years before their doctors diagnosed the condition. Women who have had their thyroid glands removed or those found to have Hashimoto's thyroiditis are well aware of the need for thyroid supplementation; the greatest danger lies in women whose hypothyroidism or subclinical hypothyroidism is undiagnosed, or those with normal thyroid levels but a high level of antibodies indicative of autoimmune thyroiditis.

Baby IQ problems result because the mother supplies all thyroid hormones for growth and development of the fetus for the first twelve weeks of pregnancy. After twelve weeks, the fetus develops its own thyroid gland; however, the mother-to-be is still the source of thyroid hormone. During those first twelve weeks, a hypothyroid mother can't always assure enough thyroid hormone for proper brain development. In some cases, miscarriage occurs at this point.

The *New England Journal of Medicine* study shows how important it is to plan and act well in advance for pregnancy and nursing. Women should cooperate closely with a doctor schooled and experienced in identifying and treating hypothyroidism properly. As it is, there's too little preparation and too much Las Vegas–style risk taking in conception for many American couples—a sad fact, because most people don't win in Las Vegas!

24

COPING WITH FIBROMYALGIA

ibromyalgia is a stubborn and enduring pain in muscles, ligaments and tendons—even bones—coupled with extreme fatigue. A researcher named L. H. Sigal characterizes the pain of fibromyalgia colorfully. When fibromyalgia sufferers are asked how they feel in the morning, they give what Dr. Sigal calls "the eighteen-wheeler response": "I feel like I was hit by a Mack truck!"

The odds of being stricken with fibromyalgia are estimated at roughly twenty to one. These odds aren't fair, but 80 percent of those who develop this disorder are women from twenty to fifty years of age.

A few fibromyalgia patients have made a lasting impression on me. For instance, a young woman in her twenties, an assistant purchasing agent for an electronics firm, was totally frank, as patients should be: "Doctor, my fatigue is so bad that I have to flog myself to go to work. At night, I just fall into bed with my clothes on. I sleep poorly, because my muscles and bones feel as if someone has driven a knife into them. When the bedsheet touches tender points on my back, buttocks, elbows, knees, neck, rib cage, and thighs, I want to scream."

I had her take the Barnes Basal Temperature test and found her well below the minimum: 97.8 F. Various other symptoms indicated that she was hypothyroid. I started her on a quarter grain daily of Armour desiccated thyroid and asked her to be patient for good results.

"Why not?" she responded. "No other treatment has helped."

Two weeks later, I raised her to one-half grain. Then, within a month, she reported less pain, better sleep, a small increase in energy, and some hope that she would recover. Three months after that, she seemed like a new person. "I can't thank you enough, doctor," she said. "I haven't felt this well in years."

Three out of four fibromyalgia patients I treated responded the same to a similar regimen, but I regarded the relationship between fibromyalgia and hypothyroidism as just a coincidence until an article in the *Annals of Rheumatic Disease* caught my attention. Biochemist J. B. Shiroky and associates wrote that some 12 percent of fibromyalgia cases are triggered by low thyroid function. They suggest a test for thyroid-stimulating hormone (TSH) to see if fibromyalgia patients are actually hypothyroid.[1]

Dr. John C. Lowe, Director of Research for the Fibromyalgia Research Foundation, considers the percentage named by Shiroky and associates too low.[2] Based on in-depth study and treatment of more than a thousand fibromyalgia patients, Dr. Lowe told Jim Scheer that in many instances fibromyalgia is actually untreated hypothyroidism. "Inadequate tissue regulation by thyroid hormones results from two causes: (1) a deficiency of thyroid hormone, and (2) a cellular resistance to thyroid hormone."

One study Dr. Lowe conducted of thirty-eight fibromyalgia patients revealed that twenty-four (63.2 percent) were deficient in thyroid hormones and reported symptoms such as slow-wave sleep, decreased brain blood flow, impeded carbohydrate metabolism, fatigue, aches and pains, cold sensitivity, dysmenorrhea (difficult or painful menstruation), depression, and problems in learning.[3] Says Dr. Lowe, "These symptoms and hormone, neurotransmitter, and other objective findings in thyroid-deficient patients are also typical of fibromyalgia patients. So when I refer to fibromyalgia, I'm referring to a certain set of symptoms and signs of too little thyroid hormone regulation of tissues."

Dr. Lowe feels that fibromyalgia patients should be tested for a deficiency of thyroid-releasing hormone (TRH) and for triiodothyronine (T_3), as well as for TSH deficiency. Even if your TSH is within the so-called "normal range," Dr. Lowe is convinced that you could still be suffering from one or more of sixty-four major symptoms of hypothyroidism, including fibromyalgic aches and pains and energy depletion.

In a publication in the *Clinical Bulletin of Myofascial Therapy*, Dr. Lowe and his associates write that, in a double-blind study, some patients with normal thyroid function had hypothyroid-fibromyalgia symptoms that seemed to result from partial cellular resistance to thyroid hormone. Seven patients alternately treated with T_3 (dosages from 95.75 micrograms to 150 micrograms) and with a placebo over eight months were shown to experience "significant therapeutic effects in their T_3 phases on all measures of fibromyalgia status."[4] Their improvement was maintained even in a two-month follow-up. These dosages were significantly effective, although they produced thyroid function tests that indicated hyperthyroidism. However, the patients experienced no ill effects from this condition.

Four false beliefs held by most doctors make it possible for you to be in what is called "the normal range" and still be hypothyroid:

1. That the sole cause of thyroid deficiency symptoms is hypothyroidism;

2. That only individuals with primary hypothyroidism (insufficient secretion of thyroid hormones) should be permitted to use thyroid hormone;

3. That hypothyroid patients should only be permitted to use synthetic T_4 (levothyroxine formulas such as Synthroid and Levoxyl);

4. That patients' replacement dosages should be limited only to amounts that keep the TSH within normal range.[5]

Dr. Lowe maintains that these unproven guidelines followed by most physicians cause inadequate thyroid hormone regulation of many patients to remain untreated. In other words, if synthetic T_4 fails to correct the symptoms of hypothyroidism, the limitations of this treatment are not blamed; rather, the illness is regarded as something different, such as fibromyalgia or chronic fatigue syndrome.

Dr. Lowe is not surprised when stressed hypothyroids start suffering fibromyalgia-like symptoms, such as muscle aches and pains and insomnia. "Over time, hypometabolism imposes a lifestyle that can further complicate hypothyroidism," he told Mary Shomon, writer-editor of the About.com Guide to Thyroid Disease.[6] "As an illustration, the hypothyroid patient may not be able to take part in enough physical activity to maintain normal muscle mass. Metabolic status is critically dependent on muscle mass. The lower an individual's muscle mass, the lower the metabolic rate."

Stress of various kinds, such as a death in the family, loss of a job, depression, poor diet, and extreme fear, seems to trigger fibromyalgia. Most authorities admit not knowing the actual cause or causes of fibromyalgia. However, Dr. Lowe finds that many patients who develop symptoms of fibromyalgia after some traumatic experience were already hypometabolic:

> After learning what the various symptoms and signs of hypothyroidism are, many fibromyalgia patients say such things as, "You know, come to think of it, I remember having these symptoms off and on since I was in my early teens." A short period of physical inactivity after the trauma appears to decrease their muscle mass and further lower their metabolic rate. After enough time passes to permit a significant loss of muscle mass, many people develop posttraumatic fibromyalgia . . . . In many cases, the patients' metabolic insufficiency was probably worsened by the typical American diet and not taking nutritional supplements. To shorten a potentially long story, factors such as hypothyroidism (even borderline), nutritional insufficiencies, and inadequate physical activity become intertwined and interactive in impeding

the person's metabolism . . . . By the time I've seen some patients, the probable interactions of factors that have contributed to their disabled conditions have become impossible to comprehend. The best I've been able to do with such patients is start working with multiple factors that may be currently sustaining their fibromyalgia, making recommendations. Usually I've asked such patients to try and generate a few months of faith. It may take that long before they feel better subjectively and before our objective measures show that their fibromyalgia is improving.[7]

In order for you to find a health practitioner who approaches hypothyroidism and fibromyalgia like Dr. Lowe, it is best to enlist help from a holistically oriented medical doctor, a doctor of osteopathy, or a naturopath in a state that licenses naturopaths.[8] These categories of physicians are usually willing to spend the time necessary to do the clinical detective work that most, for all practical purposes, have abandoned.

Hypothyroid patients following Dr. Lowe's treatment protocol have reported a high degree of success. Dr. Lowe typically starts hypothyroid patients with Armour desiccated thyroid, which he uses because it has a higher T_3 content than that in synthetic T_4/T_3 preparations.

"I have found that many hypothyroid patients also have cellular resistance to thyroid hormone," states Dr. Lowe. "Most of these patients don't benefit from T_4 alone, but some of them do from desiccated thyroid, presumably because of the relatively high T_3 content . . . . Some we do switch to synthetic T_3 when they don't benefit from desiccated thyroid. However, we've stopped altogether giving patients T_4 alone."

With every new fibromyalgia patient, Dr. Lowe has the point driven home to him that fibromyalgia is actually a manifestation of hypothyroidism. "I'm so certain of that that I would put my neck on the chopping block!" he told us. Currently, there's no research to counter Dr. Lowe's findings, and no opposing researcher who would risk her neck!

25

MENOPAUSE OR LOW THYROID FUNCTION?

Fibromyalgia and hypothyroidism have much in common with menopause.

Distinguishing the influences of menopause from those of hypothyroidism relative to symptoms of middle-aged women is not unlike trying to perform surgery to part Siamese twins—it is extremely difficult.

Not long ago, the American Association of Clinical Endocrinologists (AACE) made such an attempt. The AACE alerted its nearly four thousand members and the world to what seemed to be a startling fact: Millions of American women are not successfully managing menopausal-like symptoms even by taking estrogen as hormone replacement therapy (HRT).[1]

These women may be suffering from undiagnosed hypothyroidism, as indicated by symptoms usually attributed to meno-pause: fatigue, mood swings, depression, and sleeplessness. Most women are not aware of the all-encompassing influence of the thyroid gland on every cell in every body system and should be alerted to it by their doctors, because otherwise, their basic problems will go untreated and contribute to long-term health complications.

AACE urges all menopausal women to add thyroid hormone to the list of hormones they discuss with a physician, "because many of the symptoms of thyroid disease and menopause over-lap," observes AACE president Helena Rodbard, M.D., F.A.C.E. "As women approach menopause, many symptoms may be quickly attributed to this milestone in a woman's life without complete discussion of other easily treatable disorders, such as thyroid disease, that often mimic or accompany menopause."

Another facet of the subject not mentioned by AACE in this connection is the possible danger of breast cancer and other cancers that may result from female hormone replacement. "As endocrinologists and hormone experts, we are very concerned that the patient-physician dialogue on menopause be broadened to include discussion of thyroid hormone," states AACE past-president Stanley Feld, M.D., M.A.C.E.[2] "Fewer than 25 percent of the nearly fifty million women reaching menopause are on HRT, and we know that as many as one in three of these women continue to experience symptoms that could be a direct result of an underlying thyroid disorder . . . . Consider the fact that the incidence of thyroid disease increases to almost 20 percent for women over age sixty, and one can understand the seriousness of this situation."

The AACE states that, in addition to female hormones active during menopause, thyroid hormones play a basic role in com-plete body function. They regulate the rate of speed at which the body produces energy from nutrients, and influence the heart, brain, kidneys, liver, skin, muscle strength, reproductive functions, and appetite. Untreated, thyroid disease can diminish the quality of life, worsening osteoporosis and increasing the risk of heart disease. Many Americans have thyroid disease and do not even know it.

"As a woman is affected simultaneously by an onset of meno-pause, the increased risk of thyroid disease, and the natural aging process, the need for hormone management is essential," says Dr. Rodbard. "By recognizing the signs and symptoms of these processes as they appear, patients and doctors can reduce the long-term health risks that threaten women."

A public education program, "Thyroid: The Missing T in HRT," has been launched by the AACE to make women and physicians more aware that they need to include the thyroid hormone in their discussion of menopause. In this connection, the AACE is encouraging patients with menopausal symptoms—even if now on HRT—to perform a simple self-examination to see if they need to consult with their doctor about thyroid disease. This is to observe if they have an enlarged or irregular thyroid gland, indicating a thyroid condition that needs further examination by their physician.[3]

A glass of water and a hand mirror are the only required objects. Here's how to do it:

Step 1: Focus the mirror on your neck just beneath the Adam's apple and right above the collar bone, where your thyroid gland is located.

Step 2: Tilt your head back.

Step 3: Swallow some water.

Step 4: While swallowing, observe your neck for bulges or protrusions. Repeat this process a few times to make certain your observation is correct.

Step 5: If you detect bulges or protrusions, see your doctor at once. You may have an enlarged thyroid gland or a thyroid nodule. Have your doctor check you to determine if you need treatment for thyroid disease or whether or not cancer may be present.

If properly treated, patients with thyroid disease can lead normal and active lives!

26

TOBACCO AND ALCOHOL: THYROID GLAND ENEMIES

All sorts of charges have been launched against smoking and how it sabotages health by constricting arteries, limiting blood circulation, and contributing to strokes, heart attacks, asthma, and lung cancer—and all of them are well founded. Now we know that smoking can also undermine the thyroid gland.

Researchers at University Hospital in Basel, Switzerland, studied women in the Netherlands, Sweden, and Switzerland and discovered that smoking does two harmful things to the thyroid gland: (1) decreases its ability to secrete hormones, and (2) then limits the hormones' action. In the *New England Journal of Medicine*, Dr. Beat Mueller announced that smoking may contribute to the "high incidence of subclinical hypothyroidism (diminished synthesis of thyroid hormone) and aggravate the clinical manifestations of subclinical hypothyroidism."[1] Critiquing the Mueller study in the same issue of this magazine, Robert D. Utiger, M.D., states that smoking was not found to cause hypothyroidism, only to make it more severe and to aggravate its various symptoms.[2] The evidence against smoking is compelling, in either case.

One of many harmful ingredients of cigarette smoke is cyanide, which is converted to thiocyanate in the body. We mentioned earlier in this book that thiocyanate is a suppressor of the thyroid gland. Dr. Utiger comments that thiocyanate lessens the gland's ability to absorb iodine and to synthesize its hormones from raw materials, and actually causes much iodine to escape the gland.

Another study focused on smoking and Hashimoto's Autoimmune Thyroiditis, a condition in which the immune system attacks the thyroid gland, causing inflammation and low thyroid function. (This usually responds to treatment with Armour natural thyroid supplement.[3]) A retrospective study of 387 women with Hashimoto's Thyroiditis, averaging 50.5 years of age, included 256 nonsmokers, 110 smokers, and 21 former smokers. Hypothyroids among nonsmokers totaled 34.8 percent, among former smokers, 61.9 (suggesting that quitting smoking doesn't appear to reverse hypothyroidism), and among smokers, 76.4 percent. The percentages of smokers in the hypothyroid group, the subclinical thyroid group, and the euthyroid group (the group with normal thyroid function) were 45.2 percent, 18 percent, and 11.3 percent, respectively.

The researchers found that blood serum levels of thiocyanate, the thyroid gland suppressor, were highest in hypothyroid smokers and ex-smokers. "An increase in serum thiocyanate concentration from smoking may contribute to the development of hypothyroidism in patient's with Hashimoto's thyroiditis," write the researchers. "Our results suggest that smoking may increase the risk of hypothyroidism in patients with Hashimoto's thyroiditis."

An article by David S. Cooper, M.D., F.A.C.P., in the Thyroid Foundation of America's newsletter, "The Bridge," shows that smoking affects thyroid efficiency by introducing harmful substances into the body.[4] Further, smokers are more prone to have an enlarged thyroid gland than nonsmokers, a sign of at least subclinical hypothyroidism. It is imperative for smokers to quit at once, for life preservation, health promotion, and longevity. However, determining to quit and actually quitting are two different things.

Nicotine gum helps some people to quit smoking by degrees. However, some can quit cold turkey when made to realize that their smoke is not only jeopardizing their own health but also that of loved ones who live with them. Herbal and homeopathic remedies can also help some individuals to quit smoking.

One of the most popular antismoking herbs in Australia is coltsfoot. This was popularized by Hans Wagner, a television nutritionist. Dried leaves of coltsfoot, available in many health food stores, are crushed to granules and added to pipe tobacco or roll-your-own cigarette tobacco. When smoked, coltsfoot gives off such an offensive odor and the taste is so repellent that some people develop an aversion to it. If it doesn't work at first, some individuals keep increasing the amount of colts-foot until it does. Good luck!

My patients have had some success with a homeopathic remedy that includes lobellia inflata, nux vomica, staphisagria, and tabacum. Each of these ingredients supposedly helps to curb the desire for tobacco. In addition, lobelia inflata is said to enhance breathing, particularly in asthmatics. Nux vomica supposedly helps smoking quitters to overcome irritability. Staphisagria also works to banish irritability. Tabacum, derived from tobacco leaves before their flowers bloom, is said to reduce the powerful desire for tobacco and relieve jitteriness and trembling hands.

In the on-line About.com Guide to Thyroid Disease, writer/editor Mary Shomon writes about herself and subscribers to her free Internet thyroid newsletter and their response to quitting smoking.[5] She and some of her subscribers were diagnosed as hypothyroid after quitting smoking. They also gained weight. Like these persons, most of my patients who are former smokers gained weight when they quit. However, my literature search reveals that no study supports the position that quitting causes hypothyroidism. In most cases, my patients explained this phenomenon as follows: tobacco is an appetite suppressant and tends to rev up metabolism and the adrenal system to activate sugar stored in the liver to rev up energy.

As Mary Shomon writes: "My theory is that smoking/nicotine creates an artificially high metabolism that masks the fatigue/lethargy commonly seen in hypothyroidism. When the smoker quits, this masking is removed, and the full effects of hypothyroidism on the metabolism and thyroid are felt. . . . And for smokers with undiagnosed thyroid dysfunction, without proper thyroid hormone treatment, stopping seems to be a metabolic/weight gain double whammy, as they lose the appetite suppressant, metabolism-upping effects of nicotine, and experience the full effects of the hypothyroidism."[6]

Mary advocates that those who experience this should have a thyroid-stimulating hormone (TSH) test to establish or rule out hypothyroidism. I go a few steps further, recommending that they have the full panel of thyroid tests, a history of health, and questioning by their doctor to catalogue their symptoms.

Heavy smoking is not the only harmful habit that can reduce the effectiveness of thyroid function. A high intake of alcoholic beverages can do this as well. As a highly refined carbohydrate, alcohol demands the whole family of B vitamins—particularly vitamin B_1 (thiamin)—for its metabolizing. This leaves little, if any, vitamin B_1 to extract energy from foods.

In natural products such as liver and brewer's yeast, B-vitamin family members appear together, and they work together. As people age, they can't metabolize vitamin B_1 efficiently, so they must compensate by taking more.

Aging and alcoholism combine to drain vitamin B_1 and other B family members away. Depletion of vitamin B_1 is a prime cause of cardiomyopathy, inability of the heart to contract and pump blood forcefully to our farthest extremities. Could it be coincidence that, in hypothyroidism, the heart cannot pump with enough vigor?

Isobel Jennings (see chapter 3) found that a deficiency of vitamin B_2 depresses the function of various glands and organs, including the thyroid. She also discovered that a deficiency of vitamin B_6 reduces the thyroid gland's ability to convert iodine efficiently into thyroid hormone.

Various animal and human studies show that chronic alcohol drinking and food deprivation can negatively influence three related glands—the hypothalamus, pituitary, and thyroid. A rat experiment described in the journal *Endocrine* revealed that alcohol at 10 percent of total intake along with too little food produced a decrease in TSH. At the same time, this increased thyrotropin-releasing hormone, TRH, a chemical that tells the pituitary gland to produce TSH to induce the thyroid gland to synthesize and release hormone.[7]

An article in *Clinical Experimental Research* indicates in a human study that alcoholism sometimes blunts the response of TSH to thyrotropin-releasing hormone.[8] Researchers are not certain whether this is due to alcohol-related harm that reduces the pituitary gland's ability to secrete TSH, to genetic vulnerability, or to the toxic effects of prolonged alcohol abuse.

As there is little doubt that alcohol reduces thyroid function, along with other damage it produces in the body, can something be done to counteract it?

The intake of additional vitamin B complex—as much as 100 milligrams of the major family members daily—has helped many of my patients. Those who drink heavily and find it difficult to quit may profit by a discovery of the late Roger J. Williams, Ph.D., longtime director of the Clayton Foundation Biochemical Institute, the researcher who isolated pantothenic acid, and a Hall of Fame biochemical researcher.[9] Dr. Williams experimented with L-glutamine—not glutamic acid—and found that, when given to rats, it decreases their voluntary drinking of alcohol.

How does it work? Dr. Williams theorized that L-glutamine gets into the rats' brains and protects cells in the appetite center so that they lose their desire to drink more alcohol. Enough human trials have been made to encourage its use by alcohol-addicted individuals. An interesting case study is described by Dr. Williams in *Nutrition Against Disease*. A friend was given a supply of L-glutamine to try on an alcoholic acquaintance. Dr. Williams writes that "the result was dramatic"—and due entirely to the supplement, rather than to any placebo effect. The person voluntarily stopped drinking, found work, and two years later still did not crave alcohol.

Dr. Williams got positive results from just 2 grams of L-glutamine daily. However, he sometimes needed 4 grams daily to turn an individual around. Naturally, in my practice over the years, I have used from 2 to 4 grams of L-glutamine daily for alcoholic patients. It actually worked in sixteen patients out of twenty— all hypothyroids. Not a bad record!

27

ENVIRONMENTAL PROBLEMS

Once upon a time, the environment was our friend. Today, pollutants assail us in the air we breathe, the food we eat, and the water we drink. Metropolitan smog has turned many a blue sky into a dirty gray. Insecticides have all but done away with once-common yellow clouds of butterflies, as well as with some of us. Additives in processed foods extend their shelf life, but not our lives.

One of the worst chemicals in the environment is fluoride, a known thyroid gland inhibitor since 1854, as we discuss on page 35. A waste product from the aluminum and synthetic fertilizer industries and a former rat poison, fluoride is added to the water of many cities as a preventive for cavities. By authority of the Environmental Protection Agency (EPA), public water supplies can exceed one part per million of fluoride—up to four parts per million. Reputable medical and technical publications, however, state that it does not contribute to better teeth and that it can cause deterioration of bones and even bone cancer. These are typical excerpts from a newsletter by fluoride authority Walter Miller:[1]

". . . [T]he current decline in caries in the United States and other western industrialized nations has been observed in both fluoridated and nonfluoridated communities with the percentage reduction about the same." (*Journal of the American Dental Association*, April 1988.)

"Our committee had access to a recent dental screening of 26,000 elementary school children, and it was found that the more fluoride a child drank, the more cavities appeared in the teeth." (*Chemical and Engineering News*, July 27, 1992.)

"We found a small but significant increase in the risk of hip fracture in both men and women exposed to artificial fluoridation at one part per million, suggesting that low levels of fluoride may increase the risk of hip fracture in the elderly." (*Journal of the American Medical Association*, August 12, 1992.)

A study found that the central nervous system is "vulnerable to fluoride and that fluoride accumulates in brain tissue and that the neurotoxic risks can be indicative of a potential for motor dysfunction, IQ deficits, and/or learning disabilities in humans."[2]

Similar reputable publications reveal that fluoride can cause nausea and vomiting, kidney failure, and a type of bone cancer.

An article in the *Journal of the International Society for Fluoride Research* states that fluoride is an antagonist to the mineral magnesium, essential to the function of more than three hundred enzyme systems.[3] "The amount of fluoride assimilated by living organisms constantly increases, and magnesium absorption diminishes as a consequence of progressively advancing industrialization. An increased intake of magnesium plays a protective role by countering and reducing toxic effects of fluoride."

Generally the accepted ratio of magnesium to calcium is one to two. However, several authorities now advocate a one-to-one ratio: 1,000 milligrams of magnesium to 1,000 milligrams of calcium, for example.

Fluoride enters us from many more sources than city water:

soft drinks, fruit juices, jellies, beer, various processed foods, many TV dinners, mouthwashes, and toothpastes, as well as in any other products that utilize tap water in fluoridated communities, and accumulates in our systems. Not only do we swallow it, we breathe it if we are in areas where aluminum is processed or synthetic fertilizers are produced. So, our intake of fluoride can be frighteningly high—far above the one to four parts per million authorized by the EPA. Inasmuch as fluoride inhibits thyroid function, is it any wonder that there is so much undiagnosed hypothyroidism?

Another potent environmental toxin is perchlorate, which the EPA says inhibits the thyroid gland from absorbing iodine. You've never heard of perchlorate? Many people haven't. Still, you may be unknowingly ingesting it.

Its sources are mainly the by-products of synthetic fertilizers and solid propellants for rockets, missiles, and fireworks. Perchlorate salts are also used as a component of air bag inflators. Ever since 1950, perchlorate wastes have been stored without appropriate care and monitoring, so it has invaded surface and underground water supplies. Thanks to watchdog organizations such as Zero Waste America, which promotes the elimination of waste, toxins, and pollution, we have been alerted to its dangers.

Why didn't the EPA warn us of perchlorate's dangers and order city water suppliers to test for this hazardous chemical? The EPA informed Zero Waste America that, because perchlorate is used in military applications, secrecy was necessary.[4] Defense contractors and fertilizer makers in forty-four of the fifty states use perchlorate, so the time has come for water companies to develop appropriate tests and ways to eliminate it. The EPA's stated safe limit for adults is thirty-two parts per billion—much less for children and infants. However, far more testing is necessary to establish that this figure is valid.

Still another source for possible thyroid suppression are the pesticides used on domestic and international airline flights, supposedly to discourage insects and rodents from coming aboard. It may also discourage you and me from coming aboard for any more flights than necessary.

So much emphasis is placed on dangers from radiation exposure in high-altitude flights that little was known about hazards from airplane insecticide spraying until a few years ago when Karin Winegar wrote a revealing article on this subject for *Mother Jones* magazine. This unfair practice is being carried on without a federal agency requirement and without warning to passengers. Dozens of studies—including some by the National Research Council and the National Institute of Environmental Health Sciences—link pesticide ingredients to many ailments, including respiratory illnesses, allergic skin reactions, nervous system damage, sexual dysfunction, cancer, and glandular disorders.

Becky Riley, spokesperson for the National Coalition for Alternatives to Pesticides, based in Portland, Oregon, reveals that pesticides, health hazardous on land, are even more so in the air, inasmuch as 50 percent of the air in airplane cabins is recycled. She is quoted in Karin Winegar's *Mother Jones* magazine article as saying, "Pesticides break down slowly in the enclosed, poorly ventilated aircraft. Passengers are sealed in a chamber that has been gassed, and sit there for hours."[5]

Airline representatives insist that this practice is carried on for the safety and protection of passengers. Although the sight of a mouse or insect on an airplane could upset passengers, it is more likely that spraying is done for public relations purposes.

Many toxicologists quoted in the *Mother Jones* article take exception to this practice, relating it to many common medical ailments. Jack Thrasher, Ph.D., an immunotoxicologist in Alto, New Mexico, told writer Winegar, "This practice is insanity. Tralomethrin (a commonly used airline spray) contains bromide." Bromide has been shown in animal studies to cause thyroid disease, states Dr. Thrasher. Other chemicals in Tralomethrin create allergic reactions and worsen asthma. "They have no business spraying pesticide. I don't care if it's .05 percent," he said.

Winegar writes that Sheila Daar, director of the Bio-Integral Resource Center in Berkeley, California, a developer of non-poisonous ways of controlling pests and weeds, insists that cleaning crews for aircraft follow safe procedures.

First, they should check each airplane with sticky or pheromone traps to determine if there actually is an insect problem: "Affected planes can be treated in a number of inexpensive ways that don't involve volatile materials, or (that use) only low-toxic methods such as caulking cracks, traps, boric acid gels, or paste in a bait station at entry points or hiding places." Daar also notes that insects quickly develop resistance to pesticides.

Periodically the EPA meets with industry to determine how environmental chemicals impact on secretions of various glands. In one conclave, participants focused on thyroid hormones. Unfortunately, the only conclusions reached were that environmental chemicals do three things to thyroid hormones: block their synthesis, change serum transport proteins (the delivery system), or increase their catabolizing (breaking down).

28

SOME THINGS YOU OUGHT
TO KNOW . . .

1. ANTIDEPRESSANTS CAN DEPRESS THE THYROID

Beware of antidepressants if you are hypothyroid and are on a synthetic thyroid hormone! A study in the *New England Journal of Medicine* shows that if you take synthetic levothyroxine sodium such as Euthyrox, Levothyroid, Levoxyl, or the most familiar brand, Synthroid, the antidepressant Zoloft, which contains sertraline, can reduce the effectiveness of your thyroid formula.[1] The manufacturer of Zoloft claims that the same results have been observed in patients using other treatments for illness, such as carbazepine, lithium, and certain serotonin-reuptake and tricyclic antidepressants. If you take antidepressants, let your doctor know about the results of the

New England Journal of Medicine study so he will check you with periodic tests to make certain your thyroid function isn't too low.[2]

2. SEPARATE CALCIUM AND SYNTHETIC THYROID INTAKE

To prevent or to cope with bone-riddling osteoporosis, many hypothyroid women take a calcium supplement. They often take it at the wrong time, however—along with their synthetic thyroid hormone, levothyroxine.

Results of a small sampling (three patients) motivated Christine Schneyer, M.D., of the Sinai Hospital of Baltimore, the Johns Hopkins School of Medicine, to share her findings in a letter to the *Journal of the American Medical Association.*[3] The calcium supplement reduced thyroid function, as shown in an increase of thyroid-stimulating hormone (TSH) levels and symptoms of fatigue and weight gain. One patient stopped taking calcium, continued with her thyroid hormone, and within three weeks, her TSH level declined markedly. Rather than discontinue needed calcium, the other two patients changed their supplementation pattern. They took their thyroid hormone in the morning and their calcium after lunch and dinner. This restored the effectiveness of their thyroid function. (Numerous studies demonstrate that calcium is best absorbed before bedtime.)

Dr. Schneyer also comments that simultaneous ingestion of synthetic thyroid hormone with aluminum-containing antacids, cholestyramine (a cholesterol-lowering chemical), and iron also may diminish the efficacy of the hormone. Separating the intake of calcium supplements and medicines from synthetic thyroid hormone by at least four hours should help maintain the desired level of thyroid function. Dr. Schneyer felt it necessary to share experiences of her three patients because suppression of thyroid gland efficiency by calcium and other supplements and drugs is likely to be a "widespread phenomenon."

3. BE AWARE OF THE RELATIONSHIP BETWEEN SYNTHETIC HORMONES AND ALLERGIES.

A little-considered aspect of taking synthetic thyroid hormone is the fact that it can cause allergies in some patients, as I have observed in thirty years of practice. These allergies, often thought to be caused by foods or environmental pollutants, can be triggered by the various coloring agents included in some synthetic thyroid hormones, such as red and yellow dyes, or even by lactose (milk sugar). This is yet another argument in favor of taking a natural supplement such as Armour desiccated thyroid (see chapter 21 for others).

4. HYPOTHYROIDISM MAY CAUSE SLEEP APNEA.

A frightening ailment, sleep apnea (the stopping of breathing during sleep, sometimes for long periods) has many causes. Rita Wittman, Ph.D., a sleep specialist at the University of British Columbia, reports that hypothyroidism has been found to bring on sleep apnea in a small number of patients.[4] Dr. Wittman and associates conducted the largest retrospective study on this subject and discovered that 4.2 percent of 833 obstructive sleep apnea patients tested were found to be hypothyroid.

Even more revealing is the fact that almost every hypothyroid patient had sleep apnea. The more extreme the condition, the more likely the person was to be hypothyroid, said Dr. Wittman.

5. BE SURE YOU'RE TESTED FOR HAIT.

Sometimes a patient will have so many symptoms that it is difficult to make an accurate diagnosis. This is especially true in the case of Hashimoto's Autoimmune Thyroiditis (HAIT).

In HAIT, the thyroid gland is a bit enlarged, with little or no pain. However, the autoimmune system is involved, because the body unleashes antibodies against its own thyroid gland, as if it is a threatening enemy.

HAIT runs in families, and most individuals afflicted are between the ages of thirteen and forty-three. Symptoms range from mental to physical: a faulty memory; difficulty in thinking; depression; nervousness; allergies; irregular heartbeat; palpitations; muscle and joint pains (as in fibromyalgia); disturbed sleep; wakefulness in bed while the mind races and the heart beats fast; diminished interest in sex; menstrual problems such as too little flow, too much flow, or shortened periods; frequent headaches; digestive disorders and intestinal ailments, ranging from constipation to diarrhea; and the feeling that there's a lump in the throat (a slightly swollen thyroid gland).

Many of these symptoms cause me to routinely order tests of the patient's antibodies. Sadly, most physicians don't insist on these tests, so they fail to make the proper diagnosis. If you have many such symptoms, please insist upon testing. Thyroid antibody tests should be run on anyone with chronic health problems. T_4 and TSH may be normal, so they don't reveal autoimmune thyroiditis. Even a low elevation of thyroid antibodies will prompt me to start the patient on a low dose of thyroid hormone, despite the fact that her blood thyroid hormone levels give a reading of normal.

In an article in the magazine *Alternative Medicine*, a leading health publication, I mentioned the case of Theodora, aged forty-three, who had a medical book full of symptoms.[5] Theodora had numerous upper respiratory infections, many sore throats, one cold that merged into another, nasal blockage, heart palpitations, irregular periods, intestinal bloating, indigestion, and alternating constipation and diarrhea, pain in joints and muscles throughout her body, headaches, and sleeplessness. Although her thyroid hormone levels were in the normal range, her level of thyroid antibodies was sky high.

As with most patients, I started her on a quarter grain of Armour natural desiccated thyroid daily and, over the next year, gradually increased it to three grains. One of her lab tests indicated she was deficient in three amino acids, as well as other nutrients: vitamin B_5 (pantothenic acid), inositol, and the mineral zinc. Instead of prescribing these individual amino acids, I had her increase her protein intake—more fish, lean meat, and poultry—and take a high-potency multiple vitamin and a multiple mineral formula.

I also found that Theodora had an elevated *Candida albicans* yeast infection in her intestines, so I started her on a high–

complex carbohydrate diet and had her avoid refined sugars, sweets, and fruits. Theodora began rotating her foods so that her system did not always have to process the same foods. Through allergy testing, I determined that she was sensitive to a lengthy list of foods: kidney beans, rye grain, cheddar cheese, egg yolk, wheat, almonds, figs, and kale. She avoided these foods.

Additionally, I gave her three supplements to detoxify her intestines: grapefruit seed extract (500 milligrams, three times daily); Acidophilus capsules (two capsules, three times daily to recolonize her intestines with friendly bacteria); and a high-potency, odor-free, aged garlic tablet twice daily.

Six months later, Theodora's symptoms were reduced in intensity, and, after a year, she was almost symptom free. Her energy level was much higher. For the first time in her memory, her upper respiratory infections were gone with no signs of a cold or the flu.

Her pains were so diminished that she could exercise again. Her digestion was almost normal.

HAIT is no easy ailment to control and eliminate. It takes patience from both the patient and the doctor, because progress is slow. However, when treated correctly it improves steadily, and that can be encouraging.

29

LIVE LONGER, HEALTHIER,
AND YOUNGER

An all-time high in long living was set by a fellow named
Methuselah—969 years. He isn't mentioned in the *Guinness
Book of World Records*, but you *can* find him in the Book
of Genesis.

You may not expect to dethrone Methuselah, but wouldn't it
be great to live several decades longer than average with great
health and a sharp mind?

You *can*.

First, however, you should be armed with the latest solid
information on this subject—psychological, social, physical, and
biochemical.

Staying young starts with thinking and acting young. A positive attitude helps because, sooner or later, signs of aging appear

somewhere between the top of the head and the soles of the feet. It is essential not to let an unwelcome wrinkle, a gray hair, or a joint's worth of arthritis send negativism richocheting through your mind, causing you to give in to aging.

Accentuating the negative only accelerates the aging process, as it did in the forty-five-year-old father of a school acquaintance of mine back east. His frequent comment was, "I'm getting old fast."

Returning after a decade away, I was shocked at how cruelly the years had treated him. Yet there was grim justice in the physical response to his self-image. A comparatively youthful, vigorous, middle-aged man had become bent, faltering, and stiff legged, his hands locked like claws with arthritis. Poor self-image and negative programming were surely not the only factors in his rapid deterioration, but they were powerful determinants.

Certain psychological and social factors contribute strongly to staying young, says Dr. G. Z. Pitskhelauri, a noted gerontologist, based on in-depth studies in the Republic of Georgia, reputedly the home of more hundred-year-olds (and older) than any other area in the world.[1]

Following are his major requirements for longevity, many of which can be applied in the United States: (1) close family ties—the branch should always remain a part of the family tree; if possible, several generations should live under a single roof; (2) a continuous daily work routine within the body's capabilities; (3) continued physical activity, not vegetative retirement; (4) independent pursuits within the close family structure; (5) periods of relaxation.

Dr. Pitskhelauri would take exception to Oliver Wendell Holmes's classic witticism that the best way to live long is to select your grandparents wisely. Environment is more important than heredity, at least so far as the Republic of Georgia is concerned, he maintains. In answer to the argument that many long-living Georgians also have long-living ancestors, he states that this is to be expected, because they are products of the same environment.

Dr. Pitskhelauri also says that a key to longevity is the typical Georgian diet, one that gives the back of the hand to the low-cholesterol diet; fatty meats, whole milk products, native sauces, herbs, and other greens, and moderate amounts of wine.

His final words of advice are to eat in moderation; avoid hard liquor and tobacco; be active, with a lively interest in family and the community; and, of crucial importance, follow regular life patterns (including work) to try to stay free of excess stress.

Another longevity program—this one in the United States—is based on a comprehensive survey by the California State Department of Public Health.[2] Several thousand individuals were interviewed initially and then nine years later. Persons who adhered to at least six of the following rules experienced better health and more years to enjoy it than those who complied with fewer than four:

1. Sleep seven to eight hours a night.

2. Always eat breakfast.

3. Snack infrequently.

4. Keep weight to between 5 percent under and 20 percent over desirable standard weight (for males) and less than 10 percent over desirable standard (for females).

5. Exercise frequently: do some physical work such as gardening, pursue sports (swimming, golf, calisthenics), and take long walks.

6. Always keep alcoholic consumption low.

7. Do not smoke.

Such guidelines offer a helpful pattern for longevity. However, certain bits of misinformation still mislead and discourage the young on their way to advanced years, as well as those who are already there. One of them is the moss-covered cliche, "You can't teach an old dog new tricks." Another is the belief that we inevitably begin losing irreplaceable brain cells at age twenty-six and with them essential mental capacity.

More than a generation ago, studies by Dr. Irving Lorge of Columbia University proved conclusively that old dogs not only learn new tricks but learn them well. A remarkable research project conducted by Dr. William A. Owens, Jr., while he was head of the psychology department at Iowa State University, exploded the "old dogs" cliche again. He happened upon a musty treasure in the attic of a college building—scores of 179 freshmen who, in 1919, had taken the Army Alpha test, one of the first comprehensive means of measuring mental ability. Aware that he could make a tremendous contribution to psychological knowledge, Dr. Owens managed to track down 127 of these then middle-aged individuals and administered the same test, comparing performances.

What impressed him most was that, after four years of college and three decades of experience, these individuals scored higher on general information and far higher on questions requiring judgment and logic. Unquestionably, the fifty-year-olds demonstrated superior thinking ability when compared with their younger selves.

A few decades ago, the then Soviet Union issued a report to the United Nations, *The Right to Old Age*, based on tested physical and mental abilities of 21,000 elderly individuals. Its conclusion was, "The more brains and muscles are used, the less they age."

Many similar studies have been published in the past fifty years, and now scientists in laboratories are learning underlying reasons for previous findings.

One of the leaders of this alluring field of research is Professor Marian Diamond, a neuroanatomist at the University of California at Berkeley. Results of her twenty years of experiments with rats have given the world enlightenment and new hope. She says that if we seek stimulation and challenge all of our lives, we can delay and even defeat mental aging. She has also shattered the misconception that we necessarily lose thousands of brain cells daily, that there is nothing we can do to replace them, and that therefore our mental capacity declines steadily and inevitably.[3]

To skeptics who might say, "All of this is helpful if you're a rat," Professor Diamond responds that brains are big clumps of nerve cells, and that nerve cells of rats and human beings have the same basic constituents. In the Gertrude Stein tradition, she says, "A nerve cell is a nerve cell is a nerve cell."

It is not true that the brain settles on a comfortable plateau of accomplishment in early life and declines after that. Professor Diamond learned that there can be brain growth even in rats who are in their eighties and nineties in human years. In one experiment, she moved rats who had lived boring lives in uninteresting cages with only a few companions into what she called "enriched quarters," with larger cages, a choice of toys, and sometimes twelve other rats for companionship. Toys were changed every day. She compared this group's progress with that of a control group, rats in standard dull cages with no toys and only two companions. Without stimulation or challenge, the control rats stayed in their rut, keeping to themselves, hardly moving, moping, and acting as old as they were. It was just the opposite for the rats in the enriched environment. They socialized, played with their new toys, and seemed to look forward to the next day's toys.

At the end of the experiment, when the rats were more than 120 years old in human terms, those in the enriched environment had actually increased their number of brain cells. Their cerebral cortexes were 6 percent thicker than those of the unstimulated rats. Further, their brains showed 9 percent less lipofuscin (aging pigment).

Nerve cells were designed to receive stimuli. They will react positively to stimuli at any age, Professor Diamond says. Brains which meet challenges positively don't lose cells; they gain some. Professor Diamond sees a lesson for human beings in the rat studies. We can socialize, keep our minds stimulated, and stay young or isolate ourselves, vegetate, and age rapidly. The decision is up to us. It's a question of using or losing our brain power.

Other scientists worldwide are also uncovering secrets to keep us physically young for productive living. Most gerontologists agree that there's no point in extending life only to give ourselves an additional fifteen or twenty years to be ravaged by disease and degeneration.

Dr. Allan Goldstein, chairman of the biochemistry department of George Washington University Medical School, Washington, D.C., one of the foremost researchers in longevity, feels that scientists will soon discover how to use immune system energy, just as researchers decades ago learned how to release energy by splitting the atom. Effervescent with optimism, Dr. Goldstein feels that within a decade we will know how to live to age one hundred or beyond. It will be up to us to learn how to use this information.

How can immune system energy be utilized for our benefit?

Before we answer, let us review what the immune system is and what it does. The immune system is an inner guard that protects us from threats to our existence, from anything that's foreign or abnormal, whether it is a transplanted organ or malaria germs, viruses, or cancer cells.

A popular theory holds that when the immune system begins to decline, that is the beginning of the end. The decline appears to start in the thymus gland, a twin-lobed, gray-pink organ located at the top of the chest. Dr. Goldstein calls the thymus (thought to be useless until the early 1960s) the immune system's master gland. Unlike other glands whose peak productivity continues for many years, the thymus slows down when we are about fourteen years old.

Protective white blood cells called T-cells pass through the thymus gland to be modified and matured for action. These cells fight for our lives. Like soldiers, they have various missions—annihilating invaders, stimulating certain immune functions, shutting down others, enhancing the ability of antibodies (cells which provide immunity against disease) to recognize enemies. As a person ages, the immune system cells lose their power to protect against infection as well as their ability to distinguish between friends and enemies. Then they sometimes mistake their own body tissues for enemies, and attack. This is what happens in autoimmune disease.

When we reach the age of fifty, the immune system is operating on something like 15 percent of full efficiency. A weakened immune system loses its ability to monitor and kill abnormal cells; this is a cause for the growing threat of cancer as we grow older, according to some authorities.

As the thymus gland weakens, it is important that we supplement this organ as we do the lazy or weak thyroid gland. The main thrust of thymus research is therefore the synthesizing of a family of hormones named thymosins. The co-discoverer of thymosin, Dr. Allan Goldstein, says scientific evidence indicates that the immune system probably can be rejuvenated by thymosin. In experiments at the National Institutes of Health, these hormones proved effective in blocking, delaying, and even curing certain cancers that seem to be age related—those of the kidney, lung, and prostate.

A controlled study of fifty-five patients afflicted with inoperable oat cell lung cancer brought rewarding results. Thymosin supplementation doubled survival time. Twenty-one subjects received extremely high doses of this hormone and were cleared of cancer. Two years later they are still free of it.

Another authority on thymosin, Dr. William Regelson, Professor of Medicine and Microbiology at the Medical College of Virginia, has had some encouragement in experiments with these hormones against rheumatoid arthritis and multiple sclerosis. He says that this approach is a fundamental one, aimed at the heart of the problem, not at the edges.

Thus far, the side effects of thymosin supplementation seem negligible. The body appears to use what is required from what is injected and excretes the rest.

Not all the world's best gerontologists agree by any means that the declining immune system is the sole cause of aging, important though it is. Some maintain that the individual cells gradually lose their ability to repair DNA, the complex chemical of heredity. Still another group feels that a buildup of free radicals accelerates aging. Free radicals are atoms with an unpaired or odd electron, or clusters of such atoms. They originate from chemicals in food, water, and air, from radiation, and from oxidation, which goes on ceaselessly in the cells. Highly charged with energy and as unpredictable as a violent person, they run amuck and attack, damage, or destroy healthy cells.

Protection of body cells, in which an estimated thousand chemical processes go on, is accomplished by antioxidants, including vitamin C, a water-soluble nutrient; vitamins A and E, fat-soluble vitamins; selenium, a trace mineral which cooperates with vitamin E; and iodine.

The late Dr. Benjamin Frank believed that supplementary nucleic acids—DNA and RNA—protect cell integrity, too, and even reverse aging. The best sources of nucleic acids, which he advised taking with plenty of fluids, are brewer's yeast, sardines, and leafy green vegetables. Nucleic acids supposedly minimize production of free radicals within cells.

Various authorities feel that high-quality nutrition, regular exercise, and care of the heart and arteries contribute to longer life.

Dr. Linus Pauling favored taking in 8 to 10 grams of vitamin C daily, a practice which he believed may extend lifespan by twenty-four years. His own daily intake of vitamin C was 18 grams.

Dr. Roy L. Walford of the University of California at Los Angeles advocates a severe restriction of food as one of the best ways to prolong life, particularly starting in the early years. His experiments with mice demonstrate the validity of his thesis.[4] While the Walford system appears to work, it is doubtful whether most individuals could endure his Spartan limitations without divine intervention. Furthermore, the pleasure of eating (not overeating) is part of our enjoyment of life.

Aside from deficiencies in critically needed vitamins, minerals, nucleic acids, and sometimes proteins, the greatest problem in nutrition for longer life is overeating and its natural consequence, obesity. As fat accumulates in all the old familiar places, chances of becoming a victim of brain disease, cancer, diabetes, gallbladder trouble, heart disease, and liver ailments soar, says Dr. Grant Gwinup, Professor of Medicine at the University of California, Irvine.

"Stay active physically if you want to live long," insist advocates of daily exercise. Dr. Lawrence Morehouse, professor of exercise physiology at UCLA, states in his book *Total Fitness in 30 Minutes a Week* that 80 percent of the adult American population doesn't exercise properly or sufficiently to stop physical decay.

Although many authorities find that we benefit most from a lifetime of physical exercise, Dr. Herbert deVries, exercise physiologist at the University of Southern California Gerontology Center, insists that older people can also profit from exercise even if they start late in life. Men between the ages of fifty-two and eighty-eight at Leisure World, a retirement colony at Laguna Hills, California, were put through carefully monitored exercise routines by Dr. deVries and showed surprising improvement: 35 percent greater breathing capacity and 30 percent increased ability of the blood to transport oxygen to tissues. They also realized greater ability to relax and to release pent-up feelings of frustration, aggression, and hostility.

All too often, individuals who are indifferent to the needs of their bodies for exercise, rest, and proper diet receive painful reminders in the form of degenerative diseases, including arthritis, one of the most exquisite tortures ever to twist and gnarl the human frame and appendages.

As early as the late nineteenth century, researchers found thyroid supplements effective in managing arthritis in hypothyroids. They came to this knowledge by accident. In subnormal thyroid function, when the thyroid gland became enlarged and choked off the windpipe and breathing and doctors surgically removed the entire gland, they discovered that arthritis usually became worse. This valuable information was buried under the landslide of new scientific information. A Harvard University study showed that two-thirds of 312 patients with arthritis were hypothyroid. Dr. Loring P. Swaim, who was in charge of the project, suggested that arthritis develops in persons with low metabolism.[5]

Dr. Broda Barnes, following Dr. Swaim's lead, made a similar discovery in his study of three hundred arthritics, and published his findings in a prestigious medical journal.[6]

"There is a characteristic pattern marking the patient with crippling arthritis," he once told me. "First, it is poor circulation, then repeated infections throughout the years, and other symptoms that come from low thyroid function. In the late stage of this disease, thyroid therapy alone may not be entirely effective against arthritis, even though other characteristic symptoms of hypothyroidism may respond satisfactorily," he says.

Stubborn cases have responded to Dr. Barnes's daily administration of as little as 5 mg of prednisone, the least harmful of the corticosteroids. Aware of the dangers of corticosteroids, I approached this treatment carefully. However, I have had excellent results with it, too.

One convincing fact arises from various research projects: the best time to treat arthritis by thyroid therapy is before you have it or in its earliest stages.

Hypothyroidism is not the cause of an illness. In diagnosis, however, it should be considered as a possible basic cause until ruled out by accurate testing, a check of symptoms, and a complete medical history.

Efficiency of your thyroid gland is not something to take for granted. Everyone's status can change, as we pointed out when discussing the thyroid's many subtle suppressants mentioned throughout this book, particularly in chapter 3, Care and Feeding of the Thyroid.

With enough thyroid hormone circulating in your five quarts of blood, you can fend off life-shortening infections, allergies, and a negative outlook. You can stall or even stop debilitating degenerative diseases such as cardiovascular ailments.

Your heart will beat vigorously and regularly and pump a rich volume of blood through resilient, clean, and smooth arteries to nearby and distant destinations, efficiently delivering food and oxygen to every cell and carrying off wastes.

All the information in this chapter and in previous ones will prove valuable in assuring that you live longer, healthier, and younger. It would be well to remember, however, that even a normal thyroid gland slows down with the passing years, although at a much lesser rate than the thymus. Then, perhaps, it will need a little help from its friend: you!

Best of luck!

30

FOR DOCTORS ONLY

Aside from references cited, information in this chapter is based on standard, recognized books: *The Thyroid*, edited by Sidney C. Werner and Sidney H. Ingbar, Harper & Row, New York, 1971; *Vitamins in Endocrine Metabolism* by Isobel Jennings, Charles C Thomas, Springfield, Illinois, 1970; and *Victory over Diabetes* by William H. Philpott, Keats Publishing, Inc., New Canaan, Connecticut, 1983.

There's an often unsuspected cause for many chronic health problems in the field of clinical medicine. I am referring to hypothyroidism, which affects every major organ and profoundly influences the efficiency of metabolism of every cell. Its symptoms are numerous and protean.

Suffice it to say that there is no clear-cut hypothyroid

syndrome. The symptoms of hypothyroidism can mimic many of the physiologic disturbances we see on a day-to-day basis. To ignore the thyroid connection, however, is merely to treat our patients symptomatically and not to treat the underlying causative factors of their illnesses.

Simple examples of this are patients with recurrent infections who are chronically treated with antibiotics. These patients are frequently hypothyroid. As noted later in this chapter, this is in part due to the thyroid hormone's control of certain immune functions. I can cite many other examples but these are included in the section on thyroid physiology.

An accurate way to diagnose hypothyroidism is by means of the Barnes Basal Temperature Test. More than a hundred years of research has established a definite relationship between subnormal temperature, no matter how slight, and hypothyroidism. Broda O. Barnes, M.D., Ph.D., refined the test. A clinical researcher in hypothyroidism for half a century, Dr. Barnes published more than a hundred papers on his investigations in the most reputable medical journals. He has had a strong influence on my career as a physician.

Initially, I approached his work with more than a tincture of skepticism, despite the fact that full details of how he evolved the test and proved its reliability had been published in the respected *Journal of the American Medical Association.*[1]

Over several years, Dr. Barnes had correlated the basal temperature of more than two thousand individuals with metabolic rate (BMR) tests which he had performed himself to minimize the possibility of skewing results, and with thyroid blood chemistry results. Through the years, he found a much higher correlation of negative BMR results and clinical hypothyroidism with basal metabolic temperature than with results of any other test. In addition, Dr. Barnes learned that many of these clinically hypothyroid patients actually had euthyroid blood tests.

Even the additional fact that the basal temperature test had appeared in the *Physician's Desk Reference* for years failed to satisfy my reservations about its validity. However, in the interest of fairness, I kept an open mind toward the test, which is carried out as follows: Shake down a thermometer before going to bed at night and leave it on the bedside table. Immediately upon awakening in the morning, insert the thermometer snugly in your armpit for ten minutes as you lie quietly in bed. In normal thyroid function, the temperature range reads 97.8 to 98.2 degrees. A lower temperature indicates probable hypothyroidism. The test should be done on two consecutive days. Women obtain the most accurate readings if not menstruating or on the second and third day of menstruation.

In 1978, shortly after a long-distance telephone interview with Dr. Barnes on the medical talk show I then hosted on a San Francisco radio station, I tried the test on myself, discovered a low basal temperature, and each day took a small amount of natural desiccated thyroid. (Dr. Barnes and his more than one hundred followers used the natural form, as I do, on the premise that nature should know better than man, with all his synthetic chemicals, what is best for the body.) My energy level increased. My ability to concentrate improved dramatically, and many minor, nagging symptoms disappeared.

Next, I began using the basal temperature test on a number of problem patients who had failed to respond to the usual medications. When indicated, I gave them thyroid supplementation. Their quick, positive responses dissipated the last vestiges of my skepticism.

I will frequently start a new patient on thyroid therapy even if the thyroid lab work is normal, and I believe there is scientific justification to use it. Thyroid medication given to carefully screened patients is, in my experience, almost always helpful. I start all my patients on the equivalent of one-fourth to one-half grain of the Armour desiccated thyroid preparation, and increase their dosage in one-fourth to one-half grain increments every seven to ten days until a level that achieves the desired clinical results is obtained.

The dosage I use most commonly in adults is one to two grains. I have never put a patient on more than four grains of thyroid hormone per day, as in most of these patients we achieved the desired result with the smaller one to two grain dosage.

During the time my patients are titrated with a thyroid preparation, I have them check their basal temperatures regularly. I also test their thyroid hormone levels regularly. I refrain from increasing their dosage if their basal temperature goes above 98.2, if their resting heartbeat is above 85 per minute, if on history they relate episodes of either constant jitteryness or palpitations, or if their lab results indicate they're taking too much thyroid.

Fortunately, these symptoms are encountered infrequently. Once my patients are titrated on a proper dosage of the thyroid hormone and they are symptomatically improved, I see them a minimum of once every two to three months for a year to make sure they are still doing well clinically. This also rules out a placebo response. Although in most instances the use of thyroid medication alone is sufficient to correct many of the symptoms I will discuss, the effects are greatly amplified by the judicious use of applied clinical nutrition.

The main complaint I encounter from physicians is that the basal temperature test is unscientific; they feel that hypothyroidism can be diagnosed only by the standard laboratory blood work. That is exactly what I once thought. Now the basal temperature test is invariably the starting point of my three-pronged diagnostic approach. I relate temperature to patient symptoms and, of course, to medical history.

Today, the vast majority of physicians rely heavily on results of blood tests for diagnosing thyroid function, perhaps too heavily. I make this statement because many of my patients—and those of Dr. Barnes—have been declared euthyroid by blood tests and proved to be conclusively hypothyroid according to the basal temperature test, symptoms, and medical history.

A Mayo Clinic study by Drs. Joseph C. Scott, Jr., and Elizabeth Mussey determined that the diagnosis of thyroid function should be done carefully and judiciously to avoid errors.[2] A patient considered to be mildly hypothyroid by one doctor may be regarded as euthyroid by a second physician, if conclusions are based on just one interview or test.

"No single test procedure will define the status of the thyroid gland," they write. "Further, any combination of methods may lead to erroneous interpretation or to inconsistent results. The clinician must have the faculty of correlating the clinical appearance of the patient with laboratory findings."

The subtle development of hypothyroidism, too, makes diagnosis difficult; this is graphically reported in an article by Drs. Mark Gold, H. Rowland Pearsall, and A. Carter Pottash in *Diagnosis*.[3] Dr. Gold and his associates studied 250 consecutive inpatients admitted to a psychiatric hospital for evaluation and discovered that an often undetected cause of depression is hypothyroidism, whose symptoms overlap those of depression. They state that thyroid hypofunction first appears in subclinical form (grade three) manifested by decreased energy and depressed mood. Next, the condition deteriorates to mild hypothyroidism (grade two) whose symptoms are fatigue, dry skin, and constipation. Blood levels of thyroid hormone are usually still normal, however. Then comes overt hypothyroidism (grade one) which presents the classical signs: a measurable decrease in circulating thyroid hormone, extreme weakness, dry skin, coarsening of hair, constipation, lethargy, memory impairment, a sensation of cold, slowed speech, and weight gain.

"It is not correct to say that hypothyroidism is present or absent; rather, that there are grades of thyroid function," write the doctors. They conclude that one of every ten patients with initial complaints of depressed mood or decreased energy may have subclinical hypothyroidism.

"In our experience, thyroid hormone replacement is more effective therapy for such patients than antidepressant drugs," they state.

These physicians stress the need for careful evaluation of depressed patients who have not responded to conventional treatment or those with a family history of thyroid disease to determine if they are suffering from either hyperthyroidism or hypothyroidism.

Hypothyroidism is often such an extremely subtle disease that physicians misinterpret its symptoms, states Gerald S. Levey, M.D., an endocrinologist and chief of medicine at the University of Pittsburgh School of Medicine, in an article "Hypothyroidism: A Treacherous Masquerader" in *Acute Care Medicine* (May, 1984).

The correct diagnosis is frequently missed, because a broad range of symptoms is generally not associated with hypothyroidism, he says: musculoskeletal disorders such as severe muscle cramps, particularly at night; long-standing low back pain; hematologic disturbances (one-third to one-half of hypothyroids show some loss of blood cell mass, resulting in anemia); coagulability ailments: easy bruising, minor bleeding, and menorrhagia; rheumatologic conditions: stiffness, arthralgias, and paresthesias in hands and feet with accent on stiffness, rather than pain; myalgic complaints and synovial effusions, mainly in the knees; hyperuricemia; and a decrease in heart muscle contractility.

These conditions can be improved or reversed with thyroid hormone replacement, he says. Relative to routine screening for thyroid function, Dr. Levey states that this would not be cost effective, inasmuch as numerous factors, among them drugs and systemic states, affect such tests.

In my opinion, it is prudent for medical clinicians to be suspicious of any patient with a chronically low basal temperature and treat him or her for underactive thyroid before using toxic drugs and irreversible surgical procedures.

The importance of thyroid function to good health should not be underestimated. The thyroid gland is the largest endocrine gland in the human body. It weighs less than an ounce, secretes less than a teaspoon of hormone substance a year and controls the metabolic activity of all of our cells. As Dr. Barnes said, "Cellular health depends on three factors, a steady supply of nutrients, oxygen, and thyroid hormones." The thyroid hormones stimulate oxidative metabolism, thereby increasing the oxygen consumption of every cell.

Thyroid hormone also stimulates protein synthesis; that is, the buildup of protein from amino acids. Protein is necessary for replacing worn-out cells and for the manufacture of enzymes, which moderate the speed at which biochemical reactions take place within the cells. Thyroid hormone potentiates the effect of other body hormones such as adrenaline, is necessary for the secretion of the sex-activating hormones such as the gonadotrophins of the pituitary gland, and is, in large part, responsible for controlling the rate of absorption of nutrients in the gastrointestinal tract.

In hypothyroidism, blood cholesterol and triglycerides are higher than average, a condition often predictive of cardiovascular disorders. Thyroid supplementation causes them to decrease.

Thyroid hormone is partly responsible for production of a compound known as retinine, essential for visual acuity at night. It is also necessary for the synthesis or activation of specific enzymatic proteins within cells and for the translation and transcription of nucleic acids. The major sites of thyroid hormone activity are the cell membranes, mitochondria, ribosomes, and nuclei.

Thyroid hormone stimulates both the sodium pump and the glycolytic pathways, leading to oxidative phosphorylation in tissues such as the liver, kidneys, and muscles.

Hypothyroids characteristically have thick and puffy skin, due to an accumulation of a mucinlike substance called hyaluronic acid, which binds water. The most frequent complaint of such patients is that they accumulate fluid. Powerful diuretics rid the body of this substance, but it returns as soon as the water pills are discontinued. Low-thyroid individuals are usually the patients who can't lose weight unless they subject their bodies to the rigors of spas, exercise, and a very low calorie diet.

The swollen features of hypothyroids are characteristically nonpitting fluid accumulations around the eyes, hands, ankles, and feet. The skin is usually pale and cool, as a result of generalized blood vessel constriction. Low thyroid patients often complain of an inability to sweat even in great heat, and of being cold all the time. Their skin is often dry and coarse, because of decreased secretion of the sebaceous glands. As a result of diminished blood supply and decreased skin metabolism, their wounds heal slowly. This is particularly true in diabetics, many of whom tend to be hypothyroid.

Low-thyroid patients will frequently have severe hair loss. In the differential diagnosis of alopecia, hypothyroidism should always be a prime suspect. Nails grow slowly, tend to be weak and brittle, and are usually striated both longitudinally and transversely.

The hypothyroid patient's heart is characterized by a low stroke volume and decreased cardiac output. To compensate for this, the body increases blood vessel resistance in the skin, resulting in the coolness and pallor already described. There may also be a compensatory increase in blood pressure and this, coupled with an increased cholesterol and triglyceride level, often predisposes the patients to an greater incidence of coronary artery disease.

Hypothyroidism may also cause EKG and blood chemistry changes mimicking heart attacks and other cardiovascular disorders. The most common electrocardiographic changes are flattening or inversion of the T-wave, particularly in lead 2, along with generalized low P-wave, QRS, and T-wave amplitude. Nonspecific T-wave flattening and sinus bradycardia are frequently seen.

Cerebral blood flow and oxygen consumption may be decreased in hypothyroidism. Renal and glomerular blood flow is slightly decreased.

The digestive changes in the low-thyroid patient are quite common and reflect the general sluggishness of every tissue, cell, and organ. The hypothyroid's common problems are loss of appetite with either no weight loss or an actual weight increase and decreased peristaltic activity of all gastrointestinal cells, often resulting in chronic constipation.

Gaseous distention is another frequent complaint. Should this be accompanied by colicky pain, indigestion, and vomiting, it may be mistaken for a mechanical ileus or other related GI problems, and result in unnecessary surgery.

In certain cases, hypothyroidism may also contribute to an inability of the stomach to secrete enough acid for proper digestion, causing a general inability to resorb and utilize the essential nutrients calcium and vitamin B_{12}. It has been estimated that true pernicious anemia occurs in 12 percent of the hypothyroid population.

Serum chemistry determinations of SGOT, LDH, and CPK are frequently increased in hypothyroidism. These blood chemistries will generally return to normal in two to four weeks after thyroid hormone therapy is begun. They are thought to represent changes in enzyme metabolism and not hepatic or cardiovascular damage. Serum amylase levels may likewise be increased. This is often accompanied by a decrease in gallbladder motility. All too frequently gallbladder disease is diagnosed in these cases, and may again result in unnecessary surgery.

The digestive change in hypothyroidism may, in many cases, leave an investigating clinician with a false sense that GI absorption is normal or even increased, due to the fact that decreased absorption is often offset by a decrease in the patient's intestinal motility.

Neurologically, the hypothyroid individual often suffers decreased circulation to the brain, which may contribute to a generalized slowing of all intellectual functions, including speech. These persons frequently lack initiative and may even be described as slow witted. Memory frequently appears impaired, with a decrease in the powers of retention and desire to think, and, frequently, an increased level of irritability. Reasoning power, however, is generally good. Questions may be answered slowly but with enthusiasm. Sleepiness is another common symptom.

Behavior in the hypothyroid patient may run the gamut from hyperactivity to lethargy, depending on how he or she responds to profound mental fatigue. Hypothyroidism should always be considered in the differential diagnosis of children who are hyperactive. Low-thyroid patients are often classified psychiatrically as paranoid personalities or depressive types. Thyroid hormone therapy has been studied intensively in depressed patients.

Hypothyroid individuals show a characteristic electroencephalogram: abnormally flat, low voltage or lacking alpha waves. They may therefore be diagnosed as suffering from a primary brain dysfunction or neurological disorder. Such EEG changes will generally revert to normal once the patients are treated with thyroid hormone. In severe cases of hypothyroidism, patients may be predisposed to epileptic seizure. Hypothyroidism should always be included in any differential diagnosis of epilepsy.

Many low-thyroid patients complain of night blindness. This condition is generally caused by a deficiency of the vitamin A metabolized retinine A, which requires thyroid hormone for its generation, and is generally reversible following the administration of vitamin A and thyroid hormone.

Slurred speech and hoarseness are likewise found occasionally in hypothyroidism, due to a buildup of mucopolysaccharides in the tongue and the larynx.

Vertigo, sensory neural hearing loss, and Ménière's disease may also accompany hypothyroidism. Dry ears often occur because of decreased activity of the cerumen glands. Sore throats, dysphagia, nasal congestion, and headaches are likewise frequent.

Women are particularly vulnerable to undetected hypothyroidism. Complaints of diminished libido and menstrual irregularities such as menorrhagia and metrorrhagia are common, as are menstrual cramping and amenorrhea. As a result, these women may be subjected to unnecessary D & Cs as well as hysterectomies.

Hypothyroidism in the prepubertal girl may be associated with delayed growth or delay of menarche, and, if prolonged, may give rise to premature vaginal bleeding and premature breast development.

Diagnosis of hypothyroidism during pregnancy is essential, inasmuch as animal studies and clinical investigations strongly indicate that thyroid hormone is essential to normal fetal brain development. It is likewise essential to rule out hypothyroidism in patients with either chronic undiagnosed infertility or multiple miscarriages, as first-trimester fetal loss in hypothyroidism is common, approaching 50 percent or more in certain studies.

Thyroid hormone deficiency in the prepubertal male may result in delayed gonadic development, delayed sexual maturation, and, in the adult, a decrease in sperm count and sperm motility. Men with decreased sperm motility who have hypothyroidism diagnosed as the underlying causative factor should never be treated with human chorionic gonadotropin (HCG) or testosterone unless hypothyroidism has been effectively ruled out and the symptoms persist despite a year or more of adequate hormone replacement. Premature use of androgen therapy in the preadolescent may mask or further delay the onset of normal puberty. The most common complaint of the hypothyroid adult male involving the reproductive system is a general diminution of sex drive and libido. Suspect hypothyroidism in anyone who complains of a diminished libido.

Carbohydrate metabolism in hypothyroidism is characterized by a decreased release of glycerol from adipose tissue, diminished glucose absorption, and a decreased availability of amino acids and glycerol for gluconeogenesis. There is also frequently a characteristic flat glucose tolerance curve in these people because of their inability to absorb glucose from the GI tract.

In addition, a high serum amylase level is found in severely hypothyroid patients and is considered to reflect chronic pancreatitis. The mechanism is thought to be related to hypothermia, which is known to be a cause of pancreatitis. Thus, diabetes mellitus, which has long been attributed to an insulin imbalance, should, by definition, encompass a concept of generalized pancreatic insufficiency which may be due in no small part to chronic hypothyroidism and superimposed nutritional imbalances, leading to a breakdown of pancreas production of bicarbonate, secretion of proteolytic enzymes, and insulin production.

The possible mechanism of diabetes and the chronic metabolic disturbances of pancreatic insufficiency caused by an unsuspected hypothyroid condition have been elucidated by William Philpott, M.D., in his book *Victory over Diabetes*, in the following terms: Hypothyroidism (1) → gives rise to pancreatitis → gives rise to pancreatic insufficiency; which results in insufficiency of proteolytic enzymes → gives rise to amino acid deficiencies → contributing to greater deficiency of proteolytic enzymes which are manufactured from amino acids; (2) decreases the quality and quantity of insulin which is, in fact, built from amino acids; (3) decreases lipase activity → gives rise to increased fatty acids in the blood → increased arteriosclerosis and heart disease; (4) increases absorption through the gut of poorly digested protein particles → yields kinin or inflammatory reactions in body tissues and organs, giving possible rise to atherosclerosis and/or severe mental changes, if the reactions take place in the brain, and also an increased absorption of circulating blood lipids into the arterial intima, possibly resulting in arteriosclerotic plaque; (5) decreases the production of pancreatic bicarbonate which is necessary for the alkaline medium of the small intestine → giving rise to metabolic acidosis after meals, since the pancreatic bicarbonate or HCO_3 has not neutralized the stomach acid as it empties into the duodenum → giving rise to further effective reduction of any pancreatic proteolytic enzymes, as they require an alkaline medium in the small intestine to function best.

More than 80 percent of insulin-dependent diabetics had abnormal output of proteolytic enzymes, and most diabetics of more than five years' duration had an abnormal bicarbonate secretory response.

Drug metabolism is frequently changed in hypothyroidism. Such drugs as Digoxin are increased in the plasma, due to an increase in the half-life caused by a decreased glomerular filtration, as well as a decrease in peripheral metabolism. Drug therapy in hypothyroid patients should be undertaken with particular judiciousness. In fact, caution should be exercised with any patient, because so much hidden hypothyroidism exists.

Decreased thyroid function retards growth and delays maturation of the skeletal system, and this can be largely prevented or corrected by administration of the desiccated thyroid preparation.

Hypothyroid patients may complain of vague muscular and articular pains as well as coldness and stiffness of the extremities that resemble fibrositis and rheumatoid arthritis. Clinically, they may present with a laxity of the ligament capsules and tendons, causing joint instability, aching on motion, joint stiffness, and pain. Symptoms are often worse in the morning or after immobilization and are exacerbated by cold and dampness. Infrequently, the hypothyroid patient presenting with musculoskeletal problems is found to have the characteristic articular deterioration of the person who has rheumatoid arthritis.

One study of hypothyroid patients in regard to the musculoskeletal system shows that nine of eleven test subjects had generalized osteoporosis. Another study revealed that 10 percent of persons with low thyroid function had an increased incidence of carpal tunnel syndrome. There tends to be an increased uric acid level in hypothyroid patients with musculoskeletal problems and generally an increase in their sedimentation rate, so these lab studies, although abnormal, may be misleading.

Muscle condition in hypothyroids may differ appreciably, from normal strength and firm to weak and flabby. Transient pain, stiffness, and cramps—frequent complaints—are often due to mineral imbalances caused by this ailment.

A high percentage of hypothyroid patients suffer from iron-deficiency anemia. The hypoplastic anemia of the low-thyroid patient is brought about by decreased production of circulating blood cells as an adaptive response to decreased tissue oxygen needs. In other words, diminished tissue oxygen consumption gives rise to a decrease in tissue hypoxia, which is a normal trigger for erythropoetin, which, under normal circumstances, increases the number of circulating red blood cells. There is, therefore, a decrease in iron turnover.

This type of anemia strongly resembles an adaptive anemia

and the protein-calorie malnutrition which is frequently super-imposed on it, and may further cloud the clinical picture. In general, though, the hypoplastic anemia of hypothyroidism is mild, with hemoglobin levels about 9 grams per 100 mls. A hemoglobin below 9 should cause suspicion that the anemia of the hypothyroid patient is perhaps superimposed on another type of anemia.

Environmental factors play a large role in thyroid functioning. Sulfonamide drugs have a potent antithyroid effect, as do all antidiabetic drugs. These inhibit the formation of thyroid hormone by inhibiting iodine uptake. Adrenal corticosteroids, too, have a depressing effect on thyroid function. Again, corticosteroids, Prednisone and the like, should be used judiciously in the patient with known hypothyroidism or with a suspected hypothyroid condition.

Defining hypothyroidism as purely an endocrine dysfunction is narrow and myopic in that the primary problem may not be in the glandular secretions themselves, but rather due to impaired cell surface binding, so that the physiology of these cells is abnormal even with a normal range of thyroid hormone.

In addition, different tissue types often have different responses to the same level of thyroid hormone so that, due to biochemical individuality, a thyroid hormone level within normal limits may be adequate for the smooth physiological function of a person's skeletal muscle, but inadequate for optimal cardiac physiology. Also, the symptoms of subclinical hypothyroidism such as chronic fatigue, depression, mild anemias, inability to lose weight, and the like, may be easily mistaken for a host of other disorders and written off as neurotic or psychosomatic complaints.

Thyroid hormone is secreted into the bloodstream predominantly bound to three proteins: thyroid-binding protein, thyroid binding-prealbumin, and albumin. Only a minuscule percentage of the thyroid hormone is active at the peripheral tissues in a free form. It is therefore possible, because of biochemical individuality, for the body to have an adequate total output of thyroid hormone but to be hypothyroid, because more than the optimal amount of hormone for a particular individual is bound by protein and therefore inactive. It is also possible, because of the liver's role in the T_4 to T_3 conversion, to have an over-

or underconversion of T_4 as a result of liver function. Patients with conditions such as hepatitis or the nephrotic syndrome will often have an accompanying thyroid dysfunction. In short, there is a difference in the output of thyroid by the gland and the level of activity of that hormone.

It is probably true that the parameters of normal that we now use in the diagnosis of thyroid illness are not wide enough to pick up the vast amount of hypothyroid pathology that exists. Some researchers suggest that the lower unit of the total T_4 range be around 65 to 70 mcg per liter rather than the present 50, because of what was found to be a five times greater prevalence of hypothyroidism at the level of 65 mcg. This same determination has been made with all other commonly measured parameters of thyroid hormone with the same results.

It is apparent, therefore, that the blood test criterion for thyroid disease should never be the be-all or end-all in the diagnosis of hypothyroidism, but rather just one parameter.

Elsewhere in this book, it was explained that the body's basal temperature is one of the most sensitive indicators of thyroid hypofunction. It is therefore clinically more accurate than blood tests in those patients whose symptoms are highly indicative of low thyroid but whose blood work says otherwise.

In accordance with research by biochemist Dr. Jeffrey Bland's group, there are certain other blood test criteria to corroborate the hypothyroid diagnosis with the Barnes Basal Temperature Test: (1) cholesterol in excess of 252; (2) a triglyceride level greater than 200; (3) a total CPK level above 30; (4) a BUN-to-creatinine ratio less than 12; (5) an LDH level greater than 40; (6) a cholesterol-to-HDL level greater than 5; and (7) an increased B-2 fraction in lipoprotein electrophoresis.

Pharmacologic doses of estrogen depress the secretion of thyroid hormone by suppressing TSH. This is very important in the population of women on oral contraceptive pills. Dr. Barnes's research indicated that many women who are taking birth control pills develop cardiovascular difficulties because of their underactive thyroid conditions and not as a result of the side effects of the birth control medication itself.

The biologic reducing agents cystine and glutathione can markedly inhibit the thyroid gland's function. Cystine and glutathione are two of the major components of the glucose tolerance factor molecule, which is necessary for carbohydrate metabolism.

There is some clinical evidence to show that massive doses of vitamin C can inhibit the thyroid by changing the ionization reactions in the thyroid gland proper. The B vitamin PABA, likewise, if taken in large doses, has an inhibitory effect on the thyroid gland.

The cyanide molecule is a potent inhibitor of the thyroid. Cigarette smoking can increase the body's concentration of certain cyanide-containing molecules. So cigarette smoking, in addition to all the other things we know about, can, in some cases, cause a fairly powerful inhibition of the thyroid gland.

31

CONCLUSION

olved: The Riddle of Illness has established that hypothyroidism and HAIT are the two most common undiagnosed
causes of chronic medical problems in the United States
today. Sadly, undertreatment of diagnosed hypothyroidism and
HAIT is also widespread. These patients have been placed on
thyroid medication, and when their levels of thyroid hormones
and the TSH are somewhere in the normal range, they are told
they're on adequate doses of thyroid hormones.

This is often far from the truth, and these unfortunate people
often suffer unnecessarily for years with many of the same
symptoms (although less extreme) and are often dismissed with
such remarks as, "It's all in your head," "Go home and live with
it," "You're depressed," "You're under stress," "It's just middle

age," "This happens to the elderly," or "Everyone has the same complaints." Even worse, some are started on antidepressants or tranquilizers—a practice not unlike removing a flashing red light from your car's dashboard and feeling that the mechanical problem indicated has been solved.

There are a few important scenarios to consider if you're already being treated for hypothyroidism or HAIT but still have many of the same symptoms you had before.

1. You're not getting enough thyroid hormone. Most doctors monitor your medical progress by taking a blood level of TSH (thyroid-stimulating hormone), the normal range of which in many labs is 0.4–5.5.

Too often, a posttreatment TSH level anywhere within normal limits is considered acceptable. TSH is produced by the pituitary gland and controls the output of thyroid hormones. The higher the blood level of thyroid hormone—from your own thyroid gland and from what the doctor has given you—the lower the TSH level. Many patients don't begin to feel well until their TSH levels are at the low end of the normal range and they are on higher doses of thyroid medication.

So, if your symptoms persist, and your TSH is in the high-normal range, it's not "all in your head." You may still be undertreated and should work with your physician to increase the level of your thyroid supplementation.

2. Your TSH is in the low-normal range, but you're still suffering with symptoms. Many patients in this category are being treated with synthetic T_4 only, and are not getting the therapeutic benefit of T_3 found in the natural hormone. In such cases, I slowly change patients' medication to natural thyroid. Remember this conversion: 0.1 milligran of T_4 equals one grain (60 milligrams) of natural thyroid.

3. If you're on an adequate dose of natural thyroid and still have symptoms, make sure you're taking the brand name thyroid— Armour (my favorite), Westhroid, or NaturThroid—as generic thyroid.

4. If your thyroid condition is sufficiently treated and you're still having symptoms, you're probably suffering from another problem.

Remember, it's always best to have your thyroid medication adjusted in conjunction with a complete holistic medical evaluation, including nutritional status, food and environmental allergy evaluation, bowel function, environmental toxicity, and adrenal gland status, as well as a complete history and physical evaluation.

5. If nothing seems to work, get a fresh point of view by seeking a second opinion to rule out a wide range of other body/mind imbalances that can keep you from experiencing complete wellness.

The best of health to you!

AFTERWORD

There are always some people whose symptoms seem to indicate hypothyroidism but whose physical exam, clinical lab results, and Barnes Basal Temperature Test are all within normal limits.

You may be one of them. Should you then consult your nearest psychiatrist? The answer is, "Possibly." We all have unfinished business psychologically. In certain instances, these problems may be converted into physical complaints. A purely psychological diagnosis is always one of exclusion. I will never tell a patient, "It's all in your mind," before attempting to rule out as many of the unsuspected causes of illness as I can, because—let's face it—a psychiatric diagnosis follows you around forever. Unfortunately, there are no recovered schizophrenics in the eyes of many employers. Once you've had a "nervous breakdown," you're always suspect by the narrow minds that pass uneducated judgment about everything.

The following are the main unsuspected causes of illness that I have encountered professionally. These should be checked into if the thyroid solution discussed in the book does not solve your own particular clinical problems.

A major unsuspected cause of clinical problems is food and environmental allergies. These allergies, beyond any doubt, mimic most of the disorders discussed elsewhere in this book. If treatment of patients' hypothyroidism, coupled with an optimal nutritional program, is not getting the proper clinical results, I always test them for food and environmental allergies and sensitivities or refer them to a physician who specializes exclusively in this area, a clinical ecologist. You may get more information about clinical ecologists in your area by writing to me c/o Solved-Ecology, P.O. Box 1549, Lafayette, CA 94549-1549.

Candida albicans is an insidious yeast infection which is growing in epidemic proportions. It affects mainly women in their childbearing years but can strike anyone—even infants. It assumes a wide variety of symptoms and can cause untold distress. Common major symptoms of chronic yeast infection include fatigue, poor memory, "spacy" feelings, depression, joint swelling or pain, constipation, diarrhea, bloating, impotence, endometriosis, and premenstrual tension.

Candida victims can fight back by using a combination of diet, food supplements, and drugs. You may obtain more information about yeast infections and how to deal with them by reading either *Candida Albicans* by Wunderlich and Kalita, one of Keats Publishing's Good Health Guides, or *The Yeast Connection* by William G. Crook, published by Professional Books, P.O. Box 3494, Jackson, Tenn. 38301.

Adrenal exhaustion is a condition which may preclude substantive improvement of your symptoms. Your own nutritionally oriented physician may be able to help strengthen your adrenals by placing you on a small amount of hydrocortisone (5 mg four times a day, after meals and at bedtime). This regimen has been clinically tested for twenty-five years by William McKendree

Jeffries, M.D., and I urge you to have your doctor read Professor Jeffries' book, *The Safe Uses of Cortisone*, published by Charles C Thomas, which documents why and how to use cortisone to help restore you to peak health.

REFERENCES

Chapter 1

1. Herman H. Rubin, *Glands, Sex, and Personality* (New York: Wilfred Funk, Inc., 1952), 36.

2. Louis Berman, *The Glands Regulating Personality* (New York: The Macmillan Company, 1921), 55.

3. J. C. Scott, Jr., and Elizabeth Mussey, "Menstrual Patterns in Myxedema," *American Journal of Obstetrics and Gynecology* (1965): 90:161.

4. B. Stone, *American Medical News*: May 23, 1980.

5. E. R. Pinckney, "The Accuracy and Significance of Medical Testing," *Archives of Internal Medicine* (March, 1983): 143:3, 512.

6. A. S. Jackson, "Hypothyroidism," *Journal of the American Medical Association* (1957): 121–165.

7. Roger J. Williams, *Free and Unequal* (Austin, Tex.: University of Texas Press, 1953), 19.

8. J. C. Wren, "Thyroid Function and Coronary Atherosclerosis," *Journal of the American Geriatric Society* (1968): 16:696–704.

9. H. L. Newbold, *Dr. Newbold's Revolutionary New Discoveries About Weight Loss* (New York: Rawson Associates Publishers, Inc., 1977), 220–221.

Chapter 2

1. News Story, University of Mississippi Medical Center, Jackson, Miss., May, 1983.

2. Roger J. Williams, *Free and Unequal* (Austin, Tex.: University of Texas Press, 1953), 19.

3. Nathan Masor, *The New Psychiatry* (New York: Philosophical Library, 1959), 99–100.

4. *Ibid.*, 102, 103.

5. *Ibid.*, 105.

6. "Age and the Thyroid Gland," *Prevention* (August, 1971): 166.

Chapter 3

1. Isobel W. Jennings, *Vitamins in Endocrine Metabolism* (Springfield, Ill.: Charles C Thomas, 1970), 41.

2. *Ibid.*

3. *Ibid.*, 45.

4. *Ibid.*, 65.

5. *Ibid.*

6. *Ibid.*

7. *Ibid.*, 75.

8. *Ibid.*, 80

9. *Ibid.*, 69.

10. *Ibid.*, 47.

11. *Ibid.*, 62.

12. *Ibid.*, 62.

13. *Ibid.*, 80.

14. *Ibid.*, 92.

15. *Ibid.*, 99.

16. *Ibid.*, 109.

Chapter 4

1. Janet Raloff, "Geologically Induced Goiters," *Science News* (May 3, 1986).

2. *Encyclopedia of Common Diseases* (Emmaus, Pa.: Rodale Press, 1976), 754–755.

3. Janet Raloff, "Goiter? Do You Eat Millet?" *Science News* (May 3, 1986).

Chapter 5

1. *Complete Book of Vitamins* (Emmaus, Pa.: Rodale Press, 1976), 507.

2. *Ibid.*, 507, 508.

3. *Encyclopedia of Common Diseases* (Emmaus, Pa.: Rodale Press, 1976), 44.

4. Noel K. Marshall, "A Chilling Effect," *Psychology Today* (February, 1982): 92.

5. *Ibid.*

6. Boris Sokoloff, *Middle Age Is What You Make It* (Garden City, N.Y.: Garden City Publishing Company, 1942), 124.

7. E. Atkins, "Fever—New Perspectives on an Old Phenomenon," *New England Journal of Medicine* (April 21, 1983): 308:16, 958.

8. *Ibid.*

9. *Ibid.*, 958, 959.

10. *Ibid.*, 959.

11. Broda O. Barnes and Lawrence Galton, *Hypothyroidism: The Unsuspected Illness* (New York: Thomas Y. Crowell Company, 1976), 102.

Chapter 6

1. A. H. Curtis and John W. Huffman, *A Textbook of Gynecology* (Philadelphia and London: W. B. Saunders Company, 1950), 148.

2. E. S. Taylor, *Essentials of Gynecology* (Philadelphia: Lea & Febiger, 1969), 462.

3. *The Thyroid Gland* (Chicago: Armour Laboratories, 1945), 71.

4. P. Ylostalu et al., "Amenorrhea with Low Normal Thyroid Function and Thyroxine Treatment," *International Journal of Gynecological Obstetrics* (1980): 18:3, 176–80.

5. L. S. Matveewa, "Effect of Thyroliberin on the Prolactin Level in the Blood Serum of Primary Hypothyroid Patients," *Problems of Endokrinology* (1980): 26:5, 22–25.

6. P. Peczely et al., "Interrelationship Between Thyroid and Gonadal Function in Female Japanese Quail Kept Under Short and Long Photoperiods," *Journal of Endocrinology* (1980): 87 (1), 55–63.

7. B. K. Vonderhaar and A. E. Greco, "Lobulo-Alveolar Development of Mouse Mammary Glands Is Regulated by Thyroid Hormones," *Endocrinology* (February, 1979): 104 (2), 409–418.

8. Broda O. Barnes and Lawrence Galton, *Hypothyroidism: The Unsuspected Illness* (New York: Thomas Y. Crowell, 1976), 135.

9. Emil Novak, *Gynecology and Female Endocrinology* (Boston: Little, Brown and Company, 1941), 465.

10. Broda O. Barnes, "Making the Pill Safer with Thyroid." *Federation Proceedings* (March, 1970): 29:2.

11. Kaufman, David W. et al., "The Effects of Different Types of Intrauterine Devices on the Risk of Pelvic Inflammatory Disease," *Journal of the American Medical Association* (Aug. 12, 1983): 250:6, 759–762.

Chapter 7

1. Webster-Barnes Foundation Conference on Thyroid (Dallas, June 6, 7, 8, 1980).

2. *Ibid.*

3. *Ibid.*

4. *Ibid.*

5. *Ibid.*

6. A. Aakvaag et al., "Hormonal Changes in Serum in Young Men During Prolonged Physical Stress," *European Journal of Applied Physiology* (October 20, 1978): 39:4, 283–91.

7. Sidney C. Werner and Sidney H. Ingbar, eds., *The Thyroid* (New York: Harper & Row, 1965), 765.

8. Peter A. Singer, "Effects of Hypothyroidism and Hyperthyroidism on Sexual Function," *Medical Aspects of Human Sexuality* (August, 1981): 15:8, 56R.

Chapter 8

1. Broda O. Barnes and Lawrence Galton, *Hypothyroidism: The Unsuspected Illness* (New York: Thomas Y. Crowell Company, 1976), 110.

2. News Feature, Royal Hallamshire Hospital, Sheffield, England, April, 1988.

Chapter 9

1. Roy G. Hoskins, *The Biology of Schizophrenia* (New York: W. W. Norton & Company, Inc., 1946), 110.

2. Broda O. Barnes and Lawrence Galton, *Hypothyroidism: The Unsuspected Illness* (New York: Thomas Y. Crowell Company, 1976), 79.

3. Nathan Masor, *The New Psychiatry* (New York: Philosophical Library, Inc., 1959), 45.

4. Edward R. Pinckney and Cathey Pinckney, *The Fallacy of Freud and Psychoanalysis* (Englewood Cliffs, N.J.: Prentice-Hall, Inc., 1965), 101–102.

5. M. B. Whybrow et al., "Mental Changes Accompanying Thyroid Gland Dysfunction," *Archives of General Psychiatry* (1969): 20:48.

6. Barnes and Galton, *Hypothyroidism*, 82.

7. Masor, *Psychiatry*, 21.

8. Cathryn Elwood, *Feel Like a Million* (New York: Devin-Adair Co., 1956), 235.

9. J. M. Holmes, *British Medical Journal:* 5006: 1394–98.

10. Masor, *Psychiatry*, 20.

Chapter 10

1. Mark Gold, "Significant Number of Depressives May Have Hypothyroidism," *Family Practice News* (November, 1982): 1.

2. A. Coppen, P. C. Whybrow et al., "The Comparative Antidepressant Value of L-Tryptophan and Imipramine With and Without Attempted Potentiation by Liothyronine," *Archives of General Psychiatry* (1972): 26:234–241.

3. K. Jensen et al., "Depression," *Lancet* (November 8, 1975): 920.

4. P. L. Rabin and D. C. Evans, "Exophthalmus and Elevated Thyroxine Levels in Association with Lithium Therapy," *Journal of Clinical Psychiatry* (October, 1981): 398–400.

Chapter 11

1. Carlton Fredericks and Herman Goodman, *Low Blood Sugar and You* (New York: Constellation International), 18–23.

Chapter 12

1. *Encyclopedia of Common Diseases* (Emmaus, Pa.: Rodale Press, 1976), 461.

2. "Conference on Diabetes and Obesity," *The Sciences* (June, 1967): 7:1, 13, 14.

3. "Diabetes," United Press International release (November 21, 1981).

4. "Roles of Nutrition, Obesity, and Estrogen in Diabetes Mellitus: Human Leads to an Experimental Approach to Prevention," *Preventive Medicine* (1981): 10, 577–589.

5. William H. Philpott and Dwight K. Kalita, *Victory over Diabetes* (New Canaan, Conn.: Keats Publishing, Inc., 1983), 56–65.

6. C. D. Eaton, "Co-Existence of Hypothyroidism with Diabetes Mellitus," *The Journal of the Michigan Medical Society* (1954): 53:1101.

Chapter 14

1. *Time* (March 26, 1984), 58–59.

2. *Modern Medicine* (March 1, 1984), 268.

3. L. V. Malysheva, "Tissue Respiration Rate in Certain Organs in Experimental Hypercholesteremia in Atherosclerosis," *Federation Proceedings* Translation Supplement (1964): 23:T562.

4. I. B. Friedland, "Investigations on the Influence of Thyroid Preparations on Experimental Hypercholesterolemia and Atherosclerosis," *Zeitung Ges. Exp. Med.* (1933): 87:683.

5. Broda O. Barnes and Charlotte W. Barnes, *Heart Attack Rareness in Thyroid-Treated Patients* (Springfield, Ill.: Charles C Thomas Publisher, 1972), 75.

6. *Ibid.*, 76.

7. Edward R. Pinckney and Cathey Pinckney, *The Cholesterol Controversy* (Los Angeles: Sherbourne Press, 1973), 7–8.

8. *Los Angeles Times* (October 2, 1975): Section 1, page 2.

9. Richard Passwater, *Supernutrition for Healthy Hearts* (New York: Dial Press, 1976), 57.

10. M. K. Gersovitz, K. Motil, H. N. Munro, N. S. Scrimshaw, and V. R. Young, *American Journal of Clinical Nutrition* (1982): 35(1): 6–14.

11. Pinckney, E. and C., *Cholesterol*, 36.

12. *Journal of the American Medical Association* (June 8, 1964): 188:845.

13. Pinckney, E. and C., *Cholesterol*, 33.

14. *Ibid.*

Chapter 15

1. Broda O. Barnes and Charlotte W. Barnes, *Heart Attack Rareness*

in Thyroid-Treated Patients (Springfield, Ill.: Charles C Thomas, 1972), 25–27.

2. Frank Chappell, "Obesity Rather Than Diet Blamed in High Cholesterol," American Medical Association news story (October 25, 1976).

3. L. M. Hurxthal, "Blood Cholesterol and Thyroid Disease," *Archives of Internal Medicine* (1934): 53:825.

4. Meyer Bodansky and Oscar Bodansky, *The Biochemistry of Disease* (New York: The Macmillan Company, 1940), 341.

5. J. D. Wilson et al., "Influence of Dietary Cholesterol in Cholesterol Metabolism," *Annals of New York Academy of Science* (1968): 149:808–821.

6. Timothy G. Johnson and Stephen Goldfinger, *The Harvard Medical School Health Letter Book* (New York: Warner Books, 1981), 229–230.

7. William B. Kountz, *Thyroid Function and Its Possible Role in Vascular Degeneration* (Springfield, Ill.: Charles C Thomas, 1951).

8. Matthias Rath, "How Vitamin C Prevents Heart Attack and Stroke," a publication of the Linus Pauling Heart Foundation, 1992.

9. Mark Bricklin, *The Practical Encyclopedia of Natural Healing* (Emmaus, Pa.: Rodale Press, 1976), 196.

10. *The Complete Book of Vitamins* (Emmaus, Pa.: Rodale Press, 1977), 314–315.

11. *Ibid.*, 315–316.

12. *Ibid.*, 198.

13. Bricklin, *Practical Encyclopedia*, 310–311.

Chapter 16

1. *The Encyclopedia of Common Diseases* (Emmaus, Pa.: Rodale Press, 1976), 667–670.

2. *Ibid.*

Chapter 17

1. J. G. C. Spencer, "The Influence of the Thyroid in Malignant Disease," *British Journal of Cancer* (1954): 8:393.

2. *The Encyclopedia of Common Diseases* (Emmaus, Pa.: Rodale Press, 1976), 294–295.

3. H. Vorheer, "Thyroid Disease in Relation to Breast Cancer," *Klinical Wochenschr.* (December, 1978): 23–56, 1139–45.

4. D. P. Rose and T. E. Davis, "Plasma Triiodothyronine Concentration in Breast Cancer," *Cancer* (April, 1979): 43–4, 1434–8.

5. S. Shapiro et al., "Use of Thyroid Supplements in Relation to the Risk of Breast Cancer," *Journal of the American Medical Association* (October 10, 1980): 15–244, 1685–7.

6. J. C. Pita, Jr. et al., "Diminution of Large Pituitary Tumor After Replacement Therapy for Primary Hypothyroidism," *Neurology* (August 29, 1979): 29:8, 1169–72.

7. L. A. Guerrero and R. Carnovale, "Regression of Pituitary Tumor After Thyroid Replacement in Primary Hypothyroidism," *Southern Medical Journal* (April, 1983): 76:4, 529–31.

8. John A. Myers with Carl H. Schutte, *Metabolic Aspects of Health: Nutritional Elements in Health and Disease* (Kentfield, Cal.: Discovery Press, 1979).

Chapter 19

1. R. R. Brenner, "Metabolism of Endogenous Substrates by Microsomes," *Drug Metabolism Review* (1977): 6:155–212, and D. F. Horrobin, "A Biochemical Basis for Alcoholism-Induced Damage," *Medical Hypotheses* (1980): 6:929–42.

2. "Essential Fatty Acids (EFAs)—Measuring Deficiency," *Technical Information Bulletin #2*: Health from the Sun Products, Inc., New York, 1.

3. *Ibid.*, 2.

4. S. Kunkel and R. B. Zurier, "Treatment of Adjuvant Arthritis with Evening Primrose Oil," *Progress in Lipid Research*, in press.

5. M. G. Brush, "Efamol in Treatment of the Premenstrual Syndrome," Report for St. Thomas Hospital Medical School, London.

6. N. L. Pashby et al., "A Clinical Trial of Evening Primrose Oil (Efamol) in Mastalgia," presented at British Surgical Research Society, Cardiff (Wales) Meeting, July, 1981.

7. K. S. Vaddadi and D. F. Horrobin, "Weight Loss Produced by Eve-

ning Primrose Oil Administration in Normal and Schizophrenic Individuals," *IRCS Journal of Medical Science* (1979): 7:52.

8. D. F. Horrobin, "A Biochemical Basis for Alcoholism and Alcohol-Induced Damage," *Medical Hypothesis* (1980): 6:929–942, and Horrobin and M. S. Manku, "Possible Role of Prostaglandin E1 in the Affective Disorders and in Alcoholism," *British Medical Journal* (1980): 1:1363–6.

9. J. Rotrosen, D. Mandio, D. Segarich et al., "Ethanol and Prostaglandin E1: Biochemical and Behavioral Interaction," *Life Science* (1980): 26: 1867–76.

10. "Essential Fatty Acids and Hyperactivity," *Technical Information Bulletin #8:* Health from the Sun Products, Inc., New York, 1.

11. A. J. Houtsmuller et al., "Favourable Influence of Linoleic Acid on the Progression of Diabetes Micro- and Macroangiopathy," *Nutrition Metabolism* (1980): 24 (Supp. 1) 105–18.

12. A. E. Hansen, "Serum Lipid Changes and Therapeutic Effects of Various Oils in Infantile Eczema," *Proceedings of the Society of Experimental Biological Medicine* (1933): 31: 160–161, and A. E. Hansen and M. E. Haggard et al., "Essential Fatty Acids in Human Nutrition," *Journal of Nutrition* (1958): 565–76.

13. C. R. Lovell, J. L. Burton, and D. F. Horrobin, "Treatment of Atopic Eczema with Evening Primrose Oil," *Lancet* (1981): 1:278.

14. A. C. Campbell and G. C. MacEwen, "Treatment of Brittle Nails and Dry Eyes," *British Journal of Dermatology*, in press.

15. *Lancet*, Vol. 1 (1981), 278.

Chapter 20

1. Allen C. Alfrey et al., "The Dialysis Encephalopathy Syndrome: Possible Aluminum Intoxication," *New England Journal of Medicine* (January 22, 1976), 185–6.

2. Robert J. Johnson, "Aluminum: A Threat to Mental Health." *Bestways* (December 1986), 28.

3. *Science News*, "A Reason for Alzheimer's Disease?" (September 15, 1984), 167.

4. Personal Communication with Richard Casdorph, M.D.

5. Edna Zeavin, "Foods That Influence Human Behavior," *Bestways* (September, 1985), 11.

6. Abram Hoffer, *Orthomolecular Medicine for Physicians* (New Canaan, CT: Keats Publishing, Inc., 1989), 204–206.

7. Blair Justice, *Who Gets Sick* (Houston: Peak Press, 1987), 79–80.

8. Personal Communication, November 14, 1994.

Chapter 21

1. Robertas Bunevicius et al., "Effects of Thyroxine Compared with Thyroxine Plus Triiodythyronine in Patients with Hypothyroidism," *New England Journal of Medicine*, February 11, 1999.

2. Arem Riha, M.D., *The Thyroid Solution* (New York, Ballantine Books, 1999), 244.

3. Michael Schachter, M.D., "The Diagnosis and Treatment of Hypothyroidism," Health World Online.

4. Mary Shomon, "Research Finds Most Patients Feel Better with Addition of T_3, Not Levothyroxine (Synthroid) Alone," About.com Guide to Thyroid Disease, February 12, 1999.

Chapter 22

1. Richard Passwater, Ph.D., "New Discoveries Expand Our Knowledge About Selenium's Importance," *Whole Foods Magazine*, May 1999.

2. Harold D. Foster, Ph.D., "Selenium and Cancer: A Geographic Perspective," *Journal of Orthomolecular Medicine*, First Quarter, 1998, p. 8.

3. Patrick Quillin, Ph.D., *Healing Nutrients* (Chicago, Contemporary Books, 1987), 9, 129.

Chapter 23

1. "Iodine's Role in Learning," *Science News*, June 29, 1996, 410.

2. Elson M. Haas, M.D., "Minerals: Iodine," from Staying with Nutrition, Reported in Health World Online.

3. Stephen Langer, M.D., and James F. Scheer, *Super Smarts* (New York. Kensington Books, 1999), 165.

4. Weston A. Price, D.D.S., *Nutrition and Physical Degeneration.* (Los Angeles: Keats Publishing, Inc. 6th Edition, 1997), 401.

5. James E. Haddow, M.D. et al, "Babies Born to Mothers with Untreated Hypothyroidism Have Lower I.Q.s," *New England Journal of Medicine*, August 19, 1999.

Chapter 24

1. J.B. Shiroky et al., "Thyroid Dysfunction in Rheumatoid Arthritis," *Annals of Rheumatic Diseases* 52 (1993):454–56.

2. Dr. John C. Lowe, Personal Communication, July, 1999.

3. Dr. John C. Lowe, "Thyroid Status of 38 Fibromyalgia Patients: Implications for the Etiology of Fibromyalgia," *Clinical Bulletin of Myofascial Therapy*, 1997: 2(1):47–64.

4. Dr. John C. Lowe et al., "Effectiveness and Safety of T_3 (Triiodothyronine) Therapy for Euthyroid Fibromyalgia: A Double-Blind Placebo-Controlled Response-Driven Crossover Study," *Clinical Bulletin of Myofascial Therapy*, 1997: 2(2/3):31–57.

5. Dr. John C. Lowe, Personal Communication, July 1999.

6. Mary Shomon, "Fibromyalgia Aches and Pains as a 'Symptom' of Hypothyroidism: A Look at the Theories of Dr. John Lowe," About.com Guide to Thyroid Disease, April 27, 1999.

7. *Ibid.*

8. Dr. John Lowe, Personal Communication, July, 1999.

Chapter 25

1. "Thyroid Hormone Missing from Menopause Discussion for Millions of Women," news release from the American of Association of Clinical Endocrinologists, January 13, 1999.

2. *Ibid.*

3. "Give Yourself the Thyroid 'Neck Check!' It Could Save Your Life," news release from the American Association of Clinical Endocrinologists, January 13, 1999.

Chapter 26

1. Beat Mueller, M.D., et al., "Impaired Action of Thyroid Hormone Associated with Smoking in Women with Hypothyroidism," *New England Journal of Medicine*, October 12, 1995: 333 (15): 964–969.

2. Robert D. Utiger, M.D., "Cigarette Smoking and the Thyroid," *New England Journal of Medicine*, October 12, 1995: 333 (15): 1001–1002.

3. S. Fukata, et al., "Relationship Between Cigarette Smoking and Hypothyroidism in Patients with Hashimoto's Thyroiditis," *Journal of Endocrinological Investigation*, October, 1996: 19(9): 697–12.

4. David S. Cooper, M.D., F.A.C.P., "Smoking and the Thyroid," *The Bridge* (newsletter of the Thyroid Foundation of America), Spring, 1993, Vol. 8, Number 1.

5. Mary Shomon, "Does Quitting Smoking Trigger Thyroid Disease?" About.com Guide to Thyroid Disease, October 13, 1997.

6. *Ibid.*

7. M. Nikodemov et al., "Chronic Ethanol Drinking and Food Deprivation Affect Rat Hypothalmic-Pituitary-Thyroid Axis and TRH in Septum," *Endocrine*, October, 1998: 9: 213–218.

8. V. Coiro and P.P. Vescovi, "Effect of Pyridostigmine on the Thyroid-Stimulating Hormone in Abstinent Alcoholics," *Clinical Experimental Research*, October, 1997: 21: 1308–1311.

9. Roger J. Williams, Ph.D., *Nutrition Against Disease* (New York. Bantam Books, 1981), 177–178.

Chapter 27

1. Walter Miller, "Health Risks From Fluoridation," newsletter, August, 1997.

2. Phyllis J. Mullenix et al., "Neurotoxicity and Teratology," *Trends in Neuroscience*: 17: 2, 1995.

3. A. Machoy-Mokrzynska, "Fluoride-Magnesium Interaction," *Journal of the International Society for Fluoride Research*: 28: 24, November, 1995: 175–177.

4. "Perchlorate: The Quiet Contaminant," news release from Zero Waste America, December 5, 1998.

5. Karin Winegar, "Danger in the Air," *Mother Jones* magazine, July/August, 1998.

Chapter 28

1. K.C. McCowen et al., "Elevated Serum Thyrotropin in Thyroxine-Treated Patients with Hypothyroidism Given Sertraline," *The New England Journal of Medicine*, Oct. 2, 1997: (14):1010–1011.

2. *Ibid.*

3. Christine R. Schneyer, "Calcium Carbonate and Reduction of Levothyroxine Efficacy," *Journal of the American Medical Association*, March 11, 1998.

4. Barbara Baker, "Hypothyroidism, Allergic Rhinitis Tied to Apnea," *Family Practice News*, August 1, 1999.

5. Stephen E. Langer, M.D., "The Reason Behind Weight Gain, Fatigue, Muscle Pain, Depression, Food Allergies, Infections . . .", *Alternative Medicine*: 16, 1998.

Chapter 29

1. G. Z. Pitskhelauri, "The Long-Living of Soviet Georgia," *The Gerontologist* (February, 1982): 22:2, 117–118.

2. *Nutrition and the M.D.* (October, 1981): 7:10, 5.

3. "Keep Your Brain Young at Any Age," *Los Angeles Times* (April 26, 1983): Part 3, 1–4.

4. "Of Life Extension, Mice, and Men," *Los Angeles Times* (June 21, 1982).

5. L. P. Swaim, "Chronic Arthritis," *Journal of the American Medical Association* (1929): 93:259.

6. Broda O. Barnes and Lawrence Galton, *Hypothyroidism: The Unsuspected Illness* (New York: Thomas Y. Crowell Company, 1976), 204, 205.

Chapter 30

1. B. O. Barnes, "Basal Temperature versus Basal Metabolism," *Journal of the American Medical Association* (August, 1942): 119:1072.

2. J. C. Scott, Jr., and Elizabeth Mussey, "Menstrual Patterns and Myxedema," *American Journal of Obstetrics and Gynecology* (1965): 90:161.

3. M. S. Gold, H. R. Pearsall, and A. C. Pottash, "Hypothyroidism and Depression: The Causal Connection," *Diagnosis* (December, 1983): 77–80.

BIBLIOGRAPHY

Adams, Ruth. *The Complete Home Guide to All the Vitamins*. New York: Larchmont Books, 1976.

Balch, James F. and Phyllis A. *Prescription for Nutritional Healing*. Garden City Park, N.Y.: Avery Publishing Group, Inc., 1990.

Bricklin, Mark. *The Practical Encyclopedia of Natural Healing*. Emmaus, Pa.: Rodale Press, Inc., 1976.

Clark, Guy W. *A Vitamin Digest*. Springfield, Ill.: Charles C Thomas, 1953.

Davies, Stephen, and Alan Stewart. *Nutritional Medicine*. London: Pan Books, 1987.

Davis, Adelle. *Let's Get Well*. New York: Harcourt Brace & World, Inc., 1965.

Elwood, Catharyn. *Feel Like a Million*. New York: The Devin-Adair Company, 1952.

Fredericks, Carlton. *Psycho-Nutrition*. New York: Grosset & Dunlap, 1976.

Fredericks, Carlton, and Herman Goodman. *Low Blood Sugar and You*. New York: Constellations International, 1969.

Gerras, Charles. *The Complete Book of Vitamins*. Emmaus, Pa.: Rodale Press, Inc., 1977.

Justice, Blair. *Who Gets Sick*. Houston: Peak Press, 1987.

Kugler, Hans, et al. *Life Extenders and Memory Boosters*. Reno, Nev.: Health Quest Publications, 1993.

Langer, Stephen, and James F. Scheer. *Raise Your I.Q.* New York: Kensington Books, 1999.

———. *Solved: The Riddle of Weight Loss*. Rochester, Vt.: Healing Arts Press, 1989.

Mandell, Marshall, and Lynne Waller Scanlon. *Dr. Mandell's 5-Day Allergy Relief System*. New York: Pocket Books, 1980.

Masor, Nathan. *The New Psychiatry*. New York: Philosophical Library, 1959.

Newbold, H. L. *Dr. Newbold's Revolutionary New Discoveries About Weight Loss*. New York: Rawson Associates Publishers, Inc., 1977.

Passwater, Richard. *Supernutrition for Healthy Hearts*. New York: The Dial Press, 1977.

Philpott, William H., and Dwight K. Kalita. *Victory over Diabetes*. New Canaan, Conn.: Keats Publishing, Inc., 1983.

Pinckney, Cathey, and Edward R. Pinckney. *Do-It-Yourself Medical Testing*. New York: Facts on File, 1983.

Pinckney, Edward R., and Cathey Pinckney. *The Fallacy of Freud and Psychoanalysis*. Englewood Cliffs, N.J.: Prentice-Hall, Inc., 1965.

———. *The Cholesterol Controversy*. Los Angeles: Sherbourne Press, 1973.

Price, Weston A. *Nutrition and Physical Degeneration*, 6th ed. Los Angeles: Keats Publishing, 1997.

Staff of *Prevention. The Encyclopedia of Common Diseases*. Emmaus, Pa.: Rodale Press, Inc., 1976.

Quillin, Patrick, *Healing Nutrients*. Chicago, Ill.: Contemporary Books, 1987.

Randolph, Theron G., and Ralph W. Moss. *An Alternative Approach to Allergies*. Toronto, New York: Bantam Books, 1982.

Riedman, Sarah R. *Our Hormones and How They Work*. New York: Collier Books, 1962.

Riha, Arem. *The Thyroid Solution*. New York: Ballantine Books, 1999.

Rubin, Herman H. *Glands, Sex, and Personality*. New York: Wilfred Funk, Inc., 1952.

Vogel, H.C.A. *The Nature Doctor*. New Canaan, Conn.: Keats Publishing, Inc., 1991.

Werbach, Melvyn R. *Nutritional Influences on Illness*. New Canaan, Conn.: Keats Publishing. Inc., 1988.

Williams, Roger J. *Free and Unequal*. Austin, Tex.: University of Texas Press, 1953.

———. *Biochemical Individuality*. New York: John Wiley & Sons, Inc., 1956.

———. *Nutrition Against Disease*. New York: Bantam Books, 1981.

Williams, Roger J., and Dwight K. Kalita. *A Physician's Handbook on Orthomolecular Medicine*. New York: Pergamon Press, 1977.

INDEX

A
abscesses, 140
acne, 63–65
adolescents, hypothyroidism in, 228
   See also children
adrenal exhaustion, 168, 240–241
adrenal glands, 43, 85
aerobic exercise, 75, 103
aging process
   alcoholism and, 194
   declining immune system and, 156,
      213–215
   longevity program, 210–211
   malnutrition and, 60, 156
   mental capacity in, 211–213
   protection of body cells, 215–216
   psychological factors in, 209–210
   See also Alzheimer's disease
Ahrens, Edward, 109

air pollutants. *See* environmental
   chemicals
Albrecht, William J., 27–28
alcohol addiction, 51, 153, 194–196
aligomenorrhea, 49
allergies, 103–104, 156, 205, 240
   See also food allergens
alopecia, 225
aluminum absorption, 160–162
Alzheimer's disease
   aluminum absorption and, 160–162
   reversing pseudosenility, 162–165
   senility and, 157–160
amenorrhea, 49, 228
American Association of Clinical Endocrinologists (AACE), 187–189
amino acid deficiency, 95, 228
androgen therapy, 228
anemia, iron-deficiency, 30, 40, 60, 223,
   230–231

263

ABOUT THE AUTHORS

Stephen E. Langer, M.D., received his medical training at New York College of Medicine in Buffalo, New York. He has been president of the American Nutritional Medical Association since 1982 and has a private practice, specializing in orthomolecular medicine and clinical nutrition in Berkeley, California. Over the last twenty years, Dr. Langer has had his own nationwide radio and television talk shows. In addition to this book, he is co-author of *Solved: The Riddle of Weight Loss* and over two hundred articles for major health and medical publications.

For the latest information on chronic fatigue relief, weight control, medical nutrition, and natural therapies call Dr. Langer's Super-Health Hotline at 1-900-329-4040, ext. 987; or write Dr. Langer at 3031 Telegraph Avenue, Berkeley, CA 94705.

James F. Scheer has authored a co-authored fifteen published book, many in nutrition and health. He is the co-author of *Foods That Heal*, whose sales topped a million copies. One of his books served as the basis for a David Wolper-produced 60-minute documentary, which was nominated for an Academy Award.

More than one thousand of his nutrition/health articles have appeared in leading magazines throughout the world. He has edited three health publications: *Let's LIVE*, *Food-Wise*, and *Health Freedom News*.